ADORNO'S RHINOCEROS

ALSO AVAILABLE FROM BLOOMSBURY

Adorno and the Ban on Images, Sebastian Truskolaski

Adorno and Neoliberalism: The Critique of Exchange Society, Charles A. Prusik

Understanding Adorno, Understanding Modernism, ed. Robin Truth Goodman

ADORNO'S RHINOCEROS

Art, Nature, Critique

Edited by
Antonia Hofstätter and
Daniel Steuer

BLOOMSBURY ACADEMIC
LONDON • NEW YORK • OXFORD • NEW DELHI • SYDNEY

BLOOMSBURY ACADEMIC
Bloomsbury Publishing Plc
50 Bedford Square, London, WC1B 3DP, UK
1385 Broadway, New York, NY 10018, USA
29 Earlsfort Terrace, Dublin 2, Ireland

BLOOMSBURY, BLOOMSBURY ACADEMIC and the Diana logo
are trademarks of Bloomsbury Publishing Plc

First published in Great Britain 2022
This paperback edition published 2023

Copyright © Antonia Hofstätter, Daniel Steuer, and Contributors, 2022

Antonia Hofstätter and Daniel Steuer have asserted their right under the Copyright, Designs and Patents Act, 1988, to be identified as Editors of this work.

For legal purposes the Acknowledgements on p. x constitute
an extension of this copyright page.

Cover design by Ben Anslow
Cover image: Silhouette of rhino and young small rhino. Vector illustration.
(© Kozyreva Elena / Shutterstock)

All rights reserved. No part of this publication may be reproduced or transmitted in any form or by any means, electronic or mechanical, including photocopying, recording, or any information storage or retrieval system, without prior permission in writing from the publishers.

Bloomsbury Publishing Plc does not have any control over, or responsibility for, any third-party websites referred to or in this book. All internet addresses given in this book were correct at the time of going to press. The author and publisher regret any inconvenience caused if addresses have changed or sites have ceased to exist, but can accept no responsibility for any such changes.

A catalogue record for this book is available from the British Library.

A catalog record for this book is available from the Library of Congress.

ISBN:	HB:	978-1-3501-7780-2
	PB:	978-1-3502-7317-7
	ePDF:	978-1-3501-7782-6
	eBook:	978-1-3501-7783-3

Typeset by Integra Software Services Pvt. Ltd.

To find out more about our authors and books visit www.bloomsbury.com
and sign up for our newsletters.

CONTENTS

List of Illustrations vii

Contributors viii

Acknowledgements x

1 Introduction: The Enigma of the Rhinoceros 1
 Antonia Hofstätter

2 In the Name of the Rhinoceros: Expression beyond Human Intention 19
 Camilla Flodin

3 The Rhinoceros at the Bottom of the Sea: Adorno, Dürer and the Silent Eloquence of Artworks 43
 Antonia Hofstätter

4 Just One Line: Reading T. W. Adorno on Humans, Artworks, and Animals 57
 Lydia Goehr

5 The Mute Animal 73
 Alexander García Düttmann

6 The Speaking Animal: On a Metaphor of Humanity 85
 Sebastian Tränkle

7 The Gaze of the Rhinoceros and the 'It' of *Aesthetic Theory* 119
 Daniel Steuer

8 The Muted Animal 153
 Daniel Herwitz

9 Epilogue: On the Actuality of Adorno's Rhinoceros – Extraction, Extinction, and Dignity 169
Daniel Steuer

Name Index 190

Subject Index 193

LIST OF ILLUSTRATIONS

1. Sketches for Three Rhinos, 2005. 1. Crowd Pleaser, 2. Dunce, 3. Untitled. © William Kentridge   xii

2. Rhinoceros, 1515. Albrecht Dürer. Public domain. Wikimedia Commons   42

3. Zweizehenfaultier, Unau (Choloepus didactylus), *Meyers Konversations-Lexikon*. 5th edition (1893–1897/1901). Public domain. Private scan: Sebastian Tränkle   108

4. Still from *Mine*, 1991. © William Kentridge   160

5. Rhino on Lake, Lake Nakuru, 2007. © Nick Brandt, Courtesy of Edwynn Houk Gallery, New York   168

CONTRIBUTORS

Alexander García Düttmann teaches philosophy at Universität der Künste in Berlin. Recent book publication: *In Praise of Youth* (Diaphanes, 2021).

Camilla Flodin is Associate Professor of Philosophy at the University of Agder, Norway. She has published extensively on Adorno's aesthetics and the art–nature relationship in, for example, *British Journal for the History of Philosophy* and *Adorno Studies*. She is a contributor to the edited volume *Understanding Adorno, Understanding Modernism* (Bloomsbury, 2020) as well as to the *Oxford Handbook of Adorno* (Oxford University Press, forthcoming). She is also co-editor of *Beyond Autonomy in Eighteenth-Century British and German Aesthetics* (Routledge, 2021).

Lydia Goehr is Professor of Philosophy at Columbia University. She is author of *The Imaginary Museum of Musical Works: An Essay in the Philosophy of Music* (Clarendon Press, 1992); *The Quest for Voice: Music, Politics, and the Limits of Philosophy* (Oxford University Press, 2002); *Elective Affinities: Musical Essays on the History of Aesthetic Theory* (Columbia University Press, 2011). Her forthcoming book is *Red Sea – Red Square – Red Thread: A Philosophical Detective Story* (Oxford University Press, 2021).

Daniel Herwitz is Fredric Huetwell Professor of Humanities at the University of Michigan where for a decade he directed the Institute for the Humanities. From 1996 to 2002 he was Chair in Philosophy at the University of Natal and involved in the events of the democratic transition. Among his most recent books are *Aesthetics, Arts and Politics in a Global World* (Bloomsbury, 2017), *Cosmopolitan Aesthetics* (Bloomsbury, 2019) and the forthcoming *Political Power of Visual Art* (Bloomsbury, 2021).

Antonia Hofstätter is teaching fellow in German Studies at the University of Warwick. She has published widely on Adorno's aesthetics, inter alia in *Adorno Studies* and *Zeitschrift für kritische Theorie*. Recently, she contributed to the edited volumes *Understanding Adorno, Understanding Modernism* (Bloomsbury, 2020), *Theodor W. Adorno: Ästhetische Theorie* (De Gruyter, 2021), and *The Aging of Adorno's Aesthetic Theory* (Mimesis International, 2021).

Between 1989 and 2020, **Daniel Steuer** taught European literature and social and political thought at Bangor University, Trinity College Dublin, the University of Sussex, and the University of Brighton. He has published widely on Wittgenstein and Adorno, among other topics. He co-edited, with Robert Gillett and Ernest Schonfield, *Georg Büchner: Contemporary Perspectives* (Brill Rodopi, 2017). His latest publication is a book, co-authored with Max Liljefors and Gregor Noll, *War and Algorithm* (Rowman & Littlefield, 2019). He is currently an independent scholar living in Austria.

Sebastian Tränkle is postdoctoral researcher at the Department of Philosophy at Freie Universität, Berlin. He is the author of *Nichtidentität und Unbegrifflichkeit: Philosophische Sprachkritik nach Adorno und Blumenberg* (Vittorio Klostermann, 2021) and, together with Anne Eusterschulte, co-editor of *Theodor W. Adorno: Ästhetische Theorie* (De Gruyter, 2021).

ACKNOWLEDGEMENTS

Many people have supported this project in its various stages. First of all, we would like to thank all authors for their excellent contributions and for having made it such a relaxed and pleasurable affair to be working on this volume. Thanks are also due to the reviewers of the book proposal and of the draft manuscript.

When we approached the artists William Kentridge and Nick Brandt regarding the possible use of some of their work as illustrations, our inquiries were answered immediately and in the most supportive fashion. It was very motivating to know that we would be able to have their excellent artwork as fitting companions to the written word, adding a different dimension and making this a much more attractive book. Thank you! And a special thanks to Anne McIlleron and Natalie Dembo at the William Kentridge Studio for going the extra mile just before the Christmas break.

We are also very grateful to Michael Schwarz of the Theodor W. Adorno Archive for his invaluable help with many Adorno-related queries and, in particular, for giving us permission to quote from unpublished material.

As far as the written word is concerned, the volume benefited greatly from the outstanding copy-editing of Tim Carter. His suggestions and comments very often not only improved the language but forced us to clarify the substance of our arguments.

Last but not least, it is a pleasure to thank our editors at Bloomsbury, Lucy Russell and Liza Thompson, for their good humour and advice throughout, not to forget their well-timed reminders and always prompt replies.

Antonia Hofstätter
Daniel Steuer

FIGURE 1 *Sketches for Three Rhinos, 2005. 1. Crowd Pleaser, 2. Dunce, 3. Untitled.* © *William Kentridge*

1

Introduction: The Enigma of the Rhinoceros

Antonia Hofstätter

Meeting the Rhinoceros

In the cultural history of the world, the rhinoceros has long been a source of fascination. Countless texts and artefacts, from Dürer to Dali, from Longhi to Ionesco, or, more recently, the work of William Kentridge, testify to the persistent spell that this curious creature casts over our imagination. Fascinating to us are never phenomena that we know all too well or that we do not know at all; rather, what captures our attention and elicits our curiosity is that which appears familiar but which nevertheless seems to escape our grasp, or, in reverse, that which seems unlike everything else and yet has the power to intimately move us. In short, we are fascinated by what inhabits the liminal zone of the enigmatic.

While the enigma that pertains to all that exists, as Adorno reminds us in *Aesthetic Theory*, is mostly forgotten – thanks to 'the categorical net' that people have '[spun] around what is other than subjective spirit'[1] – the rhinoceros seems to evoke the zone of the enigmatic the moment it captures an attentive gaze. Its physical appearance marks it as curiously 'other', as an awe-inspiring and almost mythical creature. Grey and heavy, yet surprisingly agile under its lined and wrinkled skin, the rhinoceros is a strong and powerful animal. Embodied by its commanding appearance seems an ancient prerogative to resist domestication, a sense that is underlined by the two sharp horns that crown its bulky head. Yet the peculiarity of these horns lends this appearance of the undomesticated a further twist of strangeness, giving credibility to the anecdotes which tell of rhinoceroses that were mistaken for unicorns or dragons.[2] Two shapely and surprisingly elegant ears – they almost remind one of petals or calyxes, if it were not for the dainty rim of spiky hair – and a soft and velvety mouth imbue its unusual figure with a peaceful and melancholic expression. The strange and curious appearance of the rhinoceros seems to mark it as a wondrous remnant of different times and different places. Indeed, this powerful and tender creature appears to rightly belong to a period when mammoths and dinosaurs were still roaming this planet.[3] If it were not for the catastrophic fact of its near extinction, the rhinoceros would perhaps inspire the hope, which Adorno expresses in an aphorism in *Minima Moralia* (which will concern us later in more detail), that because it pre-existed the rise of human civilization it might also outlive its decline. Indeed, the mesmerizing effect of the rhinoceros might be owed to the perceived distance that it puts between human history and the animal itself. For Adorno, sitting by his desk in Frankfurt am Main, the rhinoceros certainly must have appeared, in the vocabulary of his time, 'exotic': as importing a glow of otherness, of what is untamed, into urban central Europe.[4] The rhinoceros's enigmatic semblance of otherness promises a transcendence of the here and now, of the tightly woven nexus of the *ever same*. Evoking that which escapes, it unsettles the seemingly all too familiar.

The recent history of the rhinoceros is of course intricately linked with that of colonialism. The exoticism that served for thinkers and artists as a reminder of what is undomesticated in the midst of 'civilization' is inextricable from and, indeed, reinforces the gruesome history of domination and exploitation that lies at its heart (a point that, as we will see, was not lost on Adorno). This tells us that a lot more is at stake when one is touched by the enigma of the rhinoceros. Indeed, its history is but one more proof that our fascination with animals, or with the 'exotic', or the 'other', can take the form of love and rage. These responses testify to an affinity that exists, however hidden or ignored, between human beings and animals; indeed, they draw the rhinoceros, seemingly distant in time and space, into the bounds of intimate closeness. The affinity points towards the Achilles heel of civilization: towards our shared participation in the realm of nature and, thus, ultimately, towards our own mortality. Mesmerizing and enigmatic about the rhinoceros is thus its uncanny resemblance to human beings. In a famous passage in 'Why Look at Animals?' John Berger seems to capture precisely this when he speaks about the gaze of animals: 'The eyes of an animal when they consider a man are attentive and wary. [...] Other animals are held by the look. Man becomes aware of himself returning the look.'[5] The liminal zone of distance and closeness, familiarity and unfamiliarity, that the rhinoceros might evoke anticipates a possible reconciliation between humans and animals, nature and culture, past and present. Yet it recalls also the comprehensive domination of nature and the suffering to which it subjects all that exists.

Today, the rhinoceros has become a symbol of mass extinction: of finitude. The thought that this creature might outlive human civilization has given way to the sad insight that human civilization has already nearly achieved the total extinction of the rhinoceros. No amount of thought and no amount of hope can get around this fact. It calls, more than ever, for rigorous reflection on the relationship between humans and animals or nature and civilization.

Theodor W. Adorno was certainly one of those fascinated by this enigmatic animal. In unexpected yet crucial places in his work, a rhinoceros makes an appearance. In *Aesthetic Theory* – in the passage that inspires this book – it steps on to the page in the context of a discussion of the language character of works of art, a central concept of Adorno's aesthetics. Describing the resemblance to speech of the Etruscan vases exhibited in the Villa Giulia in Rome, Adorno writes that their resemblance 'depends most likely on their *Here I am* or *This is what I am*, a selfhood not first excised by identificatory thought from the interdependence of being'. He continues: 'Thus the rhinoceros, that mute animal, seems to say: I am a rhinoceros' (AT, 112, trans. modified). On the pages of *Aesthetic Theory*, the seeming declaration of selfhood by the rhinoceros becomes a metaphor for the seeming *being-in-itself* of artworks – an apparent selfhood that they mutely express but do not proclaim. In this, as Camilla Flodin lucidly elaborates in her contribution to this book, works of art imitate the expressiveness of nature and of creatures of nature: artworks mimic what Adorno also refers to as the enigmatic 'more' of natural beauty.

Inasmuch as artworks – and *Aesthetic Theory*'s rhinoceros – are imbued with the semblance of an in-itself, they anticipate the end of the domination of nature: they silently promise that the current state of universal alienation, in which the mastery of inner and outer nature has turned into the comprehensive exploitation and subjugation of nature, will not have the last word. It is here that the rhinoceros in *Aesthetic Theory* meets with the rhinoceros that Adorno lets loose on the pages of *Minima Moralia*: 'In existing without any purpose recognizable to human beings', Adorno writes in an aphorism entitled 'Toy shop', 'animals hold out, as if for expression, their own names, utterly impossible to exchange. This makes them so beloved of children, their contemplation so blissful. I am a rhinoceros, signifies the shape of the rhinoceros.'[6] Both the rhinoceros and the artwork, it is implied, point towards a world beyond universal exchangeability and anticipate a state in which subject and object are reconciled. Mass extinction, the irretrievable loss of what is unique, is its dystopian antithesis.

Rhinoceroses and artworks are enigmatic, as Adorno suggests, but what is also enigmatic is what exactly 'the rhinoceros' is doing in Adorno's texts. There is a not quite accurate version of an anecdote about a dispute between Russell and Wittgenstein over the question of whether one could say with certainty that there is not a rhinoceros in the room. The anecdote is amusing because an encounter with a living rhinoceros can leave no room for uncertainty.[7] And it is with such rhino-esque certainty that 'the rhinoceros' makes its entry in *Aesthetic Theory*. Its confidence is emphasized by the conjunction 'thus', in the sense of: 'in this way': 'Thus the rhinoceros, that mute animal, seems to say: I am a rhinoceros.' The apparent selfhood of artworks is akin to the apparent selfhood of rhinoceroses. Is that not obvious?[8]

The only thing that is obvious, however, is that nothing is obvious in *Aesthetic Theory*. It is not obvious that artworks can be compared to rhinoceroses, nor indeed that 'the rhinoceros' can or should show what is peculiar to artworks. And granted that one could plausibly liken artworks to animals, it is far from obvious why, at this point, 'the rhinoceros' is given preference over, say, 'the elephant'. Yet unsettling certainties is part and parcel of Adorno's critical writing strategy. Adorno, whose texts are meticulously composed in order to correctively lend voice to what is non-identical to their concepts, left little to chance when it came to his own writing. Of course, Adorno was not immune to language getting the better of him, to it storming away upon his approach as a rhinoceros might do when accidentally startled. But still, I read this passage not only as living off a play of hidden resemblances but also as engaging in a conscious and decisively critical play of form. Akin to the gesture of the 'Here I am', which, as Alexander García Düttmann notes in his essay in this volume, 'seems to point to itself as a gesture', 'the rhinoceros' in the text silently exposes the text *as* text – as something that is crafted and never fully identical to itself. When 'thus' 'the rhinoceros' makes its surprising and confident entrance, it does so as a caesura: as a gesture that interrupts and dissolves the self-certainty of thought. In an article on Adorno's animals and the semblance of happiness, Britta Scholze puts it well when she writes that 'Adorno's animals emphasize the ambition of an undomesticated thinking: [...] they act as irritating insertions in which a context beyond thought resonates. Adorno not only demands, as one of his famous phrases has it, a remembrance of nature in the subject; his texts also practise it through their form.'[9] A text that performs the remembrance of nature in the subject is a text whose power is manifest in its own disempowerment, a kind of writing that subverts its semblance of identity in an attempt to lend voice to what exceeds its grasp.

Zoological Musings

Given the diverse vantage points of today's global readership, which brings to Adorno's work a wide range of contemporary expectations and sensitivities, it is necessary to stress the importance of bearing in mind the specific situatedness of Adorno's thought not only within the intellectual and artistic context of the Franco-German tradition but also within the specific cultural constellations of the German bourgeoisie of the early twentieth century. Adorno's thinking proceeds always in intimate engagement with these spheres – immersing itself either with generously loving attentiveness or with equally generous acidity in their texts and artefacts – in order to test and potentially transcend their bounds by means of critical reflection. Recognizing the productive and critical potential of the role of animals in Adorno's work thus requires a familiarity not only with the commitments of his critical theory of society but also with the sociocultural parameters that it seeks to transcend. And these 'parameters', as we shall see, are often intimately entwined with Adorno's own horizon of experience.[10]

While we might regard the use of animal metaphors in Adorno's texts as an expression of his 'undomesticated thinking', it is curious to note that the animals in Adorno's writings are almost always *domesticated*. Even the wild boar of his reflections on his childhood in Amorbach is granted ferocity only within the confines of a folkloristic anecdote.[11] And the armoured rhinoceros in *Negative Dialectics* probably has more in common with Dürer's famous woodcut and the descriptions in *Brehms Tierleben* – a nineteenth-century encyclopaedia of animal life that belonged to the basic inventory of the German bourgeois home and was a valued companion of Adorno's in child- and adulthood – than with a rhinoceros that roams around the plains of Africa or Asia.[12] The likeness between artworks and animals that the rhinoceros passage in *Aesthetic Theory* proposes therefore immediately suggests a similar parallel: just as artworks may be encountered in museums, and music in concert halls, a rhinoceros might be seen in a zoo or in the pages of a nineteenth-century encyclopaedia. Indeed, intertwined with the lines of Adorno's dense philosophical writings are the traces of animals that appear to have been the rather tame and friendly companions of his sheltered childhood around 1900. This impression is heightened by the fact that the animals one encounters in his texts are often characters from German fairy tales, which Adorno would have read as a child and which reappear, for instance, in the titles of some of the aphorisms in *Minima Moralia* – such as 'Frog King' or 'Wolf as Grandmother' – or in his monograph on Mahler, where he likens a musical gesture in the *Third Symphony* to the way in which 'a fearful child identifies with the tiniest goat in the clock case that escapes the big bad wolf'.[13] Is the fearful child who identifies with the little fairy-tale goat the same one that makes an appearance years later in Adorno's correspondence with the German conservationist, and director of Frankfurt zoo, Bernhard Grzimek? In a letter from 23 April 1965, after formally declaring his intention to join the Frankfurt Zoological Society, Adorno swiftly suggests new additions to his local zoo: 'Would it not be nice', he writes, 'if the Frankfurt Zoo would acquire a wombat couple? I remember these friendly and chubby animals well from my childhood, when I identified strongly with them, and I would be happy if I could see them again.'[14] The child who identifies with animals and regards them, as Adorno puts it with reference to the babirusa, about whose survival he expresses his concern in the same letter, as 'confidant[s] of his childhood'[15] does not meaningfully distinguish between the speaking animals of fairy tales, the wombats confined behind the bars of the zoo or the rhinoceros in the wild or on the pages of *Brehms Tierleben*. In Benjamin's words, childhood is a state that is *disfigured* by resemblances.[16] The animals that re-emerge as creatures of text in the writings of Adorno are ciphers of remembrance that live off an expansive and undiscriminating affinity to the object world. As mediated remnants of this state of affinity, they lend the philosopher's hermetic writings an utopian air.

Yet not all the animals that appear in Adorno's texts seem to have a utopian glow. One has only to think of the rats on the last pages of *Negative Dialectics* which, in one more childhood memory, fall victim to the club of the innkeeper. While rats are perhaps the least domesticated creatures among the animals that inhabit Adorno's texts, it is still their close proximity to culture that lends them their significance:

> A child, fond of an innkeeper named Adam, watched him club the rats pouring out of holes in the courtyard; it was in his image that the child made its own image of the first man. That this has been forgotten, that we no longer know what we used to feel before the dogcatcher's van, is both the triumph of culture and its failure. Culture, which keeps emulating the old Adam, cannot bear to be reminded of that zone, and precisely this is not to be reconciled with the conception that culture has of itself. (ND, 366)

Keenly felt by the child is a tender affinity with creaturely life and a horror at its suffering. What culture makes one forget – 'what we used to feel before the dogcatcher's van' – is the inescapable transience that human beings share with animals. Culture 'cannot bear to be reminded of that zone'; indeed, it evolves as its antithesis. The triumph of culture is its emancipation from and control over the realm of nature; its failure is the reversal of culture into barbarism of which Adorno and Horkheimer's *Dialectic of Enlightenment* speaks so eloquently: when the mastery of inner and outer nature in the service of human emancipation turns into the total subjugation of nature and thereby, ultimately, into the enslavement of human beings themselves. Highly culturally mediated in Adorno's texts, animals become both figures of the unrealized promises of culture and reminders of its failings.

It thus should not come as a surprise that Adorno was well aware of the fact that the zoo, the museum and comparable spaces of representation and display – which are the sources of his 'utopian animals' – are deeply entangled in the dialectic of enlightenment. Crucially, the animals that Adorno invokes as exemplifying the *semblance* of an in-itself never actually *are* themselves. This might point to a limitation of Adorno's thinking – and, in his chapter on 'The Muted Animal', Daniel Herwitz suggests that it is precisely this: a clear limitation – but it is also crucially entwined with what makes Adorno's work *critical*; indeed, the limitation is inseparable from the labour of negative dialectics. We can lend this thought contours by thinking through one of *Minima Moralia*'s aphorisms, which, in a play on resemblances, pays tribute to a future fellow member of the Frankfurt Zoological Society: 'Mammoth'.[17] In this somewhat scandalous aphorism – but which true aphorism would not be truly scandalous? – Adorno credits the creation of zoological gardens with a utopian kernel: rather than being intended merely as places for recreation, we read, zoological gardens also embody the bourgeois hope 'that animal creation might survive the wrong that man has done it, if not man himself, and give rise to a better species, one that eventually succeeds. [...] They are laid out on the pattern of Noah's Ark, for since their inception the bourgeois class has been waiting for the flood' (MM, 115, trans. modified). The scandalous paradox that Adorno unfolds is that the enchanting aspect of zoological gardens is intricately entwined with the ostentatiousness of their disenchanting, if not to say inhumane, setup. Only in visibly denying freedom to animals do zoological gardens harbour a promise of freedom for the bourgeois spectator; only in explicitly showing themselves to be spaces of confinement do they lend themselves to the anticipation of an 'openness' that has been denied to nature – including human beings – so far. 'The dignity of nature is that of the not-yet-existing', Adorno writes in *Aesthetic Theory* (AT, 74). As Sebastian Tränkle reminds us in his contribution to this book: 'none escape' is the logic of the domination of nature. Not even animals that live in enclaves of wilderness are truly wild. Indeed, for Adorno, the semblance of nature as an in-itself is an ideological complement to the experience of living in a social reality that is through and through structured by economic imperatives, where everything is exchangeable and nothing is truly itself: 'What appears untamed in nature and remote from history, belongs – polemically speaking – to a historical phase in which the social web is so densely woven that the living fear death by suffocation' (AT, 65). That there is no right life in the wrong applies to the rhinoceros in the nature reserve, as it does to the tiger in the zoo. From this perspective, Adorno writes in 'Mammoth' that the once progressive Hagenbeck zoo in Hamburg, 'with trenches instead of cages [...] *betrays* the Ark by simulating the rescue that only Ararat can promise' (MM, 115, my emphasis). In other words, the false semblance of reconciliation in the here and now foresakes the possibility of a future true reconciliation. Critique remains faithful to the horizon of reconciliation in eschewing affirmation in favour of the critical labour that reveals the logic of the domination of nature. 'The tiger', which, reminiscent of Rilke's panther,

> endlessly [paces] back and forth in his cage reflects back negatively, through its insanity [*Irrsein*], something of humanity [*Humanität*], but not the one frolicking behind the pit too wide to leap. The antiquated beauty of Brehm's *Animal Life* stems from its way of describing animals as they are seen through the bars of a zoological garden even, and above all, when quoting reports by fanciful explorers on life in the wilds. The fact, however, that animals really suffer more in cages than in the open range, that Hagenbeck does in fact represent a step forward in humanity, reflects on the inescapability of imprisonment. (MM, 116, trans. modified)

While the 'frolicking' animals falsely affirm a freedom that is not, the caged animals in the zoo, pacing back and forth, express the nexus of the *ever same* – the fateful order of the domination of nature – in which human beings and animals are both entangled.[18] Yet, under the gaze of the human subject, who recognizes in the domesticated and enchained animal its own likeness, the animal becomes an allegory of a state of reconciled nature that is *not yet*. 'Through animals humanity [*Menschheit*] becomes aware of itself as impeded nature and of its activity as deluded natural history', Adorno writes in his book on Mahler.[19] In the preceding sentence, Adorno even speaks of the 'twisted human creature [*verkehrtes Menschenwesen*]', where *verkehrt* means both 'wrong' and 'inverted'. Twisted is the human creature because 'under the spell of the self-preservation of the species, [it] erodes its self and makes ready to annihilate the species by fatefully substituting the means for the end it has conjured away'.[20] When the gaze of the confined animal meets that of the unfree human subject, the latter may become aware of itself as also entangled in the nexus of first and second nature: in the recognition of like as like, it loosens the grip of domination over outer and inner nature. And it is at this point that, perhaps, something akin to freedom might make itself felt (see AT, 276).

The animals in the text, which, at times more prominently and at times less prominently, carry with them their cultural identity, are, akin to artworks, 'placeholders' for what they could be in a world that would *eventually be different*. Adorno thus pins his hopes for a changed relationship between nature and human history on the critical gesture of 'remembrance of nature in the subject', of which, as some of the chapters in this book, in particular Lydia Goehr's, carefully elaborate, artworks are exemplary. To some, Adorno's negative approach might speak of painful passivity when urgent agency seems to be required; to others, it might even speak of cruelty. Yet, to others still, it speaks of an incorruptible thinking that does not come to rest in false ideological certainties: the relentlessness of critique is its figure of hope (see ND, 406).

Synopsis

Puzzled by the enigmatic presence of the rhino in *Aesthetic Theory*, three of the authors of this volume formed a panel on the passage in question at 'The International Critical Theory Conference' in Rome in May of 2018. More than two years on from this conference and many intellectually stimulating discussions later, the conference papers, together with three further contributions, have grown into the book you hold in your hands. It lies in the nature of this project that the authors sometimes come across similar places in their excursions into the world of Adorno's rhinoceros. But even where places are repeatedly visited, they are approached from within different contexts and thus display different nuances.

None of the contributions solves the enigma of the rhinoceros – true enigmas, of course, can never be solved – but together they form constellations that address the relationship of art and nature, human and animal, through the lens of Adorno's critical thought. Let me introduce the chapters one by one.

The book opens with Camilla Flodin's 'In the Name of the Rhinoceros: Expression beyond Human Intention'. Flodin's essay unfolds the rhinoceros passage in *Aesthetic Theory* in the context of the work of art as *imago naturae*. She thereby relates the rhinoceros of *Aesthetic Theory* to Adorno's discussion of natural beauty, illuminating art's potential to remember the mastery over nature as well as to hold open the hope for its overcoming. Crucially, Flodin argues, the aesthetic experience which underlies the perception towards which art and animals gesture prompts self-reflection for the sake of that which does not yet exist: the true real, the right life, the being-in-itself of nature.

Antonia Hofstätter's essay, 'The Rhinoceros at the Bottom of the Sea', explores the figure of the rhinoceros in Adorno's thought and discusses Dürer's famous woodcut of the animal and the tale associated with it. Dürer's woodcut bears the memory of a rhinoceros that never was, or, rather, never was quite like this. The actual rhinoceros on which this work of art is based never made it to Europe. Tied to deck of the ship, it sank to the bottom of the sea off the Mediterranean coast near Rome. Drawing on Walter Benjamin's work on mimesis and memory, Hofstätter argues that the gruesome history behind Dürer's woodcut exemplifies the dialectic of remembrance that is theorized by Adorno as underlying all art. In Hofstätter's reading, Dürer's iconic work becomes an allegory for the history of civilization.

Lydia Goehr's essay, 'Just One Line: Reading T. W. Adorno on Humans, Artworks, and Animals', shows Adorno as a master of the genre of the 'one-liner', using it to question appearance and identity alike, and demanding second readings or a second look. Our central quotation is just one of many such one-liners. By zooming in on the figure of the rhinoceros, and against the backdrop of Adorno's discussion thereof in *Aesthetic Theory*, Goehr explores the affinities and tensions between the dialectic of art and the dialectic that shapes the relationship between human beings and animals. By taking us, in essayistic fashion, through the landscape of Adorno's texts, visiting a selection of them, Goehr shows us that any genuine 'selfhood' cannot but be mute.

In a minute and highly nuanced reading of our central passage in *Aesthetic Theory*, Alexander García Düttmann's 'The Mute Animal' also focuses on the question of the selfhood that is seemingly embodied by the rhinoceros. Düttmann reads Adorno's commendatory use of selfhood as an unfathomable gesture of coming into presence. This gesture of exposure – exemplified by the 'Here I am' or 'This is what I am' of the Etruscan vases – invokes the threshold of language that is shared by artworks and animals. Reflecting on the indissoluble tensions that structure this threshold and the violence that is proper to the moment of emergence, Düttmann reminds us that '[s]elfhood can only be had at the risk of art falling into chaos'. Taking the risk, however, the gesture of art and the shape of the rhinoceros converge in an emerging selfhood that does not congeal into identity.

Sebastian Tränkle's 'The Speaking Animal' also foregrounds the crucial role of language. Yet Tränkle takes us, at first, away from *Aesthetic Theory* and on to the distant island of Doctor Moreau to detail the surprising extent to which H. G. Wells's famous story captures the 'price of progress' that is associated with the dialectic of enlightenment. On Moreau's island, wild beasts are forcibly humanized and taught to speak; the failure of this experiment results in their reversion into bestiality. If Tränkle's reading of Wells's novel first tells us of the failed transformation of animals into humans, the second part of his essay shows us how the transformation of humans into animals 'capable of philosophical thought' might eventually redeem the price of progress.

In his 'The Gaze of the Rhinoceros and the "It" of *Aesthetic Theory*', Daniel Steuer unfolds Adorno's claim that fireworks are prototypical artworks by tracing the paradoxes that seem to proliferate throughout the text back to a theoretical impasse that originates in Adorno's vague use of the notion of secularization. The theological inheritance in the method of a negative dialectic always threatened the disintegration of Adorno's text, most forcefully in the case of *Aesthetic Theory*, where the centrifugal forces at times seem to exceed the centripetal ones. What holds such a text together can only be the material, but at the heart of the material is 'it', something that requires a particular gaze to be visible.

Daniel Herwitz's 'The Muted Animal' is concerned with the dialectic of civilization and barbarism too, but in his reading, Adorno is in the dock for extracting the rhinoceros from the wild on to the civilized pages of his writing: while intended as an illustration of the semblance of a utopian selfhood, the rhinoceros on the page of *Aesthetic Theory* becomes a figure subjected to philosophical use. Herwitz puts his finger on what is wrong with using animals as 'stand-ins' without, in his words, 'intellectual trepidation': he emphasizes the complicity of the philosopher in a colonial culture of removal or extraction. In a correction of this colonial gesture, Herwitz tells us of real animals in real situations, not in order to advocate naive realism, but to remind us of the difference between theoretical and practical encounters.

Notes

1 Theodor W. Adorno, *Aesthetic Theory*, ed. Gretel Adorno and Rolf Tiedemann, trans. Robert Hullot-Kentor (London: Continuum, 1997), 126. Hereafter cited in text as 'AT'.

2 The remains of a woolly rhinoceros – which inhabited Europe until the last ice age – found in the Austrian city of Klagenfurt in the Middle Ages were taken to be those of a dragon. See Lothar Frenz, *Nashörner: Ein Portrait* (Berlin: Matthes und Seitz, 2017), 22. Marco Polo, on his way back from China, famously mistook the rhinoceroses that inhabited the island of Java for unicorns: 'There are wild elephants in the country, and numerous unicorns, which are very nearly as big. They have hair like that of a buffalo, feet like those of an elephant, and a horn in the middle of the forehead, which is black and very thick. [...] The head resembles that of a wild boar, and they carry it ever bent towards the ground. They delight much to abide in mire and mud. 'Tis a passing ugly beast to look upon, and is not in the least like that which our stories tell of as being caught in the lap of a virgin; in fact, 'tis altogether different from what we fancied.' Marco Polo, *The Travels of Marco Polo: The Complete Yule-Cordier Edition in Two Volumes*, vol. 2 (New York: Dover Publications, 1993), 285. Umberto Eco uses this passage to illustrate the way our preconceptions make it impossible to recognize the new: '[Marco Polo] was unable to speak about the unknown but could only refer to what he already knew and expected to meet'. Umberto Eco, *Serendipities: Language and Lunacy*, trans. William Weaver (New York: Columbia University Press, 1998), 54.

3 Adorno draws on this association when he compares rhinoceroses to dinosaurs in *Negative Dialectics* (see ND, 180).

4 Adorno discusses the emancipatory aspect of 'exoticism', for instance, in his discussion of the fifth movement of Mahler's *Lied von der Erde*. Theodor W. Adorno, *Mahler: A Musical Physiognomy*, trans. Edmund Jephcott (Chicago: University of Chicago Press, 1996), 148f.

5 John Berger, 'Why Look at Animals?' in his *About Looking* (London: Bloomsbury, 2009), 3–27; here: 4–5.

6 Theodor W. Adorno, *Minima Moralia*, trans. E. F. N. Jephcott (London: Verso, 2005), 228 (trans. modified). Hereafter cited in text as 'MM'.

7 Indeed, the presence of a rhino is so strong that even a hippopotamus cannot avoid being pushed aside by it in the general imagination. Although it is a hippopotamus that figures in Bertrand Russell's famous account of his discussion with Wittgenstein, in the retelling of this anecdote the hippo frequently becomes a rhino: 'One of the earliest encounters between Bertrand Russell and the young Ludwig Wittgenstein involved a discussion about whether there was a rhinoceros in their room', begins Joseph F. McDonald's 'Russell, Wittgenstein and the Problem of the Rhinoceros', *The Southern Journal of Philosophy* 31, no. 4 (1993): 409–24; here: 409. Understandably, the Rhino Resource Center puts the article up on its website (www.rhinoresourcecenter.com).

For Russell's account, which speaks of a hippopotamus, see his obituary for Wittgenstein in *Mind* 50, no. 239 (1951): 297–8.

8   For Eva Geulen, the rhinoceros constitutes one of Adorno's striking examples that are themselves '*beispiellos*', 'unexampled', in the double sense of the German word: something at once unparalleled/incomparable/without example and 'unheard of'. This notion is necessitated, she argues, by *Aesthetic Theory*'s insistence on the 'absolute singularity' of the artwork, and hence need to 'forego examples' in any conventional sense. In her reconstruction of Adorno's notion of expression and of mimesis through the example of the rhinoceros, however, the animal becomes not so much a presence but an absence: 'One must first have said', she concludes, '"I am a rhinoceros" before one can discover that one is no such thing.' Eva Geulen, 'Without example: Adorno', in *Exemplarity and Singularity: Thinking Through Particulars in Philosophy, Literature, and Law*, ed. Michèle Lowrie and Susanne Lüdemann (London: Routledge, 2017), 58–67; here p. 58 and p. 65.

9   Britta Scholze, 'Der Schein des Glücks und das Erwachen der Phantasie', *Die Tageszeitung*, 11 August 2003 (accessed 2 March 2021), https://taz.de/!727091/. My translation.

10 Among the emerging body of literature that explores the role of animals in Adorno's work, let me just highlight Camilla Flodin's sustained and sophisticated engagement with this topic, particularly in the context of Adorno's aesthetics. For further reading on Adorno's animals – not just rhinoceroses but also other creatures – see her contribution to this volume.

11 Incidentally, the wild boar first has to forget its tameness and remember its true selfhood before taking the lady on its back and darting off into the wilderness. 'If', Adorno adds, 'I had a role model, it would be this boar'. Theodor W. Adorno, 'Amorbach', in *Gesammelte Schriften*, vol. 10.1, ed. Rolf Tiedemann (Frankfurt am Main: Suhrkamp Verlag, 1997), 303–9; here: 308.

12 For the rhinoceros passage in *Negative Dialectics*, see Theodor W. Adorno, *Negative Dialectics*, trans. E. B. Ashton (London: Routledge, 1973), 180. Hereafter cited in text as 'ND'.

13 Adorno, *Mahler*, 8

14 Letter from T. W. Adorno to Bernhard Grzimek, 23 April 1965, Theodor W. Adorno Archiv, Frankfurt am Main, Br 518/4.

15 Ibid.

16 See Walter Benjamin, *Berlin Childhood around 1900*, trans. Howard Eiland (Cambridge, MA: Harvard University Press, 2006), 98, trans. modified.

17 This comment refers to Max Horkheimer, also known to his friends as 'Max, the Mammoth'. On the role of the animal nicknames common among Adorno's friends and relatives, see Sebastian Tränkle's contribution to this volume.

18 The rhinoceros in *Negative Dialectics*, which appears to Adorno – albeit from an explicitly anthropocentric perspective – as if it were imprisoned in the 'hardware [*Apparatur*] of its survival' (ND, 180, trans. modified) is a variation of the same image.

19 Adorno, *Mahler*, 9.

20 Ibid., trans. modified.

Bibliography

Adorno, Theodor W. *Aesthetic Theory*. Edited by Gretel Adorno and Rolf Tiedemann. Translated by Robert Hullot-Kentor. London: Continuum, 1997.

Adorno, Theodor W. 'Amorbach'. In *Gesammelte Schriften*. Vol.10.1, edited by Rolf Tiedemann, 302–9. Frankfurt am Main: Suhrkamp Verlag, 1997.

Adorno, Theodor W. Letter to Bernhard Grzimek, 23 April 1965. Theodor W. Adorno Archiv, Frankfurt am Main, Br 518/4.

Adorno, Theodor W. *Mahler: A Musical Physiognomy*. Translated by Edmund Jephcott. Chicago: University of Chicago Press, 1996.

Adorno, Theodor W. *Minima Moralia*. Translated E. F. N. Jephcott. London: Verso, 2005.

Adorno, Theodor W. *Negative Dialectics*. Translated by E. B. Ashton. London: Routledge, 1973.

Benjamin, Walter. *Berlin Childhood around 1900*. Translated by Howard Eiland. Cambridge, MA: Harvard University Press, 2006.

Berger, John. 'Why Look at Animals?' In John Berger, *About Looking*, 3–28. London: Bloomsbury, 2009.

Eco, Umberto. *Serendipities: Language and Lunacy*. Translated by William Weaver. New York: Columbia University Press, 1998.

Frenz, Lothar. *Nashörner: Ein Portrait*. Berlin: Matthes und Seitz, 2017.

Geulen, Eva, 'Without example: Adorno'. In *Exemplarity and Singularity: Thinking through Particulars in Philosophy, Literature, and Law*, edited by Michèle Lowrie and Susanne Lüdemann, 58–67. London: Routledge, 2017.

McDonald, Joseph F. 'Russell, Wittgenstein and the Problem of the Rhinoceros'. *The Southern Journal of Philosophy* 31, no. 4 (1993): 409–24.

Polo, Marco. *The Travels of Marco Polo: The Complete Yule-Cordier Edition in Two Volumes*. Vol. 2. New York: Dover Publications, 1993.

Russell, Bertrand. 'Obituary: Ludwig Wittgenstein'. *Mind* 50, no. 239 (1951): 297–8.

Scholze, Britta. 'Der Schein des Glücks und das Erwachen der Phantasie'. *Die Tageszeitung*, 11 August 2003. Accessed 2 March 2021. https://taz.de/!727091/.

2

In the Name of the Rhinoceros: Expression beyond Human Intention

Camilla Flodin

Introduction

The expression that Adorno claims for the rhinoceros – 'I am a rhinoceros' – may at first glance appear to be a statement of mere group belonging and thus a denial of individuality. Indeed, interpreters have read the line as the rhinoceros's statement of itself 'as an interchangeable example of a particular species'.[1] If it was a statement of mere universality, it would be even broader, since *rhinoceros* is actually the genus, of which there are several species (more on which later). But we need to pay careful attention to the context in which this phrase appears. Adorno is in fact comparing the expression of the rhinoceros with the artwork's non-exchangeability qua work of *art*. A focus on this comparison will illuminate why Adorno looks to art to hold on to the possibility of a universal that does not turn the particular into a mere exemplar of the general – thus reducing it to an interchangeable entity – and why he insists on the importance of art's mediation of natural beauty. This will furthermore enable disclosure of the importance of animals for Adorno, something which has not received rightful attention among Adorno scholars, especially not when it comes to his aesthetics.

Art as *Imago Naturae*

Before turning to the rhinoceros, let me briefly address what I think is at stake in Adorno's conception of the relationship between art and nature, because this constitutes an important background to what Adorno is after in his one-liner – to speak with Lydia Goehr – on the rhinoceros. A common way of thinking about human progress is to perceive it as an increasing separation from nature. In contrast to other animals, humans have liberated themselves from immediate dependency on nature and created a sphere of their own: the realm of mind or spirit, *Geist*, to use the idealist vocabulary that Adorno also employs. In this process nature has in general been paired with the metaphysical idea of it as an object of manipulation and entirely exhaustible by scientific explanation. The development of aesthetics as a distinctive area of interest, accentuating other ways of relating to sensuous objects and phenomena, can thus be regarded as a corrective to the growing alienation from nature in the modern period. This does not mean, of course, that the aesthetic sphere – as a sphere of spirit or mind – is able to 'preserve' nature in an uncomplicated sense, nor indeed that every modern thinker interested in aesthetics and art unreservedly believes that this is what is at stake. There is certainly a simultaneous tendency to turn art and aesthetics into an utterly human affair – more in line with the general movement outside art: leaving nature behind in order to come into our own as modern and autonomous human beings. Adorno perceives such a tendency especially in post-Kantian aesthetics. But its seeds are there already in Kant. It was Kant's explicit aim to mediate between nature and freedom in his *Critique of the Power of Judgment*. The account of the subject's contemplative stance, when faced with beautiful natural objects that appear as purposive in themselves, instead of being determined by external laws, served as a counter to the formal description of nature in Kant's first *Critique*. In the description of the sublime, however, human reason again wields its authority over disruptive nature (at least in the sphere of ideas). Even if Adorno argues that Kant's description of the experience of the dynamic sublime registers the tension-filled relationship between humanity and nature, he is critical of Kant's claim that ultimately it is human reason that comes forward as sublime – as raised above nature – in this experience. Adorno also observes an expansion of this denial of nature in Hegel's removal of natural beauty from aesthetics,[2] and instead insists on the importance of natural beauty for aesthetics, even if it does not have the harmonious connotations it did for Kant but rather takes on the disruptive characteristics of the Kantian sublime: shaking human being to the core, revealing spirit as dependent on nature rather than nature as already spirit or completely governable by spirit.

Authentic art remembers nature, remembers *what has happened to nature*, so that what is otherwise marginalized in the process of rationalization is preserved in a mediated way. In *Aesthetic Theory*, Adorno writes:

> Every act of making in art is a singular effort to say what the artifact itself is not and what it does not know: precisely this is art's spirit. This is the locus of the idea of art as the idea of the reconstitution [*Wiederherstellung*] of nature that has been repressed and entangled in the dynamic of history. Nature, to whose imago art is devoted, does not yet in any way exist; what is true in art is something nonexistent [*Die Natur, deren imago Kunst nachhängt, ist noch gar nicht; wahr an der Kunst ein Nichtseiendes*]. What does not exist becomes incumbent on art in that other for which identity-positing reason, which reduced it to material, uses the word nature. This other is not concept and unity, but rather a multiplicity [*ein Vieles*]. Thus truth content presents itself in art as a multiplicity, not as the concept that

abstractly subordinates artworks. The bond of the truth content of art to its works and the multiplicity of what surpasses identification accord. (AT, 131/198–9, trans. modified)

That is to say, art – no matter how spiritualized – never leaves its presumed Other, nature, completely behind. This is why Adorno claims art as the self-reflection of the dialectic of enlightenment: art remembers the mastery of nature and the suffering this has involved. The manifold gathered under the concept of nature and subjugated as reason's other is given some kind of reconstitution in art – not art in the abstract (i.e. when treated as a cover concept, as in efforts to settle the ontology of art; 'what is art?' is not the interesting question for Adorno, but rather the historically imbued '*why* is art?') but only as instantiated in artworks. Nature 'on this sad earth' (AT, 68/107) does not exist yet, because it has been distorted by the process of rationalization, and thus far has been, and still is, unable to develop its full positive potential. But what exists of the ability of nature to be more than it is allowed to be in dominant theory and praxis, that is to say, more than material for reason (also as manifested in and by society) to work upon is mediated through individual artworks. To be more precise, it is mediated through their mimesis of natural beauty.

I believe that Adorno is referring to nature's *imago* here because of its multiple meanings. Psychoanalytically speaking, imago is an unconscious idealized image of a person or object.[3] In a similar way, art is devoted to nature's imago; that is to say, it remains loyal to ideal rather than real (ravaged) nature, and art does this unconsciously, non-intentionally. And when I say ideal nature, this is emphatically *not* the same as nature as an ideal – the latter is prone to cultural projections, often of the most nature-dominating kind, while ideal nature refers to the positive potential in nature, most often revealed *via negativa* through nature's suffering (which is an expression of the wrong state of things, simultaneously revealing the need and possibility for change).[4] It lies in art's historical essence – which is how Adorno comprehends its idea – to be tied to nature; and as the unconscious historical writing of suffering nature, art also holds on to a nature beyond deformation. This is his adaptation of Kant's conception of the artistic genius as a gift of nature,[5] with an eye to Schelling's further development of this idea in the conception of the artwork as the concrete manifestation of the union of conscious (intentional) human productivity and unconscious (non-intentional) natural productivity.[6] 'Imago' also evokes the theological concept of *Imago Dei*, human beings as created in the image of God, thus resembling what is highest. Following the description in the first chapter of Genesis, this has been interpreted as humans having the God-given right to exert dominion over nature.[7] For Adorno, art reverses this anthropocentric conception since what supposedly is the summit of *human* creativity – artworks – is devoted to nature's imago; as *imago naturae* art is devoted to nature qua imago (ideal) and is mimesis of nature as image (i.e. as potentially more than what is distorted by the process of rationalization), not as object.[8] Finally, in biology, imago refers to the last stage an insect attains in its metamorphosis, giving rise to its winged imago (if it is a winged species), leaving the husk behind, as is the case with butterflies.[9] The fulfilled end of art would in an analogous manner be the fulfilment of art's promise: reconciliation between humans and nature, which amounts to the realization of nature (as long as there are humans at least). This would entail that individual artworks no longer needed to be plenipotentiaries of nature's multiplicity beyond identification: 'The historical perspective that envisions the end of art is every work's idea. There is no artwork that does not promise that its truth content, to the extent that it merely appears in the artwork as something existing [*als daseiend bloß erscheint*], realizes itself and leaves the artwork behind simply as a husk, as Mignon's prodigious verse prophesies' (AT, 132/199, trans. modified). Mignon is one of the main female characters in Goethe's Bildungsroman *Wilhelm Meisters Lehrjahre*; Goethe is of course also famous for his work on metamorphosis, albeit more so for that on the plant rather than the insect kind.[10] All of these different connotations of imago give important perspectives on the relationship between art and nature. Note also the subtle difference between the passage on the imago, where Adorno speaks of 'what is true in art' as 'something nonexistent' – in other words, not yet realized – and the passage just quoted, where he speaks of the individual work's truth content merely *appearing* as something 'existing', referring to the semblance character of the artwork, which cannot be separated from its truth content. Read through the prism of the art–nature relation, the following is at stake: natural beauty points beyond the existing order of things, beyond the mastery of nature, and promises 'that which surpasses all human immanence', as Adorno phrases it in the section on natural beauty (AT, 73/114). Drawing on traditional mimetic theories of art, but also giving them a spin, Adorno claims art as the mimesis of 'natural beauty in itself [*an sich*]' and not of beautiful natural objects or phenomena (AT, 72/113, trans. modified). Art is thus the mimesis of natural beauty's 'more' qua the potential of being beyond existing human use and abuse of nature. Outside the sphere of art, nature is for the most part subdued, damaged and distorted. So, from the point of view of nature-dominating rationality, natural beauty's 'more' is illusory, as is its mediation by the artwork. It is not the case, however, that art is somehow 'pure' and its rescue of nature utterly non-violent: 'Nature is beautiful in that it appears to say more than it is. To wrest this more [*Mehr*] from that more's contingency, to gain control of its semblance [*Schein*], to determine it as semblance as well as to negate it as unreal: This is the idea of art' (AT, 78/122). Art has its own kind of violence against nature; it captures the more of natural beauty and incorporates it as a moment of something durable: the artwork. But the authentic artwork reflects on its own violence, as well as on the violence that turns nature's beauty – that is, nature as more than subjugated object – into something unreal, into something that *does not yet exist*.

Adorno also connects the durability of the artwork with language, and claims that language qua forming principle is what makes it possible for art to rescue nature: 'The mimetic impulses that motivate the artwork, that integrate themselves in it and once again disintegrate it, are fragile, speechless expression. They only become language through their objectivation as art. Art, the rescue of nature [*Rettung von Natur*], revolts against nature's transitoriness [*Vergänglichkeit*]' (AT, 184/274).[11] As 'the rescue of nature', that is, as the antithesis of the denial and mastery of nature outside art, art is *one*. It is through being works of *art* that artworks are able to protest against what the empirical domain has turned into because of the domination of nature: the sphere where everything is exchangeable, and so-called pristine nature turned into just another sellable thing in the tourist industry (see AT, 68/107). Art can only save nature through mediating it in a form that is more stable than nature's fragile and fleeting appearance as 'more', as beautiful. It is important that we do not understand beauty along the lines of classicism here, that is, as harmonious, but as containing something deeply uncanny, as indicated above. The rescue operation is thus not achieved by restraining artistic development (mastery over artistic material) – which is the process of spiritualization or rationalization operative in art – or by appealing to allegedly more harmonious artistic forms: 'Oppressed nature expresses itself more purely in works criticized as artificial, which with regard to the level of the technical forces of production, go to the extreme, than it does in circumspect works whose *parti pris* for nature is allied with the real domination of nature as is the nature lover with the hunt' (AT, 208/310). Art translates nature's speechless expression – which for Adorno is the distinctive mark of its beauty (AT, 70/110–11) – into a language that can be heard: 'Art attempts to imitate an expression that would not be interpolated human intention' (AT, 78/121). Imitating something which surpasses human intention with human means is akin to 'us[ing] the strength of the subject to break through the fallacy of constitutive subjectivity', as Adorno formulated his task in the preface to *Negative Dialectics*.[12] Of course, creating a rupture in the myth of subjectivity's foundational role in experience demands the greatest effort from the subject, in philosophy as well as in art.

The Shape I Am

Let us turn to the passage that contains the one-liner that inspires this volume:

> By virtue of its double character, language is a constituent of art and its mortal enemy. Etruscan vases in the Villa Giulia are eloquent [*sprechend*] in the highest degree and incommensurable with all communicative language. The true language of art is mute [*sprachlos*], and its muteness takes priority over poetry's significative element, which in music too is not altogether lacking. That aspect of the Etruscan vases that most resembles speech [*das Sprachähnliche*] depends most likely on their *Here I am* [*Da bin ich*] or *This is what I am* [*Das bin ich*], a selfhood [*Selbstheit*] not first excised by identificatory thought from the interdependence of entities [*Seienden*]. Thus, the rhinoceros, the mute [*stumme*] animal, seems to say: 'I am a rhinoceros.' (AT, 112/171–2)

The double character of language is its character as both sign (*Zeichen*) and image (*Bild*). As Adorno, together with Horkheimer, argues in *Dialectic of Enlightenment*, these aspects get increasingly separated in the process of rationalization: for science, language becomes arbitrary signs for identification *of* the other, while the image aspect of language – that is, its mimetic, sensuous and expressive qualities, which instead turn on identifying *with* the other – is preserved in the different arts.[13] In the passage above, Adorno likens the non-exchangeability of artworks to the non-exchangeability of the rhinoceros. He does this by comparing the true language of art with the expression of the rhinoceros and contrasting both with discursive, communicative language. While communicative language efficiently transports *something* to a recipient, mimetic language is more akin to the language of the things themselves. It is, as Adorno formulates it in his essay on Hölderlin, the 'eloquence of something that has no language [*Beredtheit eines Sprachlosen*]'.[14] Of course, the language of things themselves cannot be immediately comprehended; Adorno nevertheless suggests that this is the language that artworks intimate. The language of things is their 'more', their pointing beyond human immanence, beyond human intention and determination; it is their expression of being *more than mere things*. That is to say, beautiful – and uncannily so, because we are also reminded of their suffering under the reduction of them to mere things by conventional language and nature-dominating society.

What is conceived as beautiful is surely subject to historical change, but this does not mean that natural beauty is merely subjective: the 'more' of natural beauty is an 'objective expression', dependent on the recipient subject but not 'reducible' to it (AT, 71/111). Furthermore, Adorno also makes the connection to a possible non-human language: 'With human means art wants to realize the language of what is not human' (AT, 78/121). And he argues that 'art seeks to make nature's muteness eloquent' (AT, 78/121). Art can only do this through a mimesis of nature's muteness, not by forcing its own language, its forming principles, on nature. Instead, art must follow nature; it must heed the preponderance of nature if it is to stay true to its (historically formed) concept and not succumb to the domination of nature that dominates the world outside art. This domination has had very real consequences. It has muted and mutilated nature, and for that reason, art cannot claim access to a non-muted, unmutilated nature. In order to bear witness to nature's mutilation, art follows nature's muteness. Nature speaks a language other than the one that has come to count as language, and art is the mimesis of that other eloquence. Language is usually taken to imply unrestricted means of expression and characterized by being symbolic (using words, signs or gestures that stand for something other than themselves), arbitrary (the connection between the sign and what it refers to is wholly arbitrary) and conventional (we have agreed upon what these arbitrary signs stand for). Language as such a system of communication is regarded as 'species-specific to human beings'.[15] When Adorno claims that '[t]he true language of art is mute' (or actually *sprachlos*: speechless, without language) I think what he is implying is the following: the language of art is a critique of how language has come to be defined outside art (symbolic, arbitrary, conventional), and it is a critique of the view that language thus defined implies unrestricted means of expression. In other words, art remembers that language is not a strictly human affair, but in a sense, a natural gift. This is one aspect of *art as the remembrance of nature*, which is a core feature of Adorno's aesthetics. The true language of art is a mimesis of the expressiveness of nature and nature's creatures, such as the rhinoceros. The rhinoceros does not in fact speak, but it is *as if* it speaks, 'a rhinoceros *seems* [*scheint*] *to say*: 'I am a rhinoceros.'[16] The rhino does not say this in the conventional way, of course, but its whole being *is* this expression (non-symbolic, non-arbitrary, non-conventional – in other words, *beyond human intention*). The difficulty for artworks is that they have to stay true to muteness at the same time as they have to mediate it with artistic means; an artwork has to be recognizable as such and has to have a certain durability.[17] Thus, an 'element [*Moment*] of universality' is necessary (AT, 219/325). The true language of art, however, is a language not of stable judgement, but of elusive gesture, of wordless expression. 'Even in linguistic works', Adorno claims, the binding force is 'wordless' (AT, 184/274). Although a poem is made up of words in the common language (a poem cannot be written in an utterly private language, at least not wholly), what makes a poem eloquent is not the same thing that makes language, used in the ordinary way, expressive. What binds the words of a poem together, making the poem a work of art, is not primarily what they communicate qua language, but the fact that it is precisely *these* words, in *this* constellation, creating *these* sensuous-mimetic interconnections that are otherwise disregarded for the sake of arbitrariness and generality – showing us that what we humans regard as maximum expressiveness (outside art) is not the same as truly being open to the world (the way animals are for Rilke).

Since what Adorno is after is the persuasiveness of the artwork, which he connects to *selfhood*, in other words, *appearance beyond mere objecthood*, the

'Here I am' does not quite capture 'Da bin ich.' 'Here I am' is how Abraham answers God when God calls for him: 'Hier bin ich'; 'Here I am.'[18] But the rhinoceros's 'Da bin ich' is not an answer to a call. It is an expression, stating: here *I* am. This is not telling anyone where they can find me ('here'). 'Da bin ich' suggests rather '*this* is what I am'. It is, as Adorno points out, a presence that precedes identificatory thought, a selfhood 'beyond human immanence'. I announce myself: I am a rhinoceros. That is what the rhino seems to tell us, making itself present. As Alexander García Düttman, Daniel Steuer, Lydia Goehr and Antonia Hofstätter also point out in their chapters in this volume, this is not a 'pure selfhood' separated from its context – something which Adorno criticizes in *Negative Dialectics* (ND, 162/165) – but precisely a relational selfhood, hence the stress on the 'interdependence of entities', from which identification and subsumption abstract.

If the passage from *Aesthetic Theory* is put into conjunction with the strikingly similar phrasing on the rhinoceros's behalf in *Minima Moralia*, the possibility of bringing together the non-exchangeability of the artwork with the expression of the name as stating a self-identity beyond identificatory thought emerges.[19] In the aphorism 'Toy shop' Adorno writes:

> The unreality of games [*Spiele*] gives notice that reality is not yet real. Unconsciously they rehearse the right life. The relation of children to animals depends entirely on the fact that Utopia is wrapped up [*vermummt*] in the creatures whom Marx even begrudged the surplus value they contribute as workers. By existing without any purpose recognizable to men, animals present as expression, as it were, their own names, that which is utterly impossible to exchange. This makes them so beloved by children, their contemplation [*Betrachtung*] so blissful. I am a rhinoceros, is what the shape [*Figur*] of the rhinoceros means [*bedeutet*].[20]

The name is impossible to exchange because it is not an abstraction; it is not a classification under which you are sorted as a substitutable thing, like a mere exemplar of a genus or species.[21] To be able to glimpse the rhinoceros's expression of its uniqueness, of not being identical to any definition put forward by human beings – thus pointing 'beyond human immanence' – demands a certain distance. That is why we need the change of perspective that art or (child's) play is able to provide. We need another approach than the subsuming, identificatory one in order to catch a glimpse of utopia. The change of perspective allows us to hear the mute expression 'I am a rhinoceros', in which 'rhinoceros' points beyond what the animal has been turned into by us: objectified as an entertaining or killable thing. This unsettling of the habitual attitude towards non-human animals allows grown-ups to remember the wordless mutual understanding, *das sprachlose Einverständnis*, between children and animals, as well as the human being's likeness to animals (*Tierähnlichkeit*) (AT, 119/182). The changed perspective renders it possible for us to perceive 'rhinoceros' as beyond a mere universal and abstract *cover concept* for domination. Thus, through the change of perspective that art and play offer, *Nashorn*, rhinoceros – literally 'nose-horned', from the Greek *rhinokeros* (*rhinos*, 'nose', and *keras*, 'horn of an animal')[22] – appears not as an arbitrary sign made up by humans merely for purposes of identification and classification, but as a unique *name*, expressed by the shape of each individual rhinoceros. In this way, the 'I am a rhinoceros' reminds subjective thought of its dependence on that which it encounters, and can thus be said to constitute 'the model of experience', similar to the one Adorno describes in *Negative Dialectics* when discussing the possibility of metaphysical experience (again, with reference to childhood):

> To the child it is obvious that what delights it about its favorite small town is to be found only there, there alone and nowhere else; it errs, but its error creates [*stiftet*] the model of experience, that of a concept, which finally would be that of the thing [*Sache*] itself, not the poverty of that which is removed from things. [...] Solely in light of what is absolutely, indissolubly

individualized is it to be hoped, that this is how it already was and would be; only by complying with [*nachzukommen*] this, would the concept of the concept be fulfilled. (ND, 373–4/366, trans. modified)

Further guidance as to what Adorno is after with his claim that the shape of the rhinoceros means 'I am a rhinoceros' is offered by the passage from *Minima Moralia* referred to earlier, together with an episode from Lewis Carroll's *Through the Looking-Glass and What Alice Found There* (1871) – the sequel to *Alice's Adventures in Wonderland* (1865). Indeed, Adorno himself can be said to guide us in this direction, because in a previous aphorism he writes about the truth content in children's books such as *Alice* (see MM, 161/172–3).[23] In *Through the Looking-Glass*, Alice meets the egg-shaped Humpty Dumpty, who asks for her name:

'My *name* is Alice, but –'
'It's a stupid name enough!' Humpty Dumpty interrupted impatiently. 'What does it mean?'
'*Must* a name mean something?' Alice asked doubtfully.
'Of course it must', Humpty Dumpty said with a short laugh: '*my* name means the shape I am – and a good handsome shape it is, too. With a name like yours, you might be any shape, almost.'[24]

'*Must* a name mean something?' – Alice's question to Humpty Dumpty is crucial for Adorno's conception of the rhinoceros as well. If the rhinoceros seemed to say 'I am Steve' – yes, scholars have actually suggested to me that this would be a better way of stating the rhino's uniqueness – it would be ridiculous. Steve is a name for a human ('It's a stupid name enough!'). It is furthermore not tied to the individual other than through a symbolic rite (name-giving, baptism); as such, it is an empty sign, even though it of course can be meaningful to the individual and his or her relatives (for example, it might be the name of the individual human being's grandfather as well). I do not deny that the name 'Steve' also has an interesting etymology, being the shortened form of the Latin *Stephanus*, which goes back to the Greek name *Stephanos*, which in its turn stems from *stephanos*, 'crown, wreath, garland, chaplet, crown of victory'.[25] But the name itself does not *mean* anything the way 'rhinoceros' means something in expressing something fundamental about the rhino, tied as it is to the physiognomy of its bearer; as with Humpty Dumpty, the name of the rhinoceros *means* the shape it is.[26] To have a proper name is furthermore no guarantee that you will not be treated as property (and thus be exchangeable). In order not to be treated as exchangeable property, you need protection from a universal (an emphatic universal): 'I am a human being' implies a demand to be treated with respect for the person that you are qua member of the species *homo sapiens*. Adorno's utopia is that 'rhinoceros' – and the names of other genera and species, along with the even more universal 'animal' – in a similar way would entail the demand to be treated with respect for a selfhood that, while not identical to the personhood of human beings, still would amount to a demand for the freedom to flourish. This is why the claim 'it is "only an animal"' haunts us; we know it is not true, not 'even of animals' (MM, 113/118).[27] 'I am a rhinoceros' is the plenipotentiary (*Statthalter*) for the possibility of a world where 'animal' would no longer be an insult, but the opposite, where 'animal' would no longer imply moving property – live*stock* – nor moving target. (Adorno is not playing *that* game.) For Adorno, the revaluation of non-human animals is a necessary condition for the possibility of the human animal to truly come into her own.

The contemplative mode which characterizes aesthetic comportment has critical potential because it constitutes a change of perspective: it resists the dominant and dominating behaviour towards non-human animals and nature. As Adorno claims in another aphorism in *Minima Moralia*, the urge to devour the object is broken off by 'the long, contemplative gaze' (MM, 88/100 trans. modified). The contemplative gaze is not an aesthetic attitude that the individual subject may apply at will; it is something that the expressions of the artwork and the animal demand because both the artwork and the animal are looking back at you. This is also implied by their expressiveness.

Animal Gaze

Immediately after the comparison between the expressiveness of the Etruscan vases and of the rhinoceros, Adorno continues elaborating on the way artworks look at you and demand something from you, and he approvingly – as Daniel Steuer and Lydia Goehr also highlight in their respective contributions to this volume – quotes Rilke's line 'denn da ist keine Stelle, / die dich nicht sieht' ('for here there is no place / that does not see you') from 'Archaic Torso of Apollo' (I follow Goehr's and Steuer's translations). Adorno did not always appreciate Rilke, but here he is quite enthusiastic, claiming that this line 'codified the nonsignificative language of artworks in almost incomparable fashion [*kaum übertroffener Weise*]: Expression is the gaze of artworks' (AT 112/172, trans. modified).

Even if, as Goehr highlights in her contribution, the gazes of both artworks and animals wordlessly reflect human barbarism, their gazes also hold utopian potential. I would like to emphasize again that what is at stake in the expression of the rhinoceros is quite the opposite of stating a generic belonging for the sake of ordering things. In just the same way, an artwork's reflection on itself as art – that is, its acknowledgement of being semblance, fiction, unreal (from the point of view of what has come to count as real: the nature-dominating world outside art) – is not for the sake of ordering the work under a universal abstract concept. The artwork *seems to be* beyond reification, beyond exchangeability, through being a work of *art*, that is, through being without external purpose and constituting an end in itself (Adorno agrees with

Kant here). But being 'more', being beyond exchangeability, is of course an illusion, the unreality of which the artwork must expose through including a self-reflective moment, acknowledging itself as art while never abandoning its character as semblance. It must do this for the sake of that which does not yet exist: the true real, the right life, the being-in-itself of nature.[28] In other words, art must perform this balancing act for the sake of a different kind of unity: a universal or a unity which does not subjugate particulars, which does not reduce the multiplicity of the world. Art must do this in order to hold open a space for '[a] togetherness of diversity [*ein Miteinander des Verschiedenen*]', as Adorno writes regarding utopia in *Negative Dialectics* (ND, 150/153). The synthesis of the artwork through aesthetic form is still, despite everything, an intimation of this utopia, a model of reconciliation in the sphere of semblance, in that it 'appears as though it had done no violence but had been chosen by the multiplicitous itself' (AT, 134/202). For what would we humans be without non-human others to see us? Without their presence, becoming human and humane would not be possible. In contrast to what Sebastian Tränkle argues in this volume, I don't think that Adorno's remark about animals seemingly mourning that they are not human (AT, 113/172) points to a wish to liberate them from the spell of 'first nature'.[29] What Adorno is after is the possibility of salvaging them from their imprisonment in current anthropogenic second nature, which includes the idea of animals as 'mere' animals: as absolutely dumb, purposeless, bestial. A human being should strive to be 'a good animal', as he writes in *Negative Dialectics* (ND, 299/294), not an animal who makes other animals mourn that they are not human beings because we continually mark our difference from them in order to legitimize our sway over them. The mourning of animals is not absolute – that would be a foreign idea for a dialectician of Adorno's rank – it is a response to our historical and ongoing abuse of them. It is what we see, and will continue to see, in their eyes, as long as we fail to acknowledge our affinity with them, and manifest it also at the level of social practice.

Coda

The diversity in our world is, as we all know, drastically decreasing. We live in the time of the sixth mass extinction, this one caused by us humans.[30] We are dangerously close to a future where no one will be able to encounter the expression of a living rhinoceros anymore. Of five existing species of rhinoceros – white, black, greater one-horned, Sumatran and Javan – three are critically endangered: the black (consisting of four subspecies, one of which was declared extinct in 2011), the Sumatran and the Javan rhinoceros. The greater one-horned rhino is listed as vulnerable.[31] The white rhinoceros is divided into the southern and northern subspecies, and on 19 March 2018, the last male northern white rhino died at the age of forty-five. (He was euthanized, because he had been suffering from age-related health issues.) His given name was Sudan (after his country of birth). Only two females of the species still exist, Sudan's daughter, Najin, and her daughter, Sudan's granddaughter, Fatu. Born in 1973 in what is now South Sudan, the rhino Sudan was captured at a very young age and spent most of his life in a zoo in the Czech Republic. In 2009, he was moved to a wildlife conservation area in Kenya together with Najin and Fatu. Protected day and night against poachers, he spent his remaining days there.[32] Now, the only hope to save the subspecies is in vitro fertilization and surrogate gestation (as both Fatu and Najin are considered unfit for pregnancy).[33] There might still be time to mitigate this sixth great extinction and to justify the name we have given our own species: *homo sapiens*.[34]

Speculatively, the mute or, for that matter, sounding but non-communicative artwork seems to say 'I am an artwork' – not a pipe, not even a rhinoceros, but a piece of *art*: unique, non-exchangeable, belonging to a universal which is not the sum of all particulars but an idea, historical in origin. And as a historically developed idea art is for the sake of another; it is non-exchangeable for the sake of another who is not yet: nature. In the same way, Adorno's rhinoceros seems to say 'I am a rhinoceros' for the sake of others who are not yet free to do so, who are still hunted, or entrapped in zoos and laboratories, in the whole animal industrial complex. A plenipotentiary. A utopian animal, gazing at you.

Notes

1. Eva Geulen, 'Without example: Adorno', in *Exemplarity and Singularity: Thinking Through Particulars in Philosophy, Literature, and Law*, ed. Michèle Lowry and Susanne Lüdemann (London: Routledge, 2017), 63.

2. See Theodor W. Adorno, *Aesthetic Theory*, trans. and ed. Robert Hullot-Kentor (London: Continuum, 1997), 62; *Ästhetische Theorie*, in *Gesammelte Schriften*, vol. 7, ed. Rolf Tiedemann (Frankfurt am Main: Suhrkamp, 2003), 98–9. Hereafter cited in text as 'AT'. Page numbers, separated by a slash, will refer first to the English translation, then to the German original.

3. Entry 'imago' in Andrew M. Colman, *A Dictionary of Psychology*, 3rd edn. (Oxford: Oxford University Press, 2008). It was Jung who introduced the concept.

4. On this topic, see my 'Of Mice and Men: Adorno on Art and the Suffering of Animals', *Estetika: The Central European Journal of Aesthetics* 48, no. 2 (2011): 139–56 and 'The Wor(l)d of the Animal: Adorno on Art's Expression of Suffering', *Journal of Aesthetics & Culture* 3, no. 1 (2011), https://doi.org/10.3402/jac.v3i0.7987.

5. Immanuel Kant, *Critique of the Power of Judgment*, ed. Paul Guyer, trans. Paul Guyer and Eric Matthews (Cambridge: Cambridge University Press, 2000), 186 (§46) [Akademie-Ausgabe 5:307].

6. F. W. J. Schelling, *System of Transcendental Idealism*, trans. Peter Heath (Charlottesville: University Press of Virginia, 1978), 225; *System des transzendentalen Idealismus*, in *Sämmtliche Werke*, ed. K. F. A. Schelling, vol. I/3 (Stuttgart: Cotta, 1858), 619. For more on the connection between Adorno and Schelling in this regard, see Camilla Flodin, 'Adorno and Schelling on the Art–Nature Relation', *British Journal for the History of Philosophy* 26, no. 1 (2018): 176–96, doi: 10.1080/09608788.2017.1349648.

7. Gen. 1.26–8.

8. 'Like the experience of art, the aesthetic experience of nature is that of images. Nature, as appearing beauty [*Natur als erscheinendes Schönes*] is not perceived as an object of action [*Aktionsobjekt*]' (AT, 65/103). Because nature as beautiful already is image, it 'cannot be copied'; the mere imitation of beautiful nature reduces it to an object (AT, 67/105).

9. Marie L. Thompson, 'Butterflies', in *The Gale Encyclopedia of Science*, 3rd edn, ed. K. Lee Lerner and Brenda Wilmoth Lerner, vol. 1 (Detroit, MI: Gale, 2004), 651–4.

10   However, see Goethe's early entomological studies from 1796, where he describes experiments with butterflies, or, to be specific, moths (he classifies them as 'Schmetterlinge', and names the species as *Phalaena grossularia*, which is nowadays called *Abraxas grossulariata*, or the magpie moth), in different stages of development, including how he decapitates one of them just when it emerges from its shell (chrysalis). Goethe, *Die Schriften zur Naturwissenschaft*, ed. Dorothea Kuhn, vol. I:10 (Weimar: Böhlau, 1964), 170. As Eva Geulen has pointed out, this is quite far from his 'tender empiricism' (*zarte Empirie*) emphasized elsewhere. *Aus dem Leben der Form: Goethes Morphologie und die Nager* (Berlin: August, 2016), 31–3.

11   For another perspective on this quote, see Antonia Hofstätter's piece in this volume.

12   Theodor W. Adorno, *Negative Dialectics*, trans. E. B. Ashton (London: Routledge, 1990), xx; *Negative Dialektik*, in *Gesammelte Schriften*, vol. 6, ed. Rolf Tiedemann (Frankfurt am Main: Suhrkamp, 2003), 10. Hereafter cited in text as 'ND'. Page numbers, separated by a slash, will refer first to the English translation, then to the German original.

13   Max Horkheimer and Theodor W. Adorno, *Dialectic of Enlightenment: Philosophical Fragments*, ed. Gunzelin Schmid Noerr, trans. Edmund Jephcott (Stanford: Stanford University Press, 2002), 12–13; *Dialektik der Aufklärung: Philosophische Fragmente*, in Theodor W. Adorno, *Gesammelte Schriften*, vol. 3, ed. Rolf Tiedemann (Frankfurt am Main: Suhrkamp, 2003), 34. Hereafter cited in text as 'DE'. Page numbers, separated by a slash, will refer first to the English translation, then to the German original. For Adorno's description of mimesis as identifying *with* the other, see Theodor W. Adorno, *Lectures on Negative Dialectics: Fragments of a Lecture Course 1965/1966*, ed. Rolf Tiedemann, trans. Rodney Livingstone (Cambridge: Polity, 2008), 92; *Vorlesung über Negative Dialektik: Fragmente zur Vorlesung 1965/66*, in *Nachgelassene Schriften*, div. IV, vol. 16, ed. Rolf Tiedemann (Frankfurt am Main: Suhrkamp, 2007), 135.

14   Theodor W. Adorno, 'Parataxis: On Hölderlin's Late Poetry', in *Notes to Literature*, vol. 2, ed. Rolf Tiedemann, trans. Shierry Weber Nicholsen (New York: Columbia University Press, 1992), 112; 'Parataxis: Zur späten Lyrik Hölderlins', in *Noten zur Literatur*, *Gesammelte Schriften*, vol. 11, ed. Rolf Tiedemann (Frankfurt am Main: Suhrkamp, 2003), 450. I discuss Adorno's reading of Hölderlin in Flodin, '"The eloquence of something that has no language": Adorno on Hölderlin's Late Poetry', *Adorno Studies* 2, no. 1 (2018): 1–28, http://adornostudies.org/ojs/index.php/as/article/view/21.

15   David Crystal and Robert Henry Robins, 'Language', *Encyclopedia Britannica* (website), 29 October 2020, https://www.britannica.com/topic/language.

16   My italics.

17   An artwork indeed stands for something other than itself, and in some way this could be said to constitute a resemblance to language as well, but an artwork is a plenipotentiary (*Statthalter*) of the reconciliation between humans and nature, so it is a *stand-in-for* in a very specific, non-arbitrary way. It should also be stressed

that Adorno is critical of interpreting artworks as symbols along the lines of religious symbols: 'No existing, appearing artwork holds any positive control over the nonexisting. This distinguishes artworks from religious symbols, which in their appearance lay claim to the transcendence of the immediately present. The nonexisting in artworks is a constellation of the existing' (AT, 135/204).

18   Gen. 22.1.

19   Oshrat C. Silberbusch reflects on both of these rhino passages in an illuminating way that also focuses on the rhino's resistance to subjugation, albeit from the guiding perspective of the non-identical. See her *Adorno's Philosophy of the Nonidentical: Thinking as Resistance* (Basingstoke: Palgrave MacMillan, 2018), 154–9.

20   Theodor W. Adorno, *Minima Moralia: Reflections from Damaged Life*, trans. E. F. N. Jephcott (London: Verso, 2005), 242–3, trans. modified on the basis of Daniel Steuer's and Lydia Goehr's translations of parts of the same passage in their respective pieces for this volume; *Minima Moralia: Reflexionen aus dem beschädigten Leben*, in *Gesammelte Schriften*, vol. 4, ed. Rolf Tiedemann (Frankfurt am Main: Suhrkamp, 2003), 260–1. Hereafter cited in text as 'MM'. Page numbers, separated by a slash, will refer first to the English translation, then to the German original. On the connection between children, animals and art, see also AT, 119/182. I discuss this further in my 'Adorno's Utopian Animals', in *The Future of Critical Theory*, ed. Anders Bartonek and Sven-Olov Wallenstein (Huddinge: Södertörn University Press, 2021).

21   The way the rabbit is reduced to 'a mere exemplar' in the laboratory (DE, 7/26).

22   Entry 'rhinoceros (n.)', Online Etymology Dictionary, accessed 15 December 2020, https://www.etymonline.com/word/rhinoceros.

23   For discussion, see Flodin, 'Adorno's Utopian Animals'.

24   Lewis Carroll, *Through the Looking-Glass and What Alice Found There*, in *The Annotated Alice: The Definitive Edition* (New York and London: W. W. Norton & Company, 2000), 208. Thanks to Elisabeth Friis for reminding me of this episode.

25   'Stephen', Online Etymology Dictionary, accessed 15 December 2020, https://www.etymonline.com/word/stephen.

26   Interestingly, given Adorno's comparison between the expression of the Etruscan vases and the rhino's expression, there once was a rhino species called the Etruscan rhinoceros (classified by the Scottish palaeontologist Hugh Falconer in 1868), and even if this might be taking it a bit far – still I cannot resist it – its Latin name (with Greek origins) is *Stephanorhinos etruscus*, thus combining 'Stephanos' and 'rhinos' so that we may in fact *have had* a rhino saying 'I am Steve', or, physiognomically speaking, 'I am nose-crowned'. And just as with today's rhinoceros, the Stephanorhinos was a genus consisting of several species. See Luca Pandolfi and Carmelo Petronio, '*Stephanorhinus etruscus* (Falconer 1868) from Pirro Nord (Apricena, Foggia, Southern Italy) with Notes on the Other late Early Pleistocene Rhinoceros Remains of Italy', *Rivista Italiana di Paleontologia e Stratigrafia* 117, no.

1 (2011): 173–87. The Etruscan rhino was a Eurasian species that lived from the Late Pliocene (around 3.5 million years ago) to the early Late Pleistocene, and it 'survived in Italy and the Iberian Peninsula until the early-middle Galerian transition (early-middle Pleistocene transition)', that is, until ca. 1.2 million to 500,000 years ago. See Luca Pandolfi, Esperanza Cerdeño, Vlad Codrea and Tassos Kotsakis, 'Biogeography and Chronology of the Eurasian Extinct Rhinoceros *Stephanorhinus etruscus* (Mammalia, Rhinocerotidae)', *Comptes Rendus Palevol* 16 (2017): 771, http://dx.doi.org/10.1016/j.crpv.2017.06.004. The Etruscan rhino was similar in size to today's white rhino.

27 For more on Adorno's conception of animals, along with his criticism of Kant in this regard, see Flodin, 'Adorno's Utopian Animals'.

28 Adorno describes aesthetic objectivity as 'the reflection of the being-in-itself of nature', and he claims that '[t]he being-in-itself to which artworks are devoted is not the imitation of something real but rather the anticipation of a being-in-itself that does not yet exist' (AT, 77/120–1).

29 I discuss this remark further in 'Adorno's Utopian Animals'.

30 For an equally illuminating and distressing account, see Elizabeth Kolbert, *The Sixth Extinction: An Unnatural History* (New York: Henry Holt and Company, 2014).

31 'The IUCN Red List of Threatened Species', Version 2020–1, International Union for Conservation of Nature, accessed 15 December 2020, https://www.iucnredlist.org/search?query=Rhinoceroses&searchType=species. Thanks to conservation efforts, the black rhino population has seen a slow increase during the last years, see 'Conservation Efforts Bring Cautious Hope for African Rhinos – IUCN Red List', International Union for Conservation of Nature, 19 March 2020 (accessed 15 December 2020), https://www.iucn.org/news/species/202003/conservation-efforts-bring-cautious-hope-african-rhinos-iucn-red-list.

32 'Northern white rhino: Last Male Sudan Dies in Kenya', *BBC News*, 20 March 2018 (accessed 15 December 2020), https://www.bbc.com/news/world-africa-43468066.

33 Clare Spencer, 'Northern White Rhinos: The Audacious Plan That Could Save a Species', 14 April 2020 (accessed 15 April 2020), https://www.bbc.com/news/world-africa-52228181.

34 See also Flodin, 'Adorno's Utopian Animals'.

Bibliography

Adorno, Theodor W. *Aesthetic Theory*. Edited by Gretel Adorno and Rolf Tiedemann. Translated by Robert Hullot-Kentor. London: Continuum, 1997.

Adorno, Theodor W. *Gesammelte Schriften*. Edited by Rolf Tiedemann in cooperation with Gretel Adorno, Susan Buck-Morss and Klaus Schultz. 20 vols. Frankfurt am Main: Suhrkamp, 2003.

Adorno, Theodor W. *Lectures on Negative Dialectics: Fragments of a Lecture Course 1965/1966*. Edited by Rolf Tiedemann. Translated by Rodney Livingstone. Cambridge: Polity, 2008.

Adorno, Theodor W. *Minima Moralia: Reflections from Damaged Life*. Translated by E. F. N. Jephcott. London: Verso, 2005.

Adorno, Theodor W. *Negative Dialectics*. Translated by E. B Ashton. London: Routledge, 1990.

Adorno, Theodor W. 'Parataxis: On Hölderlin's Late Poetry'. In vol. 2 of *Notes to Literature*, translated by Shierry Weber Nicholsen and edited by Rolf Tiedemann, 109–49. New York: Columbia University Press, 1992.

Adorno, Theodor W. *Vorlesung über Negative Dialektik: Fragmente zur Vorlesung 1965/66*. In *Nachgelassene Schriften*. Div. IV. Vol. 16, edited by Rolf Tiedemann. Frankfurt am Main: Suhrkamp, 2007.

Carroll, Lewis. *Through the Looking-Glass and What Alice Found There*. In *The Annotated Alice: The Definitive Edition*. New York and London: W. W. Norton & Company, 2000.

Colman, Andrew M. *A Dictionary of Psychology*. 3rd edn. Oxford: Oxford University Press, 2008.

'Conservation Efforts Bring Cautious Hope for African Rhinos – IUCN Red List'. International Union for Conservation of Nature. 19 March 2020 (accessed 15 December 2020). https://www.iucn.org/news/species/202003/conservation-efforts-bring-cautious-hope-african-rhinos-iucn-red-list.

Crystal, David, and Robert Henry Robins. 'Language'. *Encyclopedia Britannica* (website). 29 October 2020. https://www.britannica.com/topic/language.

Flodin, Camilla. 'Adorno and Schelling on the Art–Nature Relation'. *British Journal for the History of Philosophy* 26, no. 1 (2018): 176–96. DOI: 10.1080/09608788.2017.1349648.

Flodin, Camilla. 'Adorno's Utopian Animals'. In *The Future of Critical Theory*, edited by Anders Bartonek and Sven-Olov Wallenstein, 103–17. Huddinge: Södertörn University Press, 2021.

Flodin, Camilla. '"The eloquence of something that has no language": Adorno on Hölderlin's Late Poetry'. *Adorno Studies* 2, no. 1 (2018): 1–28. http://adornostudies.org/ojs/index.php/as/article/view/21.

Flodin, Camilla. 'Of Mice and Men: Adorno on Art and the Suffering of Animals'. *Estetika: The Central European Journal of Aesthetics* 48, no. 2 (2011): 139–56.

Flodin, Camilla. 'The Wor(l)d of the Animal: Adorno on Art's Expression of Suffering'. *Journal of Aesthetics & Culture* 3, no. 1 (2011). https://doi.org/10.3402/jac.v3i0.7987.

Geulen, Eva. *Aus dem Leben der Form: Goethes Morphologie und die Nager*. Berlin: August, 2016.

Geulen, Eva. 'Without example: Adorno'. In *Examplarity and Singularity: Thinking Trough Particulars in Philosophy, Literature, and Law*, edited by Michèle Lowry and Susanne Lüdemann, 58–67. London: Routledge, 2017.

Goethe, Johann Wolfgang von. *Die Schriften zur Naturwissenschaft*. Vol. I:10. Edited by Dorothea Kuhn. Weimar: Böhlau, 1964.

Horkheimer, Max, and Theodor W. Adorno. *Dialectic of Enlightenment: Philosophical Fragments*. Edited by Gunzelin Schmid Noerr. Translated by Edmund Jephcott. Stanford: Stanford University Press, 2002.

'The IUCN Red List of Threatened Species', Version 2020-1, International Union for Conservation of Nature, accessed 15 December 2020, https://www.iucnredlist.org/search?query=Rhinoceroses&searchType=species.

Kant, Immanuel. *Critique of the Power of Judgment*. Edited by Paul Guyer. Translated by Paul Guyer and Eric Matthews. Cambridge: Cambridge University Press, 2000.

Kolbert, Elizabeth. *The Sixth Extinction: An Unnatural History*. New York: Henry Holt and Company, 2014.

'Northern White Rhino: Last Male Sudan Dies in Kenya', 20 March 2018. Accessed 15 December 2020. https://www.bbc.com/news/world-africa-43468066.

Pandolfi, Luca, and Carmelo Petronio. '*Stephanorhinus etruscus* (Falconer 1868) from Pirro Nord (Apricena, Foggia, Southern Italy) with Notes on the Other late Early Pleistocene Rhinoceros Remains of Italy'. *Rivista Italiana di Paleontologia e Stratigrafia* 117, no. 1 (2011): 173-87.

Pandolfi, Luca, Esperanza Cerdeño, Vlad Codrea, and Tassos Kotsakis. 'Biogeography and Chronology of the Eurasian Extinct Rhinoceros *Stephanorhinus etruscus* (Mammalia, Rhinocerotidae)'. *Comptes Rendus Palevol* 16 (2017): 762-73. http://dx.doi.org/10.1016/j.crpv.2017.06.004.

'rhinoceros (n.)'. Online Etymology Dictionary. Accessed 15 December 2020. https://www.etymonline.com/word/rhinoceros.

Schelling, F. W. J. *System des transzendentalen Idealismus*. In *Sämmtliche Werke*, edited by K. F. A. Schelling, vol. I/3. Stuttgart: Cotta, 1858.

Schelling, F. W. J. *System of Transcendental Idealism*. Translated by Peter Heath. Charlottesville: University Press of Virginia, 1978.

Silberbusch, Oshrat C. *Adorno's Philosophy of the Nonidentical: Thinking as Resistance*. Basingstoke, Hampshire: Palgrave Macmillan, 2018.

Spencer, Clare. 'Northern White Rhinos: The Audacious Plan That Could Save a Species'. 14 April 2020. Accessed 15 December 2020. https://www.bbc.com/news/world-africa-52228181.

'Stephen'. Online Etymology Dictionary. Accessed 15 December 2020. https://www.etymonline.com/word/stephen.

Thompson, Marie L. 'Butterflies'. In *The Gale Encyclopedia of Science*, 3rd ed., edited by K. Lee Lerner and Brenda Wilmoth Lerner, 651-4. Vol. 1. Detroit, MI: Gale, 2004.

FIGURE 2 *Rhinoceros, 1515. Albrecht Dürer. Public domain. Wikimedia Commons*

3

The Rhinoceros at the Bottom of the Sea: Adorno, Dürer and the Silent Eloquence of Artworks

Antonia Hofstätter

I

'I am a rhinoceros.'[1] – When reflecting on the strange selfhood that Adorno attributes in his *Aesthetic Theory* not only to artworks but also to the expression of the rhinoceros, it is almost impossible not to think of the famous Dürer woodcut from 1515. 'I am a rhinoceros', the rhinoceros in Dürer's piece seems to say. And who would care, or even dare, to doubt it? The inscription on the woodcut reads as follows: 'On the first of May in the year AD 1513, the powerful King of Portugal, Manuel of Lisbon, was brought such a living animal from India. They call it the rhinoceros. This is an accurate representation.' Yet Dürer's insistence on accuracy is immediately put into question by the rhinoceros's wondrous strangeness: indeed, it seems less like an animal that one would encounter in the wilderness (or in the zoo, for that matter) and more like a dragon or a mythical reptile. Its legs are covered in scales, and so is the lower part of its face. The encrustations, on the upper part of its face, of what seem to be layers of dead, hardened and cracked skin are suggestive of an archaic creature that has come to greet us from ancient times. And yet the rhinoceros's bulky body is enclosed in what appear to be armoured plates made of thick leather and fastened together with soldered seams or rivets, as if it were the cousin of a mediaeval knight. Certain details are almost comical, and strangely moving: the scaled legs of the rhinoceros disappear under the cuffs of its armour, which makes one wonder what the disarmed, naked rhinoceros would look like once it had taken off its protective shell at night and gone to sleep. The striking and strikingly strange impression of the rhinoceros is completed by a pair of delicate and alert ears, a hairy tail and an open, enlarged eye – telling us that, right now, it is wide awake and breathing.

It is said that Dürer never saw a rhinoceros, and he most certainly never saw *this* rhinoceros, before he painted the picture. The rhinoceros to which the inscription refers was sent to Rome by King Manuel of Lisbon – it was intended as a present for Pope Leo X – but before the ship could reach the Italian coast, it sailed into a storm and capsized. The rhinoceros, chained to the deck of the ship, sank to the bottom of the sea. In the aftermath of the event, Dürer was commissioned by the king of Portugal to create a woodcut of the animal as a posthumous portrait, to lift the rhinoceros from the bottom of the sea into immortality. Dürer's rhinoceros – part mythical creature, part animal, part human – memorializes a rhinoceros that never was, or, rather, never was quite like this. And yet, one might ask, with a nod to Adorno's essay on Eichendorff: was there ever a rhinoceros that was quite so much a rhinoceros as Dürer's?[2]

II

If the passage to Rome was cut short for the rhinoceros that King Manuel sent to Pope Leo X, Dürer's rhinoceros has been on a very long journey. Indeed, for many centuries, and despite all of its 'inaccuracies', Dürer's rhinoceros remained *the* image of *the* rhinoceros. There is a passage in Aesthetic Theory in which Adorno speaks of 'Proust's insight that Renoir transformed the perception of nature'.³ This might, with some qualifications, also apply to Dürer's woodcut. That Dürer's image might have shaped our perception of what a rhinoceros is and that it perhaps still does so today – in fact, it was the first image that came to mind when I began to think about the rhinoceros passage in Aesthetic Theory – is certainly owed to the fact that this image was, until the middle of the eighteenth century, with a few exceptions, the main representation of a rhinoceros accessible to Europeans. And accessible it has been: because it appeared in the form of a woodcut, Dürer's rhinoceros became one of the very first mass produced and reproduced images.⁴ There is something in this iconizing, in the fact that a commercial reproduction transforms our expectations of what an animal is, that anticipates the 'horror' of which Adorno writes with reference to Proust and Renoir: namely, 'that the reification of relations between humans would contaminate all experience and literally become absolute' (AT, 67). And, indeed, there is a passage in Negative Dialectics in which a rhinoceros appears and which captures this experience of reification: here the metaphor of the rhinoceros is employed to signify the unreflective priority of the subject, which, in acting on the principle of self-preservation, enslaves its own subjectivity.

> [A]nimal species like the dinosaur Triceratops or the rhinoceros drag their protective armour with them, an ingrown prison which they seem – anthropomorphically, at least – to be trying vainly to shed. The imprisonment in their survival mechanism may explain the special ferocity of rhinoceroses as well as the unacknowledged and therefore more dreadful ferocity of *homo sapiens*.⁵

'I am a rhinoceros and I dare you to doubt it', the ferocious animal seems to growl under the anthropomorphic gaze – its head bowed and its ears perked up in anticipation – ready for attack. Yet its posture of defiance and defence might as well be one of resignation: a creature with fluffy ears and melancholic eyes, weighed down by its solid outer shell. 'The armour', as Adorno writes elsewhere, 'covers the wound'.[6] The armour, which the rhinoceros, acting as a representative of the subject, appears in vain to try to shed, points back to the wound that the semblance of its firm and self-same identity seeks to cover up: the repressed knowledge that the 'self' relies on the disavowal of the 'other' that is its kin. Solidified and hardened, the coarse armoured plates of the rhinoceros seemingly render the separation between subject and object absolute, confining the subject, 'itself a piece of nature' – as Adorno likes to say – to a selfhood that comes to resemble what it has inflicted on its other: 'the solid, lasting, impenetrable side of the I mimics the outside world's impenetrability for conscious experience' (ND, 179). The boisterous confidence of the armoured creature, reflecting the anthropomorphic gaze, is hollow and, ultimately, toothless: its self-assertion – 'I am a rhinoceros' – blends into the noise of the *ever same*.

III

Let us take a step back from *Negative Dialectics*, bracket Dürer's rhinoceros for a moment and, instead, turn our attention to living rhinoceroses. If one looks more attentively at a rhinoceros, one will find that it bears a rather unusual type of 'armour'. Rather than being covered with hard plates or scales, the way Dürer imagined it, rhinoceroses actually have quite sensitive and soft skin, which is susceptible even to sunburn and insect bites. Indeed, this is why rhinoceroses have so *much* skin, lending them, where the excess skin forms deep folds, this peculiar armoured appearance. Upon closer scrutiny, then, the skin of rhinoceroses, while still thick, is far from impenetrable. Rather, rhinoceroses are, as it were, *wrapped* up in their own skin, as if they were draped in soft and delicate fabric. If the armoured rhinoceros of *Negative Dialectics* is an allegory for what has happened to the subject during the dialectic of enlightenment, rhinoceroses – by a not-too-extended stretch of the imagination – perhaps bear some resemblance to the young self whom Benjamin remembers in his *Berlin Childhood around 1900*, the young self who, in an aphorism entitled 'Mummerehlen', 'learned to *wrap* [himself] in words, which really were clouds'.⁷ 'The gift of perceiving resemblances', Benjamin continues, 'is, in fact, nothing but a weak remnant of the old compulsion to become similar and to behave mimetically. [...] I was disfigured [*entstellt*] by resemblances to all that surrounded me. Like a mollusk in its shell, I had my abode in the nineteenth century, which now lies hollow before me like an empty shell.'⁸

The mollusc-like, mimetic state in which the remembered little boy wraps himself in words and resemblances – the German term for wrapping is *mummen* – forms a counter-image to that of the hard and armoured creature, which seems to embody the price it has to pay for claiming superiority over the world of objects. Indeed, the intimate affinity that the child in *Berlin Childhood* experiences with words and objects – which, in childhood, as Adorno puts it elsewhere, are 'not yet constituted in [their] otherness'⁹ – discloses to him the specific qualities of objects in an anticipation of what they might be *in themselves*. Inasmuch as mimesis aims at what the object is like and not at what it signifies, it gestures towards the names of things in a world that is comprehensively mediated by exchange. In an aphorism in *Minima Moralia*, which Camilla Flodin discusses in detail in her chapter in this volume, Adorno establishes a close proximity between the rhinoceros and this experience of being 'wrapped':

> The relation of children to animals depends entirely on the fact that Utopia is wrapped up [*vermummt*] in the creatures whom Marx even begrudged the surplus value they contribute as workers. In existing without any purpose recognizable to men, animals present as expression, as it were, their own

names, that which is utterly impossible to exchange. This makes them so beloved of children, their contemplation [*Betrachtung*] so blissful. I am a rhinoceros, signifies the figure of the rhinoceros.[10]

Wrapping, *mummen*, crucially also entails an element of concealment (indeed, the German words *mummen* or *vermummen* suggest both 'to wrap' and 'to disguise'). The child disappears in the cloud of words or retreats behind the object he or she imitates in play. The child in 'Mummerehlen', 'disfigured by resemblances', is compared by Benjamin to a mollusc in a shell, a creature that adapts to its environment as much as it is adapted by it. Forgetful of himself, the child's behaviour attests to a state of heteronomy and with it to the rawness and vulnerability that precedes the formation of subjectivity.

IV

In the aphorism from *Berlin Childhood*, Benjamin, in a gesture of remembrance, picks up the empty shell that he has outgrown, that remnant of the century which has passed. He 'holds it to [his] ear'. Vacated, the shell seems to become eloquent. What does he hear? Benjamin, we read, does not hear in the murmur of the shell the 'noise of field artillery' or the 'fanfares announcing the changing of the guards'. Rather, he discerns the inconspicuous sounds that have left their traces in his sensorium of perception – the sound of a gas flame upon its ignition or the 'clatter of the […] cast-iron stove'.[11] Washed on to the shores of his memory are impressions which had lain latent in the depths of forgetting and which now re-emerge in altered form, with a faint utopian glow bestowed upon them: 'Images that we never saw, before we remembered them', as Benjamin wrote with reference to Proust.[12]

Dürer's rhinoceros, despite or, perhaps, even because of its grim appearance, seems to embody aspects of this fragile Proustian or, indeed,

Benjaminian perspective. This image will allow us to shed light on Adorno's remarks on mimesis and the eloquence of artworks in *Aesthetic Theory*. For Adorno, an artwork salvages as its utopian moment the remembrance of what is irretrievable. The sound of the sea, which draws one into the inner distance of the empty shell, is the same sound of absence, of forgetting, through which the artwork comes to itself and, in coming to itself, becomes eloquent. In this way, the interrupted itinerary of the rhinoceros that sank to the bottom of the sea before it opened its eyes as an artwork can help to illustrate the kernel of Adorno's aesthetics. In the following, I will unpick this thought.

When Benjamin writes in his essay on Baudelaire that a 'painting we look at reflects back at us that of which our eyes will never have their fill',[13] he captures the fleeting and ephemeral moment that is essential to artworks. His remark tells us that a picture always seems to express *more* than what it pictures. What a poem says is not (only) what its words say; what a painting says lies not (only) in what it signifies – those artworks worthy of the name do not aspire to be copies of reality. If we invert our perspective, the moment in which an artwork seems to say more than what is simply the case presents itself as if it were concealed, wrapped up – *vermummt* – in the work: as the work's silent eloquence. We can define it negatively, as that which identificatory thought – from the outside, as it were – apprehends as indeterminate and which escapes the reach of domination in its negation: 'Art as whole', as Adorno writes in one of his essays on music, 'is probably not amenable to the context of immanent explanations that asks everything that exists to show its passport'.[14] 'I am a rhinoceros', the rhinoceros seems to say. Passports do not apply.

As the suggestion of 'concealment' might already indicate, this silent eloquence is linked to mimesis. Artworks, as Adorno puts it in one of his lectures on aesthetics, attempt 'to restore by means of their gestures and their overall comportment a state in which the difference between subject and object did not really exist, where instead resemblance and thus kinship between subject and object prevailed' – a state which, as we have seen, is exemplified, both for Benjamin and Adorno, by childhood.[15]

Crucially, however, artworks perform this re-constitution 'within the bounds of the polarity of subject and object, as an act of autonomous spirit' (AT, 111). In other words, the element of concealment with which mimesis is allied does not terminate in total disfigurement (*Entstellung*), as it does in the mollusc-like state of childhood. Quite the contrary. Artworks utilize the force of mature subjectivity and, thus, an element of domination to silently lend voice, to objectivate, what must remain veiled and indeterminate to identificatory thought.

Mirroring the movement of *mummen*, of wrapping, artworks are mimetic in a rather specific sense, on Adorno's view: they are mimetic in that they comport themselves mimetically. Artworks *imitate themselves*, as he likes to say. They become eloquent or expressive in the mediation of their elements, which determine each other in the process of becoming a totality, however broken and fractured. Mimesis enters the artwork in the form of 'expressive impulses', Adorno writes, which are objectivated in the totality and thereby transcend its mere appearance.

> The mimetic impulses that motivate the artwork, that integrate themselves in it and once again disintegrate it, are fragile, speechless expression. They only become language through their objectivation as art. [...] Artworks become like language in the development of the bindingness of their elements, a wordless syntax even in linguistic works. What these works say is not what their words say. In art's intentionless language the mimetic impulses are bequeathed to the whole, which synthesizes them. In music an event or situation is able retroactively to shape a preceding development into something awesome even when it was not that in the first place. (AT, 184)

What appears *vermummt* – or, in fact, mute or silent – from the perspective of identificatory thinking, which seeks to determine what something *is* or what it is *for*, appears to the one who exercises her mimetic faculty, immersing herself in the fabric of the work, as at the same time highly individuated and determined. 'If artworks do not make themselves like something else but only like themselves, then only those who imitate them understand them' (AT, 125). What becomes discernible to mimetic comportment is the fleeting notion of 'a selfhood not first excised by identificatory thought from the interdependence of entities', as Adorno writes (AT, 112).

Yet the objectivation of expression that creates the semblance of a utopian selfhood is at the same time irredeemably entangled with forces of reification and domination: 'By wanting to give permanence to the transitory – to life – by wanting to save it from death', the work, in a paradoxical rescuing urge, 'kills it' (AT, 134). The individual elements on which expression is bestowed lose themselves in the work – their signifying aspect retreats beyond the mimetic consummation through which they gain determinacy.

Inasmuch as the eloquence of art is mute, its relationship to utopia is tied to remembrance: 'Art desires what has not yet been, though everything that art is has already been. It cannot escape the shadow of the past. But what has not yet been is the concrete', as Adorno writes (AT, 134). Its relationship to utopia is only ever to be conceived in terms of immanent transcendence, which suspends the order of the given in the constellation of its elements: 'But because for art, utopia – the yet-to-exist – is draped in black [one could also say: wrapped or concealed] it remains in all its mediations remembrance; remembrance of the possible in opposition to the actual that suppresses it' (AT, 135). As after-images of lived life, artworks are the 'anamnesis [...] of the repressed, and perhaps of what is possible' (AT, 259).

V

Let us now return to Dürer's rhinoceros. 'Proust's insight that Renoir transformed the perception of nature', which I mentioned at the beginning of this chapter, implies not only the horror of reification but also the potential for the rescue of nature. As a figure of remembrance for a state of affinity, the artwork bears the promise of a transformed existence: it is allied with the negative, transformative gesture of critique – the remembrance of nature in the subject – which, in denouncing the nexus of complicity in which it is entangled, is granted a moment of release.

'This is what I am', the rhinoceros seems to exhale, at once powerfully and tenderly, and this assertion, always in the here and now, suspends the here and now of what is simply the case. And yet, as we know, the very presence of the rhinoceros in the artwork is predicated on suffering. The gruesome history of the rhinoceros which, as a victim of domestication and domination, was tied to the deck of a ship and sank to the bottom of the sea becomes an allegory for the history of civilization, where everything that cannot show its passport must perish, a history which, as is proved to us daily, has not come to rest yet. If the artwork does justice to what had to perish, it is not because it endows the suffering which is its condition of possibility with a higher meaning – to do so would mean, at best, the artwork terminating in ideology. If we thus look at Dürer's rhinoceros, what do we see?

Oscillating between distance and closeness, familiarity and otherness, the rhinoceros charts an uncertain terrain between mythical creature, animal and human being, seemingly transforming from one to the other.[16] It suggests a resemblance between nature and history, between subject and object, myth and enlightenment – as if each pole of these binaries could answer for the other. Here, nature appears significant, and history, in turn, appears saturated with nature, with the force of what has always been.

Yet its overall expression seems to repudiate the semblance of reconciliation between human and animal, or history and its 'other': the way in which the armour of the rhinoceros seems almost artificially draped over its body, the way its face appears strapped into a mask and the very manner in which it bows its head reveal a predominance, an overweight, of history in the artwork.

This impression is heightened by the technique of the woodcut, its sparse, somewhat impoverished monochrome lines seeming to tally with the fact that it stands in the service of reproduction and capital. The frame, the tight cage that confines what it depicts, out of which the creature appears to want in vain to break, seems to lend voice not only to the history of domination of which it is an after-image but also to the very history of domination by virtue of which the work becomes eloquent: its deadliness. 'I am a picture', Dürer's image seems to say, and this other silent voice mingles with that of the rhinoceros and silences it for a second time.[17] The history of the rhinoceros that sank to the bottom of the sea, the history of civilization unveiled as the history of domination, stands accused by the force of the expressionless, which repeats its gesture in reverse: in the disintegration of the artwork, where history and nature break apart and the work of art reveals itself as a work of art, it turns its enigmaticality outward. It remains *vermummt*.

If Dürer's image still holds us captive, it might be because it also seems to ask: 'What might I become?' and 'What might you become?' And that this question remains unanswered – repudiated by the innermost force of the image itself – might be precisely why we do not want to turn our eyes away.

Notes

1   This essay is partly inspired by William Kentridge's wonderful reading of Dürer's artwork in his lecture on 'In Praise of Mistranslation' (William Kentridge, 'In Praise of Mistranslation', in *Six Drawing Lessons* (Boston: Harvard University Press, 2014), 129–56.

2   'In the fairy tales in the Grimm collection no forest is ever described or even given a characterization; but what forest was ever so much a forest as the one in the fairy tales?' Theodor W. Adorno, 'In Memory of Eichendorff', in *Notes to Literature*, vol. 1, trans. Shierry Weber Nicholsen (New York: Columbia University Press, 1991), 66.

3   Theodor W. Adorno, *Aesthetic Theory*, ed. Gretel Adorno and Rolf Tiedemann, trans. Robert Hullot-Kentor (London: Continuum, 1997), 67. Hereafter cited in text as 'AT'.

4　Elke Anna Werner, 'Pictures Migrating and Mutating', in *Double Vision: Albrecht Dürer/ William Kentridge*, ed. Klaus Krüger, Andreas Schalhorn and Elke Anna Werner (Munich: Sieveking Verlag, 2015), 80–90; here: 85–86.

5　Theodor W. Adorno, *Negative Dialectics*, trans. E. B. Ashton (London: Routledge, 2004), 180. Hereafter cited in text as 'ND'.

6　Theodor W. Adorno, 'Philosophy and Teachers', in *Critical Models: Interventions and Catchwords*, trans. Henry E. Pickford (New York: Columbia University Press, 2005), 19–36; here: 32, trans. modified.

7　Walter Benjamin, *Berlin Childhood around 1900*, trans. Howard Eiland (London: Harvard University Press, 2006), 97. My emphasis.

8　Ibid., 97–98, trans. modified.

9　Theodor W. Adorno, *Toward a Theory of Musical Reproduction*, trans. Wieland Hoban (Cambridge, MA: Polity Press, 2006), 170, trans. modified.

10　Theodor W. Adorno, *Minima Moralia*, trans. E. F. N. Jephcott (London: Verso, 2005), 228, trans. modified.

11　Benjamin, *Berlin Childhood*, 98.

12　Walter Benjamin, 'Aus einer kleinen Rede über Proust', in *Medienästhetische Schriften*, ed. Detlev Schöttker (Frankfurt am Main: Suhrkamp Verlag, 2002), 24. My translation.

13　Walter Benjamin, 'On Some Motifs in Baudelaire', in *Illuminations*, ed. Hannah Arendt, trans. Harry Zohn (New York: Schocken Books, 2007), 150–200; here: 187, trans. modified. I am grateful to Shierry Weber Nicholsen for pointing me towards this passage. For an illuminating engagement with Adorno's aesthetics in the context of Walter Benjamin's philosophy, particularly his theory of mimesis, see her *Exact Imagination, Late Work* (Cambridge MA. and London: MIT Press, 1997).

14　Theodor W. Adorno, 'On the Contemporary Relationship of Philosophy and Music', in *Essays on Music*, ed. Richard Leppert, trans. Susan H. Gillespie (London: University of California Press, 2002), 135–161; here: 138, trans. modified.

15　Theodor W. Adorno, *Aesthetics 1958/59*, ed. Eberhard Ortland, trans. Wieland Hoban (Cambridge: Polity Press, 2018), 42, trans. amended.

16　In his 'In Praise of Mistranslation', William Kentridge unfolds in detail the ambiguity of Dürer's rhinoceros along the lines suggested here. William Kentridge, 'In Praise of Mistranslation', 137–41.

17　See Daniel Herwitz's essay in this volume for an elaboration of the theme of the 'muted animal'.

Bibliography

Adorno, Theodor W. *Aesthetic Theory*. Edited by Gretel Adorno and Rolf Tiedemann, and translated by Robert Hullot-Kentor. London: Continuum, 1997.

Adorno, Theodor W. *Aesthetics 1958/59*. Edited by Eberhard Ortland and translated by Wieland Hoban. Cambridge: Polity Press, 2018.

Adorno, Theodor W. 'In Memory of Eichendorff'. In *Notes to Literature*. Vol. 1, translated by Shierry Weber Nicholsen, 37–54. New York: Columbia University Press, 1991.

Adorno, Theodor W. *Minima Moralia*. Translated by E. F. N. Jephcott. London: Verso, 2005.

Adorno, Theodor W. *Negative Dialectics*. Translated by E. B. Ashton. London: Routledge, 1973.

Adorno, Theodor W. 'On the Contemporary Relationship of Philosophy and Music'. In *Essays on Music*, edited by Richard Leppert and translated by Susan H. Gillespie, 135–61. London: University of California Press, 2002.

Adorno, Theodor W. 'Philosophy and Teachers'. In *Critical Models: Interventions and Catchwords*, translated by Henry E. Pickford, 19–36. New York: Columbia University Press, 2005.

Adorno, Theodor W. *Toward a Theory of Musical Reproduction*. Translated by Wieland Hoban. Cambridge, MA: Polity Press, 2006.

Benjamin, Walter. 'Aus einer kleinen Rede über Proust'. In *Medienästhetische Schriften*, edited by Detlev Schöttker, 24. Frankfurt am Main: Suhrkamp Verlag, 2002.

Benjamin, Walter. *Berlin Childhood around 1900*. Translated by Howard Eiland. London: Harvard University Press, 2006.

Benjamin, Walter. 'On Some Motifs in Baudelaire'. In *Illuminations*, edited by Hannah Arendt and translated by Harry Zohn, 150–200. New York: Schocken Books, 2007.

Kentridge, William. *Six Drawing Lessons*. Boston: Harvard University Press, 2014.

Weber Nicholsen, Shierry. *Exact Imagination, Late Work: On Adorno's Aesthetics*. Cambridge, MA and London: MIT Press, 1997.

Werner, Elke Anna. 'Pictures Migrating and Mutating'. In *Double Vision: Albrecht Dürer/William Kentridge*, edited by Klaus Krüger, Andreas Schalhorn and Elke Anna Werner, 80–90. Munich: Sieveking Verlag, 2015.

4

Just One Line: Reading T. W. Adorno on Humans, Artworks, and Animals

Lydia Goehr

> Nur das Tier allein ist wahrhaft unschuldig.
> (The animal alone is truly innocent.)
> Hegel, *Lectures on the Philosophy of History*

Twenty years ago in Berlin, I was invited to the home of an elderly musicologist who had known Adorno very well.[1] Sitting at the dinner table, I leaned over for him to whisper into my ear that he had always found Adorno's one-liners the best, implying, I suppose, that there was little reason to read the rest. I smiled but begged to disagree. Today, I know that in my disagreement I missed both the import and the wit in his whisper. Adorno knew the social import of one-liners dominating as much serious as popular productions. He was fascinated by the sloganizing of art and of thought as part of his reflections on the culture industry. He played on and with singular lines everywhere in his writings, always to a dialectical or critical purpose.

This essay follows from my participation in a panel in Rome devoted to a single line by Adorno from his *Aesthetic Theory*. It reads: 'So seems a rhinoceros, the mute animal, to say: I am a rhinoceros' ('*So scheint ein Nashorn, das stumme Tier, zu sagen: ich bin ein Nashorn*').[2] To prepare my reading of this line, I draw on more lines, culled from the internet, to show that, from almost any of Adorno's 'one-liners', one is pulled away from what gives the thought its meaning as it assumes any meaning of convenience. Each line is exemplary in situ. But the survival of meaning is threatened, according to the social diagnosis, by the reduction of traditions of thinking to commodified exchanges in the modern marketplace of ideals.

I hang out the lines to dry as one sees on banners, slogans, or as graffiti on a wall. The condemnation is not of graffiti but of the way we read these lines with easy thoughts of what they mean.

> To write poetry after Auschwitz is barbaric. – Wrong life cannot be lived rightly. – Freedom would not be to choose between black and white but to abjure such prescribed choices. – Every work of art is an uncommitted crime. – Auschwitz begins wherever someone looks at a slaughterhouse and thinks: they're only animals.[3]

There is much to say about each of these lines. The last, however, is most pertinent because, while everywhere repeated in English and German, it is not written as such (as far as I can tell) by Adorno. It is an Adornianer, a compression of several sentences from *Minima Moralia* about the dehumanizing human gaze. The particular passage addresses how the public's outrage towards atrocities decreases when, in a racial social schematism, persons are stripped of their humanity in a demotion to mere animality – '*es ist ja bloß ein Tier*' (MM, 105/189). On the slaughter-bench of history, those who bear the wounds on their racialized skins are assumed by those who wound them not to suffer or feel pain. Alongside the barbarism, Adorno finds an element of the parodic in the many ways of identification – *Ebenbildlichkeit* – when humans raise themselves to something god-like while demoting others to the status of animals. Yet, as we will see again, sometimes in the greatest self-contempt, humans find something in the animal not *mere* but *natural* and hence, contra civilization, akin in instinct to what is divine. But this is no less ideological, in Adorno's view, because seeking something allegedly missing from humanity, humanity remains the sole concern. Here, we confront the anthropological egotism that abuses animals and nature with equal spoonfuls of sloganized praise and condemnation.

Another of the one-liners, again from *Minima Moralia*, reads in the original: '*Jedes Kunstwerk ist eine abgedungene Untat*' (MM, 111/201). It is pertinent for its loss in translation when '*eine abgedungene Untat*' is rendered as 'an uncommitted crime'. This translation fails fully to capture the Faustian sense of the misdeed – *Untat* – that *waives* its truth by *ceding* or *passing over* into appearance. Even if art cannot do without appearance, the appearance that becomes a *directness* of communication is what Adorno declares art's 'mortal enemy' (AT, 112/171) – and especially when images and lines from great artworks hang out in cafes and supermarkets as the popular offerings of an easily digested stream of culture. Adorno provides this diagnosis in a passage he titles 'Zweite Lese' (MM, 109/198). It is usually translated not literally as 'Second Reading', but as 'Second Harvest', hence as invested with the very poetic hope on which Adorno is throwing plain water. When we read or regard great art of the tradition, we want something true or genuine to digest. But what hope have we for this when artworks are transmitted in speedy distribution through running citations or quotes, as the da-da-da-dah of Beethoven's *Fifth*? Precisely what we get is what we don't want, while what we want is forced into the dark, into a concealment that protects it from the abuse. A first reading gives us nothing, a second reading the chance to understand why so much modern art, understanding the nature of the modern exchange, sustains meaning by refusing to give anything away. The modern artwork, like a modern thought, turns mute in the face of the too easily distributed speech.

The line from *Aesthetic Theory* about the rhinoceros must be read and reread. It describes a mute animal *seeming* to convey something of the Cartesian spirit when it *seems* to say: I am a rhinoceros. '*So scheint ein Nashorn, das stumme Tier, zu sagen: ich bin ein Nashorn.*' By omitting the quotation marks around the sentence (if this is intentional on Adorno's part), subtle attention is brought to a sentence as not spoken. Stressing the *seeming* or *appearing* to speak, not an *identity* but an *affinity* is sustained between artworks and animals: artworks being what humans produce as appearances and animals being that with which humans seek to identify when confronted with the dissolution of their own identity. Affinity, identity, dissolution are three terms that Adorno takes over from Goethe and Hegel to capture the dialectical movement between the *several* fine arts and the *concept* of art. When this movement ceases, the relation of the object to the concept is severed, so that the object that seems to speak says nothing. Animals who speak without communicating to humans become witnesses to the human condition.

The rhino is an animal, alongside the ape, the cat, the cow, the elephant and the owl, with a long history in the dialectic between culture and human barbarism. A wealth of this history is offered by T. H. Clarke in his 1986 study *The Rhinoceros from Dürer to Stubbs, 1515–1799*. He retells the story from Pliny the Elder, given its impact on painters and writers, first off in the early modern period, when the single horn – *monoceros* – of the rhino was brought to a family resemblance with the unicorn. From Pliny's *Natural History*:

> At the same games the rhinoceros was also exhibited, an animal which has a single horn projecting from the nose; it has been frequently seen since then. This too is another natural-born enemy of the elephant. It prepares itself for the combat by sharpening its horn against the rocks; and in fighting directs it chiefly against the belly of its adversary, which it knows to be the softest part. The two animals are of equal length, but the legs of the rhinoceros are much the shorter: its skin is the colour of box-wood.[4]

Through strategic confusions of fact and fiction, the first Cartesian question of how one knows or tells the difference between the real and the unreal, dreamt or imagined, was transmuted into an art that, for its credibility, had to make a claim to be an accurate representation of the world. But then Clarke tells how rhinos were represented in word and image as both ugly and as an enemy in the kingdom of animals, as though perhaps, and this is my speculation, instead of finding peace with the elephant as suggested in Raphael's image in the Vatican, they entered into close alliance only with the most cantankerous of humans on Noah's ark. If art's credibility was at stake, so too the morality of art's representation.

In what is perhaps the best-known image, Dürer's woodcut of 1515, the rhino is represented as an impossible animal that cannot in truth or reality have ever existed. The woodcut is based on an anonymous but, as its inscription tells us, an allegedly 'accurate representation' of an Indian rhino that arrived in Lisbon as a gift sent by the king of Portugal to the pope. Unable to swim because chained to the deck, the rhino died on the way in a shipwreck. Dürer then accentuates the rigid armour of the beast, allowing, in the spirit of Pliny, the armour to be both a self-protection from the enemy and a cause for the enemy to shake in fear at the rhino's 'impetuous' nature or 'cunning'. But the armour is also strikingly ornamental, as though the beast of nature can always be tamed or disciplined by the masterful human hand of art. As Pliny suggests, the rhino lives its life for exhibition.

Clarke observes that those who take up Dürer's image tend to show the animal as *ambulated*, a deliberately obsolete word to capture the beast's feared extinction.[5] But even if obsolete as a living being, the animal endures as art, and for some or many the art matters much more. Clarke further quotes those who oddly say of Dürer's image that, being so accurate a representation, 'probably no other animal picture [...] exerted such a profound influence on the arts'.[6] Odd, because it was the inaccuracy, what eighteenth-century viewers noted as *exaggerated* characteristics, that most excited the colonial imagination of the Europeans, their desire for something *exotic* that looked nothing like anything they had ever seen. Adorno speaks of the desire for exogamy when addressing an emerging bourgeois opera that keeps everyone nicely settled in the sofas of comfort, viewing what is strange only at a distance on the stage.

There is a particularly influential travel narrative from which Hegel draws to expose false assumptions about the mimetic purpose of art. It is James Bruce's 1790 *Travels to Discover the Source of the Nile*. On his way to this biblical body of water, he declares Dürer's representation 'wonderfully ill-executed in all its parts' and 'the origin of all the monstrous forms under which that animal has been painted, ever since'.[7] The idea of a wonderful ill-execution is quite as incongruous as what we are also shown on the gilded porcelain vase known as the *Rhinoceros Vase*, made in 1826 in the Rockingham Works in South Yorkshire in England. For on its panels are painted miniature scenes from *Don Quixote* to bring out the incongruous battles between fictions of an obsolete nobility and the bland facts of modern life.

An exhibition from Berlin (2015/16), 'Double Vision: Albrecht Dürer & William Kentridge', brings two artists together for their experimentation in optics: how things are brought and erased from appearance. Kentridge finds a parallel in what is brought and not brought to speech or voice in a postcolonial society that still carries a colonial armour on its back. He notes the persistent threat of the rhino's natural extinction in South Africa due largely to the horn having been severed from the animal to serve as an icon in the administration of apartheid. In the exhibition catalogue, Elke Werner, one of the curators, dedicates her essay to the rhino, relating Kentridge's representations to his engagement also with Mozart's *Magic Flute*, an opera, we may note also, that Adorno regards exemplary of the brokenness of the two halves of a society that no longer add up to any peace or reconciliation. Werner reassesses the arrival of the rhino in Europe as marking 'a kind of living zoological Renaissance'.[8] She explores the conventions of scientific and artistic illustration and what it meant for Dürer to produce a 'life-like' image – IMAGO CONTRAFACTA or IMAGO AD VIVUM – given the medium of a woodcut as opposed to a drawing. She draws from Erwin Panofsky to note the anthropomorphism: how the rhino's eyes *seem to be* human eyes, where, again, the *seeming* is most significant. And then how a tiny second horn on the rhino's back points to Dürer's signature placed by the titular word written out as RHINOCERVS. In this act of titling and naming, nature is reauthorized as an image of art.

The key in my reading of Adorno's line turns on the remaking and reauthorizing of appearance. For all the appeals to the natural and the real, the rhino appears, when seeming to speak, *under the condition of art*. This means that every time Adorno speaks of the animal, he is speaking also about the social situation of art. For all his diagnoses of a warlike barbarity, the barbarism belongs not to the animal but to the art, for art is what humans make. This is brought home or on to the streets of capital cities with all the wit that Adorno sees in Surrealism and the modern theatre of the absurd. And significantly in Eugène Ionesco's play *Rhinocéros*, written in 1959, where one *red herring* of a question is whether the rhino has one or two horns, and whether then it comes from India or Africa, as if these differences really matter. Adorno knows the play, and perhaps also Salvador Dali's *Rinoceronte vestido con puntillas* from three or so years prior, where, changing the animal's clothes (for *clothes make the man*), Dali replaces Dürer's imposing armour, the heavy *armament* of the animal, with the lighter lace of ornament, as seen in Vermeer's *Lacemaker*, as another allegory of art.

When the rhino 'seems to say: I am a rhinoceros', the *seeming to say* marks a mute animal that, like music, is unable to speak because words do not belong to it. The muteness is, furthermore, an act of rescuing or taking back a meaning that has rendered obsolete the Cartesian identity between thinking and existing. *I seem to exist*, yet I have no attachment to my thoughts. To capture the detachment, Adorno describes what happens to humans when they engage the wrong sort of identifications, when they use words in such self-evident ways of conceptual mastery that their utterances effectively kill off the life or existence in the things to which their words refer. Asserting existence against speaking can be one way to reattach oneself directly to things without words, a way of offering a world of alignments and allegiances different from those of the current reality.

To rescue thinking from its positivistic tendency to conceptual mastery, Adorno turns to art's double character (*Doppelcharakter*): art needs language but not under the condition of its direct communicative function. Under this condition, language is art's mortal enemy – *ihr Todfeind* (AT, 112/171). The language that a non-compromised art wants nevertheless to take sides with does not come to direct expression or appearance. It takes the side of mute nature that, like the animal, does not speak. And yet, so siding, art does not become nature, since it must make its appearance as human-made. In affinity, without the assertion of identity, the human can say, I am, like a rhinoceros, a natural being, but also, being human, I am not like a rhinoceros.

Prior to writing his line about the rhino, Adorno describes the Etruscan vases in the Villa Giulia to be eloquent – *sprechend* – in the highest degree and hence incommensurable with all communicative language – *mit aller mitteilenden Sprache*. The true language of art is speechless, *sprachlos*, where its speechless moment – *sprachloses Moment* – he adds, with an ear open to music, takes priority over signification. The resemblance to speech – *das Sprachähnliche* – of the vases approaches the 'Here I am' or 'This I am', but where the identificatory thought – *das identifizierende Denken* – in this negative and speechless thinking of selfhood – *Selbstheit* – does *not* break the bond with what exists without thought.

Dietrich von Bothmer, former curator at the Metropolitan Museum in New York, said that the name *Etruscan* for the vases, while inaccurate, captures the desire, noticed already by Goethe, for the vases to sell for a higher price.[9] Labels matter. A Stradivarius unlabelled sells for less than one labelled. Apparently, Goethe never actually saw a real Etruscan vase and Dürer never saw a real rhino. But were one to have more luck, one would see, as von Bothmer noted, perhaps a small red-figured skyphos of a type known as a glaux after the Attic owl, or visions of mythic griffins or one-eyed Arimasps, or recognizable eagles, lions and jackals in *grim combat* with horses and deer in a world where survival depends on proving one's strength over the weak.

Adorno situates his remarks about the Etruscan vases and the rhino in the middle of a long paragraph in *Aesthetic Theory* which, like the passages in *Minima Moralia*, can be read more or less discretely. The passage of interest begins 'This mimesis' (AT, 112/171, trans. modified), to follow a previous discussion, but which we can read here as 'The true mimesis'. The *modification of mimesis* is in fact the topic, what mimesis means crudely as ape-like or as accurate representation contra its capability in art to do more than *communicate* in this way. Nothing in *true* art should be read at *face value*, but as carrying its assertion of the esoteric, the *this is so* that remains after any attempt to put its meaning into words.

Adorno then offers a quotation from Rilke's 'Archaic Torso of Apollo': not the best-known line, 'You must change your life', of which he approves, but the more challenging one just prior: 'for here there is no place that does not see you' – '*denn da ist keine Stelle, die dich nicht sieht*' (AT, 112/172, trans. modified). Everywhere we are seen while we do not see ourselves. Art stares back at us silent, like an animal looks at us. And the hardest task is not to assume that we already understand its look that we know not how to return. Artworks as mirrors, animals as mirrors of our gaze, tell us a secret history of our barbarism without words.

In Adorno's argument, there are all the echoes of Walter Benjamin's *language of things*, the language that carries the unconscious or 'physiological protohistory of spirit' – '*physiologischen Vorform des Geistes*' (AT, 113/172, trans. modified). The protohistory is carried in the grooves of musical records as little breakthroughs of the smooth surface, which he describes as a shudder or trembling – *Erzitterung*. This is not the pleasant tremolos of violin strings, but a Kantian *trembling* that mourns the lost dialectical movement between *nature* and *freedom*. It is a loss that humanity turns over to animals so that animals can seem to gaze back at humans with all the guilt of an accomplice – *Mitschuld*: oh, if only we were not as much like you as you make us seem to be.

I am fairly certain that Adorno runs the rhino, Estrucan vases and Apollo together following his visit to Rome around 1960. (There is a photograph of him lecturing at the Goethe Institute.) In the same year, he likely also sees or reads Ionesco's play. One passage from *Aesthetic Theory* supports my Roman hypothesis: he calls up the Etruscan Apollo at the Villa Giulia in Rome to address Alois Riegl's concept of artistic volition – *Kunstwollen*. While acknowledging the import into this concept of 'abstract timeless norms' (AT, 60/95), he finds too great an intentionalist assumption, where an artist's subjective intention is taken to exhaust or count for what is decisive in the work of art. His argument is not against intentionality, only against an overidentification of the objective with the subjective. The overidentification leads one to see the Etruscan Apollo only from one side, either the expressive thought or the emphatic assertion of existence. But one needs to see both sides in their antagonistic play if one wants to grasp the *eloquence* of which great art is capable.

Another intriguing passage from *Aesthetic Theory* has Adorno recalling an army joke about an orderly who one fine Sunday morning is sent by his superior to the zoo. The runner returns overexcited to declare: 'Lieutenant! Animals like that do not exist!' – '*solche Tiere gibt es nicht*'. With the necessary incredulity of a Sunday morning in play, the servant finds the animals at the zoo so transformed that he cannot believe that they exist like this for real. Though Adorno describes this joke as an *alberner Soldatenwitz*, 'an inane Wilhelminian army joke' (AT, 82/127), he does not just sit on the step of its wit, but moves quickly to abstract its philosophical point. Inspired by the deliberately semi-human creatures of Indian mythology and by Klee's *Angelus Novus*, he notes how the astonishment one experiences on seeing impossible animals is on par with how artworks, in their double character, reach a point of pure fiction or imagination while yet made, as mythological animals, out of disparate elements of the real.

A further passage from his *Negative Dialektik* describes the posture of the ideologue as when the transcendental subject who 'comes close to truth' –

'*rückt [...] dicht an die Wahrheit*'¹⁰ – is substituted with the narcissist who, with hubris, exalts his ego as the autonomous I – *Ich*. The latter plays into an exchange society, a bartering that does not preserve the species but only affirms the existence of the isolated and impotent ego that has become but one ego among others. Following many, but explicitly Hegel, Adorno sees in this subject's desperate self-exaltation a reaction to the experience of powerlessness. The powerlessness proves its impotence when trying to master nature. The subject strives not to meet nature but only to dominate it. To illustrate, Adorno describes the human attempt to shed a nature than cannot be shed – akin to an *outdated* animal whose species, having not survived, walks the earth like a dinosaur or rhinoceros dragging its protective armour – *Panzer* – that it can neither use nor discard.

Ego-weakness parading as strength produces a culture of raw instinct, unthought tweeting, for the survival of the lone self without care for the survival of humanity. Adorno finds this on display in Ionesco's play, in which 'a strong ego by resisting the bestial standardization' (ND, 293/289) can only be an *alcoholic* and *failure* at his trade. For no one knows what a strong ego is anymore. In *Minima Moralia*, Adorno describes a toy-merchant's shop – *Kaufmannsladen* – where the desensualizing of all sensory organs seems to reduce colours and tones to wares of equivalence, to the grey boredom of the ever-the-same (MM, 227–8/438–41). Yet here, there is an off-chance for a child who is still capable of sensing something more than the mere commodity. That the child can exercise the imagination to turn currents of *reality* into the *unreal* and *not yet real* – *noch nicht* – is where hope still obtains towards a life lived rightly, *zum richtigen Leben*. After this, it comes easily to Adorno to find an affinity of the child with the animal which/who can express his own name and his joy as non-exchangeable. 'I am a rhinoceros,' Adorno now writes, 'signifies the shape of the rhinoceros – '*Ich bin ein Nashorn, bedeutet die Figur des Nashorns*' (MM, 228/440–1). The reference to the *figure* is essential, as is the *likeness* achieved with the child, given what the child's game and art share: namely, the need for imagination to free itself from delivering prescriptions that leave the reality in place.

Let me turn now to Ionesco's play to note some Adornian motifs, which are otherwise expressed by John M. Valentine by reference to a broader literature. Valentine brings attention to the element of kitsch when 'unworthy goods' are passed off as art.[11] He quotes Milan Kundera on kitsch: 'the absolute denial of shit, in both the literal and the figurative senses of the word; kitsch excludes everything from its purview which is essentially unacceptable in human existence'.[12] Kundera distinguishes between a kitsch that is political and one that is philosophical. The latter dominates when one is confronted with the daily struggle between beauty and filth, life and death, being and oblivion, and even the monism of one horn set against the pluralism of two horns in an overall pursuit of a happiness that has not yet entirely capitulated to an ideology of a promised land arriving on the streets of a capital city of dreams. Valentine finds every sort of kitsch in the absurdist dialogue of Ionesco's play, brought out by the anti-heroic Berenger, who dangles unhappily between being and non-being, in a world caught between a provincial petit bourgeoisie and the mindless *dynamism* of the rhino.

As a discontent, Berenger is dishevelled, somehow not up with the times. Jean, with whom Berenger engages in a mismatched conversation, encourages Berenger to smarten himself up, to become one with the culture. Berenger prefers the oblivion of drink, to assuage his anguish, to forget the burden that he *drags around like a heavy armour*. He feels out of his own body: 'I don't even know if I *am* me.'[13] The only recognition of himself comes through intoxication, and intoxication has no need for logic. The logic of word and language coming from the mouth of the logician cannot make sense of the heavy stampede or trumpeting of the rhinos as they appear leaderless and wordless in increasing number as a mass, a common people, a democratic multitude. Nor can logic control the metamorphosis of the characters into the rhinos, for logic reaches its limits of a world transformed into the *appearance* of natural instinct. Logical order gives way to the disorder of a new tyrannical order, as sound syllogisms become fallacious. Valentine uses these observations to analyse the monism or totalizing ideology of the mass movement, the mental mutation and illusions of a fanaticism that justifies killing enemies with a good conscience. The metamorphosis is not that of a scream, but of a seduction by a beautiful and sonorous quality. The quality is of the song, as Kierkegaard described it to open *Either/Or*, when, facing Phalaris's brazen bull, the common people hear not the suffering of those burned alive, but only the sweetened song coming from the poet's lips. It takes time to hear the truth of the song, because with the first appearance of a rhino, the repeated surprise, 'Oh, a rhinoceros! [...] Well, of all things!'[14] does not translate into recognition.

What is disgusting to the ear or eye has no time to become beautiful or sweetened until one character can proclaim the rhinos now *like gods*. Valentine finds at the play's end a gesture towards a *personal kitsch*, when Berenger and Daisy, as the last surviving humans, refuse to *perpetuate* the human species. Daisy might as well then become a rhino, leaving Berenger a friendless solipsist with only his own lone image in the mirror. He says: 'I'm the last man left, and I'm staying that way until the end. I'm not capitulating!'[15] His refusal to be a rhino is tantamount to his awareness of the futility of the identification, because, after all, a human turned rhino is no rhino. No morality or immorality belongs to nature itself: the laws of the jungle are not moral or immoral laws. Human intuition is not natural instinct. Morality and its abuse have taken, so Berenger observes, 'centuries of human civilization to build up'.[16] The play is an exercise in false consolations or incongruent rationalizations that never get anywhere along the path of rescuing humanity from itself – from logic to science to poetry and philosophy. But which philosophy, Valentine asks: that of the sophisticate, the pedant, the pragmatist or the common man? The refusal to capitulate is a tragic-comic refusal of clichés, Valentine concludes, no better, I would add, than a Quixotic farce of words and images, repeated the second time around as slogans of recovery for a sickness named *rhinoceritis*.

In his draft introduction to *Aesthetic Theory*, Adorno reads Ionesco's play as staging the refusal of the metamorphosis wherein people become rhinos with a sheepish consciousness sustained by instrumental rationality. He sees a possible polemic, akin to Beckett's theatre, against Sartre's works, which 'firmly and subjectively posit the metaphysics of [the metamorphosis]' (AT, 347/517). The negation of the metaphysical metamorphosis, he continues, does not leave meaning meaningless, but incongruent regarding the relation of a work's form to its content. Whether or not Sartre really commits the crime of affirmation is as complex a question as whether Brecht's theatre really capitulates as much as Adorno sometimes says to a crude art of messaging and slogans. What Adorno says about humanity shedding its skins or armour or clothing in an attempt to be what it is not is an allegory for artworks that shed appearance when appearance is appropriated, but nevertheless appear. Animals serve as the mediating link.

Notes

1   The present essay shares some themes with my 'Form und Satz in Adornos Ästhetischer Theorie', in *Eros und Erkenntnis: 50 Jahre „Ästhetische Theorie"*, ed. Martin Endres, Axel Pichler and Claus Zittel (Berlin: De Gruyter, 2019); and my 'Stimmigkeit und Sinn', in *Theodor W. Adorno: Ästhetische Theorie*, ed. Anne Eusterschulte and Sebastian Tränkle (Berlin: De Gruyter, forthcoming).

2   Theodor W. Adorno, *Aesthetic Theory*, ed. Rolf Tiedemann, trans. Robert Hullot-Kentor (New York and London: Continuum, 1997), 112 (trans. modified). Theodor W. Adorno, *Ästhetische Theorie* in *Gesammelte Schriften*, vol. 7, ed. Rolf Tiedemann (Frankfurt am Main: Suhrkamp Verlag, 1997), 171–2. Hereafter cited in text as 'AT'. Page numbers, separated by a slash, will refer first to the English translation, then to the German original.

3   1. 'Cultural Criticism and Society', in *Prisms* (Cambridge, MA: MIT Press, 1967), 17–34; here: 34. 2. *Minima Moralia: Reflections on a Damaged Life*, trans.

E. F. N. Jephcott (London: Verso, 2005), 39; Theodor W. Adorno, *Minima Moralia: Reflexionen aus dem beschädigten Leben* (Frankfurt am Main: Suhrkamp Verlag, 1951), 59. Hereafter cited in text as 'MM'. Page numbers, separated by a slash, will refer first to the English translation, then to the German original. 3. MM, 132/245-6. 4. MM, 111/201.

4   Pliny the Elder, *The Natural History*, vol. 3, trans. H. Rackham (Cambridge, MA: Harvard University Press and London: William Heinemann LTD), 1967, 72.

5   T.H. Clarke, *The Rhinoceros from Dürer to Stubbs. 1515-1799* (London: Sotheby's Publications), 20.

6   Ibid.

7   James Bruce, *Travels to discover the source of the Nile: In the years 1768, 1769, 1770, 1771, 1772, and 1773*, vol. VII, second edition (Edinburgh: Archibald Constable and Co., and Manners and Miller, 1804), 193.

8   Elke Anna Werner, 'Pictures Migrating and Mutating', in *Double Vision: Albrecht Dürer/ William Kentridge*, ed. Klaus Krüger, Andreas Schalhorn and Elke Anna Werner (Munich: Sieveking Verlag, 2015), 20-32; here: 82.

9   Dietrich von Bothmer, 'Some Etruscan Vases', *Bulletin of the Metropolitan Museum of Art* 10, no. 5 (1952): 145-9; here: 145.

10 Theodor W. Adorno, *Negative Dialectics*, trans. E.B. Ashton (London and New York: Routledge, 1973), 178. Theodor W. Adorno, *Negative Dialektik*, in *Gesammelte Schriften*, vol. 6, ed. Rolf Tiedemann (Frankfurt am Main: Suhrkamp Verlag, 1997), 180. Hereafter cited in text as 'ND'. Page numbers, separated by a slash, will refer first to the English translation, then to the German original.

11 John M. Valentine, 'Kitsch and the Absurd in Eugène Ionesco's Rhinoceros', *Florida Philosophical Review* 11, no. 1 (2011): 54-65; here: 54.

12 Ibid.

13 Ionesco, Eugène, *Rhinoceros and Other Plays*, trans. Derek Prouse (New York: Grove Press, 1960), 18.

14 Ibid., 9-10.

15 Ibid., 107.

16 Ibid., 67.

Bibliography

Adorno, Theodor W. *Aesthetic Theory*. Translated by Robert Hullot-Kentor. New York and London: Continuum, 1997.

Adorno, Theodor W. *Ästhetische Theorie*. In *Gesammelte Schriften*. Vol. 7, edited by Rolf Tiedemann. Frankfurt am Main: Suhrkamp Verlag, 1997.

Adorno, Theodor W. *Minima Moralia: Reflections on a Damaged Life*. Translated by E. F. N. Jephcott. London and New York: Verso, 2005.

Adorno, Theodor W. *Minima Moralia: Reflexionen aus dem beschädigten Leben*. Frankfurt am Main: Suhrkamp Verlag, 1951.

Adorno, Theodor W. *Negative Dialectics*. Translated by E. B. Ashton. London and New York: Routledge, 1973.

Adorno, Theodor W. *Negative Dialektik*. In *Gesammelte Schriften*. Vol. 6, edited by Rolf Tiedemann. Frankfurt am Main: Suhrkamp Verlag, 1997.

Bruce, James, *Travels to Discover the Source of the Nile: In the Years 1768, 1769, 1770, 1771, 1772, and 1773*. Vol. VII. Second edition. Edinburgh: Archibald Constable and Co., and Manners and Miller, 1804.

Clark, T. H. *The Rhinoceros from Dürer to Stubbs. 1515-1799*. London and New York: Sotheby's Publications, 1986.

Goehr, Lydia. 'Form und Satz in Adornos Ästhetischer Theorie'. In *Eros und Erkenntnis: 50 Jahre, Ästhetische Theorie*", edited by Martin Endres, Axel Pichler and Claus Zittel. Berlin: De Gruyter, 2019, 71-9.

Goehr, Lydia. 'Stimmigkeit und Sinn'. In *Theodor W. Adorno: Ästhetische Theorie*, edited by Anne Eusterschulte and Sebastian Tränkle. Berlin: De Gruyter, forthcoming.

Ionesco, Eugène. *Rhinoceros and Other Plays*. Translated by Derek Prouse. New York: Grove Press, 1960.

Valentine, John. 'Kitsch and the Absurd in Eugène Ionesco's Rhinoceros'. *Florida Philosophical Review* 11, no. 1 (2011): 54-65.

Von Bothmer, Dietrich, 'Some Etruscan Vases'. *Bulletin of the Metropolitan Museum of Art* 10, no. 5 (1952): 145-9.

Werner, Elke Anna. 'Seeing the Uncertain'. In *Double Vision: Albrecht Dürer/ William Kentridge*, edited by Klaus Krüger, Andreas Schalhorn and Elke Anna Werner, 80-90. Munich: Sieveking Verlag, 2015.

5

The Mute Animal

Alexander García Düttmann

Here I am. This is me. Who is able to speak in such a manner, perhaps without exercising any particular ability and without communicating anything that would require words and propositional meanings?

In a paragraph of *Aesthetic Theory* devoted to the relationship between language and the expressive quality of artworks, Adorno mentions an animal. Out of nowhere, the rhinoceros makes its entrance and vanishes just as quickly. Is Adorno providing an arbitrary example, one among many possible examples, or, to the contrary, an example that imposes itself upon his line of thought because of its self-evidence? He qualifies the rhinoceros as the mute animal. Muteness and animality are both highlighted by the usage of a definite rather than an indefinite article in connection with the adjective and the noun. Adorno does not call the rhinoceros 'a mute animal' but rather 'the mute animal'.[1] Thus the reader may ask whether Adorno is not, in fact, providing two examples at the same time. On the one hand, the rhinoceros would be an example of what Adorno designates as selfhood.[2] On the other hand, it would be an example of animality and what turns an animal into a being distinguished from other beings, humans especially, namely its muteness or its inability to access language. It is precisely its deprivation of language that opens up a dimension to the rhinoceros that remains foreclosed to beings that are not 'mute animals' and that establishes its unexpected relationship to art, as if artists and animals, separated by language, were still able to communicate. Something about works of art is common to animals and artists, though not because animals would attempt to do what artists are expected to achieve and produce rudimentary samples of artworks. What is the dimension opened up to the rhinoceros and to mute animals on the basis of their deprivation of language?

It is the dimension of resemblance to language or speech. Just like an artwork, the rhinoceros appears to speak without actually speaking. Muteness, then, implies that language is inaccessible to the animal but not simply and not absolutely. Language itself has a 'double character'. Muteness, or speechlessness, is linguistic, or protolinguistic, inasmuch as language is not reducible to its 'significative' or 'signifying' aspect or function, to signification and communication based on signification. What Adorno refers to as muteness or speechlessness, *Stummheit* or *Sprachlosigkeit*, is not the opposite but a threshold of language. Language appears to be removed from itself; it precedes, announces, anticipates but also disseminates, loses and relinquishes itself in a resemblance incompatible with signification. Its 'double character' is the double character of instability and solidity, vagueness and fixation, indefiniteness and identifiability. It is on the threshold of language that mute animals and art must be situated in the first place. It is on this threshold that we encounter selfhood.

Adorno writes: 'By virtue of its double character, language is a constituent of art and its mortal enemy. Etruscan jugs in the Villa Giulia are eloquent [*sprechend*] in the highest degree and incommensurable with all communicative language. The true language of art is mute [*sprachlos*], and its muteness takes priority over poetry's significative element, which in music too is not altogether lacking' (AT, 112, trans. modified). Surprisingly, Adorno here introduces a hierarchy of art forms but does not place music at the top. Music is akin to poetry in that it partakes too much of the 'significative' or 'signifying' element of language and thereby remains at a distance from the other element or 'character' of language, muteness or speechlessness, in which an eloquence lies, something that speaks to speaking beings. Yet what allows for the conception of a hierarchy of art forms is that the two sides of language, which can both be found in art, though not always and not in equal measure, relate to it in contradictory and irreconcilable ways, so that the distinction between these sides is an asymmetrical and dynamic one, a distinction between two forces, the force of truth and the force of mortal enmity, as if art forms were constantly torn or entangled in a latent process of constitution and disintegration. That music does not come as close to art's truth as other art forms is due, paradoxically, to its more comprehensive relationship to language. It comprises within itself the two 'characters' of which language is composed. Music, at once mute, or speechless, and 'significative', or communicative, is too complete an art form. It is not partial enough. Resemblance and eloquence escape it. It is an art form that has gone too far, that has crossed the threshold of art and language, that has stepped outside art by allowing itself to be attracted by that 'character' of language that proves a deadly foe to art. Music, and even more so poetry, has succumbed to language's fight against art, against muteness or speechlessness. In what follows, Adorno suggests that the mute animal has more to do with archaic jugs and vases than with poetry and music: 'The vases' resemblance to language, or to speech [*das Sprachähnliche*], appears most clearly when related to a Here-I-am or a This-is-me, to a selfhood not first excised by identificatory thought from the interdependence of beings. Thus the rhinoceros, the mute animal, seems to say: "I am a rhinoceros"' (AT, 112, trans. modified). Four or five questions must be raised at this point. What does Adorno mean by selfhood, exactly? Why are mute animals supposed to share their selfhood with artworks and in what sense are they to be encountered on the threshold of language? What is it that prompts Adorno to name the rhinoceros and not some other animal? And does music not know of an equivalent to the gesture that seems to define selfhood and that Adorno describes by resorting to the deictic expressions 'Here I am' and 'This is me'?

Adorno is often critical of selfhood, though in different ways. He locates a principle of identity within selfhood that bestows unity upon the subject, the steadfast and imperturbable unity of what stays identical to itself, withstands its dissolution into the chaotic and indeterminate, and acts as an instrument of both inward and outward mastery and domination. The selfhood of the subject imposes a sort of ban on the individual since it imprisons it within itself. It is abstract and impassive, serves the purposes of self-preservation and borders upon tautology as it consists in the mere repetition of the personal pronoun 'I'. In truth, selfhood is deadly, as if self-preservation mobilized death against death, or as if it perpetuated a stubborn defiance that amounts to a negation of the self. In yet another critical context, Adorno considers selfhood to be the result of the power that the concept exerts over the non-identical. For the conceptual operation of identification to succeed, the concept needs to subsume the non-identical under its unity. This is why it transforms the non-identical into individual entities or existences, which it can then grasp as so many conceptual unities, or why it entraps it within selfhood. The concept creates a polarity between itself and the non-identical and it is this polarity that triggers the transformation of the non-identical into distinct entities or existences, into something endowed with selfhood. Hence the spell cast, or the ban imposed, upon the individual by selfhood is, ultimately, the ban of conceptual thought and conceptual language, of identification and unification. Since, however, the tautological nature of identity lacks articulation, language, for Adorno, is not reducible to conceptuality, or to a means to bring about selfhood. It is also an agent of non-identity and the means to undo the spell and liberate the individual from selfhood. Finally, in a further critical context, Adorno denounces selfhood as something that has isolated itself from a set of relations to which it belongs originally, dissimulating the mediation that wrests it from its arrogated autonomy. Selfhood is never the thing itself because the thing itself must be understood as a dynamic interconnectedness or interdependence whose movement continuously unhinges beings, entities and instances. It should not be conceived of as an isolated and autonomous thing, or as a thing that keeps to itself and thereby withdraws from conception.

Viewed from a sociological vantage point, selfhood is, according to Adorno, always provincial, never worldly. Viewed from an artistic vantage point, selfhood, which affirms itself, should not be confounded with whatever expresses itself, with expressiveness, which has always a passive moment to it.

But what about the non-critical, or commendatory, use Adorno makes of the concept of selfhood? In the passage of *Aesthetic Theory* quoted above selfhood is not the same as identity, does not constitute itself through an excising act of self-identification, is not 'excised by identificatory thought from the interconnectedness of beings' and does not provide the necessary condition for subjective acts of identification to take place. In other passages, selfhood can be a term that denotes something that has not been tampered with or altered. Selfhood can also indicate the authenticity and specificity of a non-ubiquitous phenomenon. It can indicate the blind spot, the singular quality of a specific experience or an individual thought, even though the mere fact of thinking, of engaging in cognitive acts of identification and resorting to conceptual language, seems to announce the collapse of a non-critical use of the term into a critical one. Thought lies on the border between the two.

A selfhood that has not been 'excised by identificatory thought from the interconnectedness of beings' consists in an expressiveness that does not solidify into the expression of something in particular, a feeling, a mood, a belief or a state of mind. It detaches itself somehow from the 'interconnectedness of beings' yet it cannot be set apart from it. It consists in an ongoing, hovering, constantly repeated, constantly suspended and never-ending gesture that signals, 'Here I am', or 'This is me', though it neither presupposes a constituted self nor evolves into such a self. It never completes the self-referential movement that it describes yet it lacks neither a conclusion nor an outcome – hence its straightforwardness, its self-evidence, its disarming simplicity and even stupidity. 'Here I am' [*Da bin ich*] or 'This is me' [*Das bin ich*], two expressions that in German can be distinguished only because of the addition of a single letter, should not be taken as claims but as signs of pure exposure. Such exposure does not withhold or promise anything. It does not draw attention to a secret and secretive inwardness or to an ineffable uniqueness. Nor does it expect acknowledgement, as if acknowledgement were due to selfhood or as if selfhood could get involved in a struggle for recognition. 'Here I am' does not mean 'I have finally made it' or 'I am here since it is my spot; I own it', just as 'This is me' does not mean 'Deal with it' or 'Do not make a mistake.' Rather than pointing to a given entity called 'self', the gesture of self-reference seems to point to itself as a gesture. Its own identity, however, its identifiability as a gesture, remains unfathomable. It does not attain the limit of cognition and recognition. The closer it approaches it, the less it can be ascertained. What is here is a gesture whose presence appears to be indistinguishable from an absence. It is all the more compelling for that, as if there were a quasi-intuitive readability that does not rest on a cognitive effort of identification, and in which clarity and opacity coincide, similar to a dream on the verge of awakening. What is here is a gesture that comes into presence and that, in so doing, signals its coming into presence. It is like a gaze that cannot be seen, from which no insight can be gained, because it abandons itself entirely.

In *Aesthetic Theory*, selfhood, as a notion of transition, as a threshold between the linguistic and the non-linguistic, as the limit concept of a speaking muteness, is related to expression, to the expressiveness of a gesture of self-reference since expression itself is a notion of transition, a threshold, a limit concept. For Adorno links the possibility of expression, its genesis, to the genesis of the subject, the self or spirit. He links it to the 'prehistory' or the 'protohistory of subjectivity' (AT, 112) and remarks that the subject does not underlie historical developments but 'begins anew in every moment of history' (AT, 113, trans. modified). Subjectivity persistently and fatally reinscribes 'prehistory' or 'protohistory' within history, and this is why it repeats again and again the gesture that seems to say 'Here I am' or 'This is me.' Could one not even wonder whether Etruscan art, the art of an obscurely archaic and at the same time inscrutably civilized people, is not a metonymy for art in general?[3] 'Prehistory' or 'protohistory' keeps crossing the threshold into 'history'. It is not left behind; it outlasts itself inasmuch as this threshold, this border, this limit cannot be crossed once and for all. It could only be crossed once and for all if the subject were able to engender and posit itself. It is to this impossibility, to the non-subjective, 'apersonal' or 'mute' aspect of subjectivity, to the semblance and resemblance of a non-significative and non-communicative language, that expressive selfhood testifies, in art, as art, but also outside of art, at least to the extent that it is conceivable that a 'mute animal' could ever appear to say 'Here I am' or 'This is me' in a world, in a pre- or in a protoworld, in which art, or artistic experience, did not exist at all. The reason why expression, a feature constitutive of art, of what is informed by the 'double character' of language, should not be amalgamated with the expression of a 'tangible content of the artist's soul' is that such amalgamation requires the soul to have already emerged and established its own domain in which more or less 'tangible' contents abound and can be distinguished from each other. Expressing is not a merely reproductive activity. It does not contribute to the production of artworks as 'blurred photographs' of the soul since the non-significative, non-communicative, expressive aspect or 'character' of language is 'older' (AT, 112) than language's signifying, communicative, propositional aspect or 'character' and cannot be translated into a meaning, a signification, a proposition, a content to be communicated. The 'language of expression is older though unfulfilled' (AT, 112), as Adorno puts it. Expression cannot be amalgamated with the expression of something, a particular content, as it is contemporary with 'ensoulment' (AT, 113), not with a formed soul. It is contemporary with an animism of the surfacing and materializing self. Yet, if the threshold between 'prehistory' or 'protohistory' and history cannot be crossed permanently, it is also impossible to oppose an 'older' aspect or character of language to a more recent one and maintain that expression is contemporary with 'ensoulment' and not with a formed soul. Rather expression erodes form from within and is both 'older' and younger than the soul. Art, in this sense, has no age.

To the extent that an artwork is an intentionally created object that proves to be a testimony, or a monument, to the impossibility of crossing the threshold of subjectivity, history and language, one could be tempted to argue that it is a 'modification' (AT, 113). Adorno borrows this term from phenomenology so as to endorse this type of argument. However, the very possibility of a 'modification' entails a chronological order, a distinction between what comes first and what comes second, what is older and what is more recent, what is an image and what is an 'afterimage' whose pertinence must be questioned in a world that is essentially a world before the world and in a history that is forever a 'prehistory' or 'protohistory'. Mute animals and artworks share selfhood and can be encountered on the threshold of language because art's expressiveness is not simply a 'modification' in the course of a historical progression. Without art or artistic experience, mute animals would cease to gesture, would recede into a muteness entirely alien to language and would fall prey to the human separation of humans and non-humans, to the denial of the non-human, of what is 'apersonal' within the human. Conversely, art that would be entirely human, as it were, that would not participate in the mute animality of the rhinoceros, would cease to be art.

Why does Adorno name the rhinoceros, though? Would not the ape, the *Menschenaffe*, to whom he also alludes after mentioning the horned animal, be a more suitable example for his argument? Is not the rhinoceros too distant from selfhood, from the threshold of art, subjectivity and history? When looking for an answer to these questions, one should not give in to the tempting compliancy with which the history of ideas tends to ward off the arduousness of thought. One should refrain from invoking a cultural affinity to Dürer's famous drawing or from emphasizing the cultural impact that Ionesco's successful play had in the late 1950s and in the early 1960s. One should not forget that, in his so-called early introduction to *Aesthetic Theory*, Adorno found this play a bit too obvious for its own good.[4] Perhaps one should turn instead to the following passage from *Negative Dialectics*:

> But philosophy's stress on the constitutive power of the subjective moment blocks the road to truth as well. Animal species like the dinosaur Triceratops or the rhinoceros drag their protective armor with them, an ingrown prison which they seem – anthropomorphically, at least – to be trying vainly to shed. The imprisonment in their survival mechanism may explain the special ferocity [*Wildheit*] of rhinoceroses as well as the unacknowledged and therefore more dreadful ferocity of *homo sapiens*.[5]

Is it not precisely the 'ferocity' or the 'savagery' of the 'mute animal' that allows Adorno to acknowledge the abyss that lies between 'pre-' or 'protohistory' on the one hand and history on the other, thus making their entanglement, the 'ferocity' or the 'savagery' of the human, far more striking than if he had resorted merely to the example of the ape, subscribed only to anthropomorphism, to the idea of an unobtainable liberation from animality or to the assumption of a mournful relationship to an unattainable humanity?[6]

By naming the rhinoceros, Adorno refuses to sketch a continuous trajectory between the two sides of the threshold. The threshold is the site of conflicting and indomitable forces. In order not to completely separate the two animals, the human and the non-human animal, and elevate one animal, the human, over the other, the non-human animal, Adorno must separate them as much as he can. Art's selfhood designates exactly this tension, the tension of a paradox. It alone accounts for the expressiveness that is tantamount to a purposeless exposure. After all, for there to be expressiveness, a coming to presence, an ensoulment or a beginning of history, a force, or a clash of forces, must unleash it. The achievement of art is to extract a semblance, an image or a resemblance from the violence inherent in the unleashed and clashing forces of expression, the semblance, the image or the resemblance of a gesture that exposes exposure by exposing itself. In this sense alone, art can be said to effect a 'modification', a modification of violence into disinterested contemplation,[7] notwithstanding the necessarily non-intentional dimension of this modification. The artist cannot exempt himself or herself from what happens on the threshold and retrace it from a distance, as it were, in the guise of a modification external to what is being modified. The expressiveness of the work he or she creates must be accomplished on the threshold. Selfhood can only be had at the risk of art falling into chaos. This occurs when the tension that traverses art has overpowering destructive consequences and the threshold is erased.

If music, just as poetry, does not partake of the creation and the advent of selfhood as much as, or in the manner of, jugs and vases of Etruscan origin, how come it still knows of an equivalent to the gesture that appears to say 'Here I am' or 'This is me'? Adorno is not a Manichean who excludes art forms from truth, or the 'true language of art', just as he is not a pedant, or a rulemonger, who indulges his keenness for compartmentalization. This is what he writes about expression in the music of Austrian composer Franz Schubert: 'Schubert's resignation has its locus not in the purported mood of his music, nor in how he was feeling – as if the music could give a clue to this – but in the It-is-thus [*So ist es*] that it announces with the gesture of letting oneself fall. This gesture is its expression' (AT, 112, trans. modified).[8] The different gestures converge as they become gestures of exposure. Yet their difference lies in the fact that the gesture that appears to say 'It is thus' must be sought in the gap that the movement of self-reference leaves open when it does not come full circle and turn selfhood into an identity. Since the gesture that appears to say 'Here I am', or 'This is me', does not become identifiable as an act establishing and confirming an identity, it collapses into a gesture that appears to say 'It is thus.' Both gestures are almost indiscernible, each one a gesture of art, or the shape of a rhinoceros.

Notes

1 Theodor W. Adorno, *Aesthetic Theory*, trans. and ed. Robert Hullot-Kentor (London: Continuum, 1997), 112, trans. modified. Hereafter cited in text as 'AT'.

2 On selfhood in Adorno, see also 'Selfhood' in Alexander García Düttmann, *Between Cultures: Tensions in the Struggle for Recognition*, trans. K. B. Woodgate (London: Verso, 2000), 214–18.

3 For another approach to art, and Etruscan art especially, based on an entwining of 'protohistory' and history that is both violent and contemplative, see Luchino Visconti's film *Vaghe stelle dell'Orsa* (1965). Visconti, in an interview with *Cahiers du Cinéma*, stresses that the beauty of the film's female protagonist is animal-like. Adriano Aprà, Jean-André Fieschi, Maurizio Ponzi, André Téchiné, 'Luchino Visconti: *Vaghe stelle dell'Orsa*', *Cahiers du Cinéma* 171 (1965): 44–46; here: 45.

4 Howard Hawks' *Hatari*, anyone? After all, Adorno did not give *Daktari* a miss …

5 Theodor W. Adorno, *Negative Dialectics*, trans. E. B. Ashton (London: Routledge, 1973), 180.

6 '[T]here is nothing so expressive than the eyes of animals, – especially apes – which seem objectively to mourn that they are not human' (AT, 113). The alleged objectivity of expression corresponds here to the muteness of the animal in the previous example of the rhinoceros.

7 As readers of Adorno are well aware, the passage about the rhinoceros in *Aesthetic Theory* has its precursor in *Minima Moralia*: 'In existing without any purpose recognisable to man, animals hold out, as if for expression, their own names, utterly impossible to exchange. This makes them so beloved to children, their contemplation so blissful [*selig*]. I am a rhinoceros, signifies the shape of the rhinoceros'. Theodor W. Adorno, *Minima Moralia*, trans. E. F. N. Jephcott (London: Verso, 2005), 228.

8 Robert Hullot-Kentor, the translator of *Aesthetic Theory*, adds a note at this point in the text and refers the reader to Beckett's 'novel' *Comment c'est* (*How it is*), first published in 1961. On Adorno's usage of the phrase 'It is thus' see also Alexander García Düttmann, *So ist es: Ein Kommentar zu Adornos 'Minima Moralia'* (Frankfurt am Main: Suhrkamp, 2004), passim.

Bibliography

Adorno, Theodor W. *Aesthetic Theory*. Translated and edited by Robert Hullot-Kentor. London: Continuum, 1997.

Adorno, Theodor W. *Minima Moralia*. Translated by E. F. N. Jephcott. London: Verso, 2005.

Adorno, Theodor W. *Negative Dialectics*. Translated by E. B. Ashton. London: Routledge, 1973.

Aprà, Adriano, Fieschi, Jean-André, Ponzi, Maurizio, Téchiné, André. 'Luchino Visconti: *Vaghe stelle dell'Orsa*'. *Cahiers du Cinéma* 171 (1965): 44–46.

Düttmann, Alexander García. *Between Cultures: Tensions in the Struggle for Recognition*. Translated by K. B. Woodgate. London: Verso, 2000.

Düttmann, Alexander García. *So ist es: Ein Kommentar zu Adornos 'Minima Moralia'*. Frankfurt am Main: Suhrkamp, 2004.

Vaghe stelle dell'Orsa. [Film] Dir. Luchino Visconti. Italy: Vides Cinematografica, 1965.

6

The Speaking Animal: On a Metaphor of Humanity

Sebastian Tränkle

For Robert Hullot-Kentor

In the 'Notes and Sketches' section of *Dialectic of Enlightenment*, Theodor W. Adorno and Max Horkheimer discuss the relationship of 'Man and Beast'.[1] In European history, so they claim, the very idea of man has been defined by his ontological difference from animals: their 'lack of reason' proves our humanity (DE, 203). Such lack of reason is quintessentially understood as a lack of words and concepts. If animals are defined by their speechlessness, becoming human is at heart a process of language acquisition. If becoming human means overcoming speechlessness, the loss of speech defines the ever-looming menace of regression to animality. Both metamorphoses have been the subjects of many myths and fairy tales. From Ovid to Kafka, the speaking animal is a recurring literary figure. Just as *Dialectic of Enlightenment* incorporates interpretations of such mythical stories, speaking animals appear time and again in early Critical Theory, especially in the works of Adorno.

The work on this article was funded by the Deutsche Forschungsgemeinschaft (DFG, German Research Foundation) under Germany's Excellence Strategy in the context of the Cluster of Excellence Temporal Communities: Doing Literature in a Global Perspective – EXC 2020 – Project ID 3900608380.

In the following, I want to trace the philosophical meaning of this figure. I take the speaking animal to be an ambivalent metaphor. It brings to mind the metamorphosis both of animals into humans and of humans into animals. In the first part, I focus on Adorno and Horkheimer's account of animals becoming civilized and autonomous human beings. This appears as a process of both emancipation from the heteronomy of nature and repression of the fact of our belonging to nature, as progress that comes at a price. This price the second part illustrates by introducing a modern fable: H. G. Wells's *The Island of Doctor Moreau* depicts the forced humanization of wild beasts by a mad scientist, culminating in the attempt to give them language, and the horrible failure of his experiments, resulting in the animals' reversion to bestiality. Thus, against the backdrop of *Dialectic of Enlightenment*, I decipher *the animal forced to speak* – but only capable of exchanging standardized phrases – as an allegory for the failure of our own humanization. The third part focuses on the metamorphosis of humans into animals. However, instead of interpreting this process unambiguously as regression, it exposes yet another meaning of it. Transforming humans into a kind of fairy-tale animal capable of philosophical thought evokes a different quality of speech: *the eloquent animal* commands refined linguistic expression crucial for the truthful and ethical use of language. I interpret the eloquent animal as a metaphor for the rational acknowledgement of our hitherto-repressed 'likeness to animals'.[2] Thereby, the figure anticipates a possible reconciliation with nature, an idea that encompasses recognizing the animal's 'likeness to man' (AT, 119, trans. modified). I discuss Adorno's attempt to locate this likeness in the speech-like expressive force that he ascribes to both artworks and animals that are mute but have an exceptional appearance, such as the rhinoceros. Such expression – even if only *symbolic* and stricken with *semblance* – may redeem the price of progress: it gives voice to what is mute in itself, to the suffering inherent in the oppression of nature and the repression of the fact of our belonging to it.

Natural History

If traditional philosophical anthropology defines humans as animals endowed with reason and language, *Dialectic of Enlightenment* offers a story of how such endowment came about. From the viewpoint of the catastrophic mid-twentieth century, it attempts a retrospective reconstruction of the unfolding of modern reason and subjectivity. Insofar as such an enquiry aims to understand what is by asking for its becoming, its perspective can be qualified as genealogical. The fact that the book pursues this enquiry not by sticking to the facts of modern history, seemingly extending its gaze all the way back to the origins of humanity, has caused much confusion. Yet it offers bits and pieces of the *Urgeschichte* (primordial history) of reason and subjectivity not in order to clarify the question of origin but to shed light on modern history. To that end, a mode of allegorical interpretation is applied to fictional texts.

Underlying the whole endeavour is the idea of *Naturgeschichte*.[3] This must be translated into *natural history* but is not to be confused with scientific endeavours such as evolutionary theory. In Adorno's sense, it constitutes a critical perspective encompassing both a historical correction of a naturalistic interpretation and a naturalistic correction of a historicist interpretation. From a natural-historical perspective, the process of humanization can be narrated neither simply as natural evolution nor as the gradual self-awakening of *Geist*, human spirit, setting off an autonomous cultural evolution.[4] Rather, from its ineffable beginnings this process must be understood in terms of the relationship of the historical to the natural world, a relationship that is itself historical and variable. Marx stressed its practical quality: it entails *working* oneself out of nature as well as an ongoing *interaction* with nature, for which he coined the apt metaphor of humanity's metabolism with nature.[5]

Furthermore, unlike the linear model suggested by both the naturalistic and the historicist account, a dialectical model highlights the ambivalence of progress. On the one hand, humanization entails emancipation from the heteronomy of nature. On the other hand, such actual progress comes at a price produced by a twofold exercise of violence: against outer nature, which we have to conquer in order to survive, and against inner nature, which – as in the case of our drives – we have to (de-)form in order to become autonomous subjects. For Adorno and Horkheimer there is no doubt about what separates us from the beasts: while they are eternally stuck in a 'world without concept' – their cognitive abilities restricted to 'vital patterns' – and an existence of 'gnawing emptiness' (DE, 205), we have escaped such captivity. The process of humanization is one of cultivating the 'liberating' agency of thought (DE, 205), the instrumental and reflexive power of concepts, in short: the force of reason. While animals have no words, language is the very 'backbone' (DE, 205) supporting our escape. And yet, under the constant threat of 'regression to animal form' (DE, 205), to a speechless, conceptless and purposeless existence, the process had to take on a violent form: 'Humanity had to inflict terrible injuries on itself before the self – the identical, purpose-directed, masculine character of human beings – was created' (DE, 26). What is alleged here of the becoming of humanity, the authors, taking up an idea of Sigmund Freud's, assume, must be repeated in the becoming of each and every human subject under modern conditions. This idea is key to understanding the allegorical quality of the *Urgeschichte* of subjectivity.

For the predicament they call 'Prix du progrès' (DE, 190–1), Adorno and Horkheimer introduce the image of vivisection, which reappears in the opening lines of 'Man and Beast'. Vivisection is a case in point of the systematic 'blindness' to suffering that figures as the 'transcendental condition of science' (DE, 191) under the spell of instrumental reason. Furthermore, Adorno and Horkheimer voice the suspicion that such blindness pertains not just to the suffering of animals but to that of all creatures, including man. They go even further, claiming that what is actually being found out in the mutilation of animal bodies tells us more about the historical life of human beings than about the natural life of animals. That is to say, it tells us more about the state of our deformation: shows us that the human animal in its everyday life functions 'in the same mechanical, blind, automatic way as the twitching movements of the bound victims' (DE, 204). Vivisection becomes a metaphor for our distorted and alienated – our mutilated – relations to the world and to ourselves. Citing their mechanical, blind and automatic quality means making a natural-historical argument which exhibits the critical implications of the method. It shows how historically adopted properties have turned into habits, finally appearing as natural, or, in the words of philosophical tradition: how they have become second nature to us. And it reveals the forgotten cost of this process: becoming second nature is both a process of emancipation and of (self-)domination.

From the insight into this price, Adorno and Horkheimer draw two conclusions whose significance I want to scrutinize in the following: first, the very violence inherent in humanization inhibits us from becoming truly human, from being more than, as they put it with a nod to the famous opening lines of Nietzsche's fragment on truth and lies, 'the cleverest animal' (DE, 211). Second, in further consequence, the violent repression of our animality triggers the tendency to revert to bestiality. In short, trying to escape first nature by replacing it with a rational system of self-preservation and (self-)domination, we end up reproducing it as second nature. This is what Adorno and Horkheimer call the 'regressive moment' (DE, xvi) of enlightenment: the attempt to autonomously make history leads (back) into a state of heteronomy. In this polemical sense, *natural history* signifies the process of history becoming (like) brute nature again.[6] In order to examine the process of self-creation, the suffering it inflicts and its self-cancelling consequences, I will turn to a literary text that exhibits a surprising resemblance to *Dialectic of Enlightenment*: H. G. Wells's *The Island of Doctor Moreau*, first published in 1896, offers an account of humanization that also employs the scenario of vivisection and gives special attention to the role of language. Thus, like the *Odyssey*, it can be read as an 'allegory of the dialectic of enlightenment' (DE, 27).

The Animal Forced to Speak

The Island of Doctor Moreau has the appearance of a rather simple story. It is purportedly recounted from memory and left to posterity by Edward Prendick, a wealthy Englishman studying natural history. The story begins with him being shipwrecked while on a research trip. The lone survivor of an arduous struggle for survival, lost on the Pacific Ocean in a fragile dinghy, he is saved by a schooner. Aboard he encounters Montgomery, another Englishman, who is in charge of transporting caged wild beasts to an isolated volcanic island in the middle of the ocean. As they reach Noble Island, the drunkard captain of the schooner insists Prendick disembark, and Prendick ends up being taken to the realm of Montgomery's master. Doctor Moreau, a notorious vivisectionist, had to flee England after his cruel experiments on living animals were exposed. Once on the island, the story slowly unfolds the process of Prendick finding out the truth about the people with strange features, bodies and habits populating the place: in his locked enclosure, Moreau mutilates and reshapes animals into human form, aiming, as he puts it, to 'burn out all the animal' in order to 'make' a purely 'rational creature'.[7] So far, the scientist–creator has not been completely successful, and the results of his experiments have been released on to the island to lead an existence torn between their animal origins and the basic human habits forced upon them. The 'Beast Men' are kept in check by 'the Law', a set of pseudo-religious rules that are to prevent them from resorting to animal behaviour. After Prendick has found out the truth, the story unfolds another gradual process: the Beast People's estrangement from the Law, triggered by a series of catastrophes, including the deaths first of Moreau and then of Montgomery. Yet again the sole human survivor, Prendick accommodates himself among the creatures until they revert to animal existence.

Despite Wells's role as a pioneer of a Culture Industry genre, *The Island of Doctor Moreau* is not simply a science-fiction novel.[8] Jorge Luis Borges aptly compared it to a classical fable.⁹ The latter licenses the inclusion of *fabulous* elements, among them, prominently, speaking animals. In Aesop's fables, the animals' appearance is meant to illustrate the *fabula docet*, the sentence at the end spelling out the lesson of the story. But Wells's modern version does not offer such a conclusion. Nor can it be reduced to a number of socio-historical lessons, despite obvious satirical allusions to pressing issues facing late-nineteenth-century England, among them class relations, the waning authority of religion, changing gender relations and the empire's colonialism. Deliberately or not, the question of human nature appears to underlie the socio-historical allusions. To be more precise, both the fable's narrative and its symbolism revolve around man's relation to and his difference from animals. Anthropological questions are of course never untainted by history. Their treatment in Wells's fable is clearly set in a world still under the influence of the shocks emitted by Darwin's revolution. Almost intuitively, so it seems, the text conflates an anthropological with a socio-historical perspective. Thus, what *Dialectic of Enlightenment* presents as the logic of natural history, *The Island of Doctor Moreau* reflects through literary, i.e. aesthetic means. In both cases, vivisection serves as a metaphor for that process's price, as it expresses the dehumanizing effects of becoming and being human under certain historical conditions. If metaphors can be taken to be condensed myths,[10] then *The Island of Doctor Moreau* reverses such condensation and turns what in *Dialectic of Enlightenment* is an image of the process of (self-)creation into a mythical narrative.

Burning out the Animal

Adorno and Horkheimer describe the violent process of forming the character of human beings as one of 'molding' (DE, 208) and 'directly imprinting' (DE, 209) on bodies and minds alike. This is literally what Moreau is doing to the animals. Their vivisection serves a 'humanizing process',[11] he explains to

Prendick, using the very same metaphors, as he speaks of the 'carving', 'grafting' and 'shaping' of 'living forms'.[12] What appears to us now as a B-movie-style absurdity, the very idea that cutting up various animals and rearranging and sowing back together the parts could ever result in a new living form, is perceived by Prendick in a similar manner. He first suspects Moreau to be vivisecting human beings, trying to turn them into animals. And it takes quite an effort on Moreau's part to convince him that the Beast Men are 'humanized animals – triumphs of vivisection'.[13]

This absurdity is meaningful. When Moreau claims to have dedicated his life to the study of the 'plasticity of living forms',[14] he alludes to adaptive plasticity as a basic principle of evolutionary theory. At the same time, the vivisectionist's treatment of living materials calls to mind an idea central to the German tradition of philosophical anthropology: plasticity is a defining feature of what Nietzsche called the 'as yet undetermined animal'.[15] Devoid of determinate orientation provided by instinct and adaption to its surroundings, the human animal is defined by its radical openness. Thus, man is forced to define and form himself. Moreau not only believes in the unlimited potential of plasticity but seeks to practically realize it. At first, the process of humanization re-enacted by Moreau is an attempt quite literally to *burn out all the animal*: a bloody bio-technical engineering process that eliminates physical animal features and treats bodies as raw material on which 'the human form' is to be stamped.[16] Now, if we read Moreau's enterprise as a metaphor for the process of human self-formation, it is clear that the physical part, the shaping of bodily structure, (logically) precedes the work of the self on the self. Thus, Moreau is characterized as a man aspiring to become the 'world's maker'.[17] The way he treats living matter as if it were a lump of clay leads the narrator to liken him to the image of God the Father.[18] Moreau can be read as the embodiment of the Creator, or His non-personal replacement in modernity, evolutionary progress.

Once the job of physical reshaping is done, the creator has to breathe a distinctly human life into his creature. Making it a rational creature of course entails altering 'the mental structure', which Moreau declares to be even 'less determinate than the bodily' structure.[19] Following brain surgery, incessant conditioning is supposed to do the trick, transforming the speechless into a speaking animal, the conceptless into a thinking animal. Moreau considers the 'artificial modification' of instincts and drives as the foundation of 'moral education', for instance the sublimation of pugnacity into self-sacrifice and sexuality into 'religious emotion'.[20] It means repressing first nature in the service of establishing second nature, grafting ethical life upon physical life, turning animal existence into human existence. But the replacement of 'inherited' and 'fixed ideas' with 'rational' ideas proves the experiments' source of failure. The educational process fails to bring about the desired results. Just as the biblical Creator, dissatisfied with the behaviour His creatures display in Paradise, tosses them into a world of self-responsibility, Moreau, upon encountering unsurpassable problems in forming his creatures' mental and moral capacities, leaves them to their fate on the island. It is only once the subjects have been released from the hands of their maker that the pivotal part of humanization, the formation of the self by the self, begins.

Two principles that condition each other govern this process of rational self-moulding. They are expressed in one of the recurring credos of the Beast People: 'Say the words, learn the Law'.[21] The first principle highlights the importance of acquiring speech. Being able to *say the words* preconditions the internalization of new ideals, which are condensed into the second formula, *learning the Law*. At the same time, language acquisition is tied to the learning and saying of the Law's words. This predefines the kind of language skills the creatures gain. Both principles coincide in the act of self-moulding, illustrated by the ritual of the Law, the key instrument of the Beast Men's (self-)education process. The creator has not simply set his subjects free. Instead, he seems to have given them a set of rules to internalize. Experienced by Prendick in the slum-like dwellings of the Beast People, the rule of the Law is confirmed in a verbal ritual led by its own high priest, the 'Sayer of the Law', a kind of dignified elder. He is chanting the formula for everyone to repeat:

> Not to go on all-fours; *that* is the Law. Are we not Men?
> Not to suck up Drink; *that* is the Law. Are we not Men?
> Not to eat Fish or Flesh; *that* is the Law. Are we not Men?
> Not to claw the Bark of Trees; *that* is the Law. Are we not Men?
> Not to chase other Men; *that* is the Law. Are we not Men?[22]

The Law's objective is clear: just like the cutting on the physical level, it is aimed at burning out the animal on the mental and affective level, directly addressing urges associated with animal behaviour. Furthermore, the reciting of prohibitions is supposed to preserve the attained state. The act of chanting the formula in unison functions as collective self-reassurance, manifested in the line: 'Are we not Men?' By saying it aloud the Beast Men reaffirm their humanity; by rhetorically questioning it they address the possibility of a negative answer. Adorno and Horkheimer interpret the reversed metamorphosis of humans into animals as a motif of 'torment', 'horror' and 'punishment' (DE, 205), which is found in myths and fairy tales across cultural and temporal boundaries. The urgency of the Law is fuelled by the actual ambiguity of this prospect: the effort to hold together the self, a cornerstone of civilization, is permanently accompanied by the 'temptation to be rid' of it (DE, 26). Such libidinous temptation haunts the Beast People, who seem to remember – and at times to resort to – the thrills of their supposedly burned-out animal existence. In other words, as much as they are perpetually repeating the Law, they are perpetually breaking it. This is the reason why the threat of reversion alone is not enough and has to be backed up by the more concrete threat the Sayer of the Law articulates: 'Evil are the punishments of those who break the law. None escape.'[23]

While Moreau has seemingly given up dominion over what he considers his failed experiments, their Law actually continues to appeal to his authority. Following the Ten-Commandments-like formula, there is a second half with a more prayer-like quality, reminiscent of the final lines of the Our Father:

His is the House of Pain.
His is the Hand that makes.
His is the Hand that wounds.
His is the Hand that heals.[24]

The formula oscillates between praising the benevolence of 'Him', the deified creator, and implanting in the Beast People the fear of his powers to inflict pain. On the one hand, the Law stands for a kind of domination that is no longer the arbitrary one of the absolute sovereign. Such direct force Moreau applies only in physically shaping his creatures in 'the House of Pain', the enclosure containing his operating table, and, at times, in using a whip to keep renegade individuals in check. On the other hand, the distance the Law introduces from such direct force does not imply that the Law is free from the purpose of domination. On the contrary, it embodies the internalized, abstract and systematic force of rationality shaping the mind, the affects, the habits. Because of such internalization, its sway is much more effective. But make no mistake: the Law only works in this way because behind it stand the *past* suffering in the House of Pain and the *constant* threat of the whip, in short, the knowledge that 'none escape' potential punishment by 'Him', an authority now itself of a more abstract and therefore universal kind.

The Island of Doctor Moreau hardly depicts saying the words and learning the Law as emancipation. Rather, just as vivisection serves as an image of the dark secret at the beginning of everything human, debunking the myth of Creation as an act of divine grace, so the Law exhibits its repressed foundations in terror and violence. From this perspective, even the laws of reason do not seem to be something man is freely giving to himself, but a corset he has to force upon himself in the painful process of self-formation. Language and rationality appear as themselves heteronomous forces, acting from within the self while subjecting the self (its urges, drives, desires) to their merciless rule. 'None escape' is the essence of this rule, as it is of the Law in the fable. It signifies exactly what Adorno and Horkheimer mean when they describe the logic of the domination of nature in almost identical terms: 'Nothing can escape' (DE, 207).

So far, I have taken *The Island of Doctor Moreau* as presenting in literary form the twofold violence involved in the process of humanization: the conquest of outer nature with the means of modern science by Moreau, the subjugation of inner nature with the means of moral education by the Beast Men. Now, I argue, the fable equally finds a way of expressing the price of this domination. The bloody operations illustrate both the suffering of animals as subjected to domination and the terrible injuries humans had to inflict on themselves in order to burn out the animal in them, a harm alleviated yet reproduced by their rational institutions, as demonstrated by the Law. Such injuries continue to be suffered, because the effort of holding the self together demands strict measures of self-denial. Furthermore, said effort demands that the suffering that springs from self-denial be denied as well. The fable spells out what follows from this: the systematic forgetting of suffering, itself a precondition for effective self-formation, is at the same time at the root of the failure of self-formation. This is the reason why the 'triumph', as Moreau sees it, of his enlightened humanizing methods descends into the 'triumphant calamity' (DE, 1) that is the subject of Adorno and Horkheimer: the failure of humanization and the reversion of humanity into bestiality. On Moreau's forsaken island the repression of suffering establishes, in the words of Walter Benjamin, a 'nexus of guilt among the living'.[25] None can escape its implications: not Moreau the creator, not the Beast Men, his creations and not even Prendick, the narrator pretending to be a mere observer.

None Escape

Moreau admits to the failure of his experiments: there is 'something that I cannot touch' in the Beast Men, 'somewhere – I cannot determine where – in the seat of the emotions'.[26] But he draws an inadequate conclusion as he tries to physically localize this untouchable something as 'a strange hidden reservoir' of instincts and desires.[27] As if he was a representative of contemporary neuroscience, he blames it all on the brain. He perceives his past failures as mere technical imperfections to be overcome by more refined methods of reshaping the brain. Thus, Moreau sees in the subject of his experiments no longer 'a fellow-creature, but a problem'[28] and declares: 'I will conquer yet'.[29] But Moreau's humanizing process does not fail because it leaves something unconquered by rational method. On the contrary, it is doomed to fail because it will not accept anything outside of its reach. His inability to acknowledge what Adorno calls the non-identical – that which remains unavailable to the rational claim to identity – is the actual source of failure. What he cannot burn out is the creaturely capacity for suffering, which he identifies as animality, thereby dismissing its relevance for humanization. What he forgets is that humans and animals share their participation in 'the natural history of suffering'.[30] In this respect, Moreau truly is the man of modern science. His attempt to decipher the laws of creation with the aim of mastering their applicability makes him blind to the suffering he inflicts. Answering Prendick's call to justify his cruel experiments, Moreau bluntly expresses his contempt for creaturely suffering: he who aims to be superior to animality, to conquer and rule over it, views pain as a mere physical issue of no metaphysical import.[31] Moreau's contempt reminds one of the 'bourgeois coldness' (DE, 57, trans. modified) Adorno and Horkheimer consider a precondition of humanity's regression into the barbarism of the twentieth century. This is best expressed when Moreau calls his enclosure 'a kind of Bluebeard's Chamber, in fact. Nothing very dreadful really – to a sane man'.[32]

Such coldblooded sanity is at the root of a historical formation of reason that descends into systematic insanity. Moreau is an allegory for enlightened scientific thinking's reversal into myth – the triumphant calamity that none and nothing can escape. Moreau himself in the end is killed in a beastly fashion by a puma creature who was supposed to be the crowning achievement of his creative endeavours.

The most impressive allegories of failed humanization are the Beast Men themselves. If learning the Law and saying the words are at the heart of humanization, the inability to embrace rationality and to express oneself verbally are at the heart of its failure. But the Law is not simply overcome by the untamed strength of the Beast Men's natural inclinations. As it is grafted upon them from the outside by an overwhelming authority, it remains, on the inside, alien to them. This structure is made obvious by them permanently reciting the Law, without actually *learning* it, that is, understanding it. For them, the Law never evolves into something they actually agree with based on experience and deliberation. The fact that its force rests solely on the threat of punishment and is not supported by actual acknowledgement weakens the Law. This weakness is exhibited once the Law is stripped of the whip.[33] Once Moreau is dead and Montgomery (who dies soon after) and Prendick fail to replace him, the sway of the Law begins to fade. It has not succeeded in rendering the creatures truly rational beings exactly because this purpose is identified with nothing but burning out the animal. Thus, in the formation of the self, reason is experienced only as an agent of repression and self-control, not as a force for the cultivation and enrichment of the self.

The failed self-cultivation is essentially a failure truly to master language, in the sense of both speaking it and understanding it. The principle *say the words* is taken quite literally by the Beast Men. In their communication, they hardly manage to go beyond the exchange of bits and pieces of predefined formulas, mostly derived from the text of the Law. This is illustrated by one creature in particular, the Ape Man. In an episode just before the Beast People's great regression, the Ape Man praises whatever he picks up from Prendick and does not understand as 'Big Thinks' – as distinguished from 'Little Thinks', the 'plain and comprehensible issues of everyday life'[34] – and memorizes them in order to preach them to his fellows. Such a limitation to the repetition of the same stock phrases can be described as an inability to find genuine expression. Where nothing beyond the pre-given is expressed, nothing can actually be understood. In accordance with this, the Beast Men's ability to understand appears limited to what Adorno calls *Einschnappen* (literally: snapping into place) (see MM, 141). This metaphorical expression signifies the resort to predefined patterns of perception, interpretation and reaction in response to stock phrases.

The Beast People's linguistic inability has grave consequences: they are themselves incapable of acknowledging and expressing their mutilated animality. In this regard, Wells's Ape Man differs fundamentally from his peer, the educated ape Red Peter in Kafka's 'A Report to an Academy'.[35] Unlike the latter, who eloquently reflects on the hardships of his education, the Beast Men lack the means for *symbolic* expression, which are indispensable for 'lend[ing] voice to suffering'.[36] Better captured by Adorno's German expression *Leiden beredt werden lassen* (literally: to let suffering become eloquent), such *lending voice* transcends what is dramatically characterized by Prendick on the occasion of Moreau's vivisection of the puma: 'It was as if all the pain in the world had found a voice.'[37] What begins with the wordless cries of the tortured creature longs for symbolic expression. Finding words for it distances one from its overwhelming immediacy, enables one to reflect upon it. Thereby, linguistic articulation aims at escaping the mythical spell: that the pain suffered pushes one to inflict pain. It is a precondition of any *actual* humanization, of finding a way out of the nexus of guilt among the living. In the end, the Beast People cannot escape. Paradoxically, it is their inability truly to understand and symbolically express both their difference from and their commonality with animals that drives their reversion.

After the deaths of Moreau and Montgomery, that is, the loss of authority on the island, the Beast Men's affective bond with civilization loosens. First, Prendick registers 'a growing difference in their speech and carriage, a growing coarseness of articulation, a growing disinclination to talk'.[38] Fascinated by these changes he recounts the spectacle of linguistic regression: meaningful sounds revert into meaningless ones, distinct articulations into shapeless muttering, clear-cut forms into amorphous matter. This is accompanied by a progressive degradation of all civilized behaviour. From upright posture, via feeding and drinking habits, to sexual decency, every single one of the holy rules falls into oblivion. In the end, as the ultimate consequence of their failed humanization, the Beast Men literally revert to bestiality, re-entering the eternal game of hunting and devouring each other.

And Prendick? He tries to keep his distance from the events. And yet, precisely because he clings to the one and only objective of salvaging the integrity of his human self, he does not escape the spreading barbarism either. Thus, Prendick is the most striking allegory of the dialectic of enlightenment in the book, resembling his famous predecessor Odysseus. Introduced in the fable as a wealthy Englishman of his time – clearly informed by social, racial and sexual prejudices – he further represents the prototypical enlightened bourgeois subject. In contrast to Moreau, who still believes in humanity's divine superiority, from the very beginning Prendick sees that, given the circumstances, humans are no less and may be even more bestial than animals. In the prologue, the events on the dinghy set the tone for what is to follow.[39] After they have run out of provisions, the two other survivors of the shipwreck say they should draw lots to decide which of them they should eat. A fight breaks out between the other two, but as the boat sways, they stumble and fall overboard. By staying out of the fight, Prendick ends up the lone survivor. This role thenceforth defines him, just as it defines Odysseus. Both equally prove wholly enlightened insofar as they are only interested in self-preservation by any means.

The suspension of boundaries between humanity and animality is a central motif of the fable, but keeping them clearly delineated is Prendick's foremost concern. Thus, he has to deny the Beast Men's humanity in order to preserve his own, constantly applying degrading semantics to these 'bestial monsters, mere grotesque travesties of men'.[40] The more blurred the boundaries actually become on the island, the more he is exposed to both the mortal danger of 'losing the self, and with it suspending the boundary between oneself and other life' (DE, 26), *and* the promise of happiness and lust attached to this potential loss. While Odysseus' sailors are seduced 'into abandoning themselves to their drive' (DE, 54, trans. modified) and turned into animals by the goddess Circe, the master of self-control is able to withstand her charms. Accordingly, Prendick's ongoing behaviour is defined by a fervent resistance to both the threat and the lure of such metamorphosis.

For this purpose, Prendick exploits the Beast Men's lack of adequate words and concepts. Like Odysseus, who yields to the demands of the mythical creatures only to utilize the loopholes in their order and subvert it, he employs cunning, 'the faculty by which the self survives adventures, throwing itself away in order to preserve itself' (DE, 39). In this manner, Prendick intentionally gives up his posture of superiority in order to salvage it. On the surface he lives as a fellow among the Beast People. However, knowing it would demonstrate his 'inability to master himself and others' (DE, 57), Prendick never lets real affection enter into his relations with them. 'Friendly tolerance' is the most he allows himself to feel towards singular individuals.[41] Yet he never forgets his objective – self-preservation – rendering all his relations purely instrumental and expressive of the same systematic coldness we find in Moreau. But Prendick has to harden himself against suffering because he has physically experienced it. The more it dawns on him that participation in the *natural history of suffering* is the common denominator of all things living, the more fervently he has to stress the animalistic inferiority of the Beast Men. It is this stubborn insistence on his exclusive humanity that makes Prendick inhuman, thereby involving him ever more deeply in the dialectic of civilization and barbarism governing the island.

This dialectic finds expression in the hunting of the Leopard Man, who has broken the Law.[42] Bestiality breaks free from collective repression, as the Beast Men, the former victims, become vicious persecutors, at times leaving it unclear who is hunting whom. In this scene of barbarization, the whole calamity of natural history becomes visible. Barbarization shows itself to be not simply the opposite of human civilization but the very logic of human civilization reverting into brute nature. It is the Law itself that sanctions the very bestial behaviour it was set up to prohibit. Prendick becomes one with the ecstatic, bloodthirsty crowd. But he not only becomes *like* the Beast Men he abhors; his cruelty even surpasses theirs. In the very end, as Prendick is alone and the Beast Men begin to lapse into animality, he develops genocidal fantasies.[43]

Just like Odysseus, every escape leads Prendick into a new calamity – but unlike the model of yore, the final flight does not bring him back to his beloved Ithaca. Paying attention to its symbolic meaning, the strange episode of Prendick's escape suggests itself as a story of *not* escaping. The boats having been destroyed by the drunken Montgomery, the bourgeois Prendick, inexperienced in physical labour, attempts and fails to build a seaworthy raft. His chance arrives when a passing boat, bearing two half-decayed corpses, becomes stranded on the beach. Thus, Prendick only gets to leave the island on a mythical death boat that seems to be Hades rather than homeward bound. In any case, he has to pay a price for his relentless self-preservation, which amounts to the loss of his humanity. After having participated in the hunting, Prendick cannot but acknowledge the actual source of the bestiality: 'I had here before me the whole balance of human life in miniature, the whole interplay of instinct, reason and fate in its simplest form.'[44] If life on the island represents nothing less than human existence, this judgement implies that such existence is a failure. Not just the Beast Men but we as well are 'grotesque caricatures of humanity'.[45]

It's All about Us

This is what I take to be the dire 'lesson' of Wells's fable: it's all about us. The Beast Men are allegories of our not-yet-realized humanity. Their story is our story, their island our world, their mock-human existence our own existence – and their bestiality is ours. That is why, in the end, Prendick experiences a twofold alienation as he returns to civilization. First, he has to accept that he himself is implicated in such all-too-human bestiality. His self-alienation amounts to the suspicion that he, 'too, was not a reasonable creature, but only an animal tormented with some strange disorder in its brain'.[46] What defines his humanity no longer appears as rational and moral order but as disorder and deformation. As Prendick looks at his fellow civilized human beings he perceives them in a similar manner: 'I could not persuade myself that the men and women I met were not also another, still passably human, Beast People, animals half-wrought into the outward image of human souls; and that they would presently begin to revert, to show first this bestial mark and then that.'[47] On the last pages, he reports having been unable to live in London again, as the very capital of civilization resembled the island most vividly. Just as on the island a 'bovine creature' reminded Prendick of a 'really human yokel trudging home from his mechanical labours', back in London the 'weary pale workers [who] go coughing by me with tired eyes and eager paces' appear as 'wounded deer dripping blood'.[48] The 'prowling women [...] mew after' him,[49] posing as much of a threat to his *identical, purpose-directed, masculine character* with their Circe-like lures as the female (often feline) creatures whose sexuality dominated his perception of them on the island. When Prendick flees from the wilderness of the crowded streets into a chapel, not even the church offers metaphysical shelter. There, 'it seemed that the preacher gibbered Big Thinks just as the Ape Man had done'.[50] The whole range of human characters in the modern world appear to be living their everyday lives in the 'mechanical, blind, automatic way' Adorno and Horkheimer compare to the twitches of vivisected animals. Both in case of the feline whore and the apish preacher, the mechanical, blind, automatic quality of their behaviour is presented as a deformation of language: they degrade it into 'advertisement slogans' (DE, 115) for the physical or metaphysical services they offer. Back in civilization, Prendick does not rediscover 'the sweet and wholesome intercourse of men' he longed for on the island.[51] Instead, just as for the Beast People's cult of the Law, being *the cleverest animal*, able automatically to repeat the same stock phrases – to mew or gibber – seems to be enough for civilization's purposes.

Prendick's alienation results in an altered understanding of humanity. We are not really – we only appear to be – human. In other words, *we* truly are *Beast Men*: such incomplete humanity is defined by our purpose-directed character's violent attempts to repress our own animality, which fails to burn it out and instead turns it into nothing more than bestiality. Thus, Prendick adopts a deeply pessimistic metaphysics revolving around the senseless suffering in which all things living are implicated: 'A blind fate, a vast pitiless mechanism, seemed to cut and shape the fabric of existence, and I, Moreau by his passion for research, Montgomery by his passion for drink, the Beast People, with their instincts and mental restrictions, were torn and crushed, ruthlessly, inevitably, amid the infinite complexity of its incessant wheels.'[52]

The fable's grim conclusion thus takes the form of an indictment of God, or His modern replacements, such as history, evolution or scientific progress. Even though this wantonly cruel God, embodied by Moreau, is dead, there is no emancipation, no salvation and not even consolation in sight. Existence on the island (that is, our existence) is compared by Prendick to 'one of those "Happy Family" cages that animal-tamers exhibit, if the tamer were to leave it forever'.[53] Where all seem bestial and none are able to escape the aimless suffering caused by the mechanical, blind, automatic way of anonymous and abstract forces, we are confronted with the triumphant calamity that is natural history.

The Eloquent Animal

Both *The Island of Doctor Moreau* and *Dialectic of Enlightenment* allegorically present the constant threat of being reduced to nothing more than a suffering creature as the metamorphosis of humans into animals. Just as 'the animal's lack of reason holds it eternally captive in its form' (DE, 206), the reversion effected by reason's aporias appears as humanity's eternal damnation to bestiality. Albeit with literary means in *Doctor Moreau* and theoretical ones in *Dialectic of Enlightenment*, both works seem to subscribe to a fatalistic philosophy of history. Yet, despite Jürgen Habermas's influential critique,[54] *Dialectic of Enlightenment* does not subscribe to but rather criticizes this fatalism, which is actually inherent in *Doctor Moreau*. The latter depicts human civilization as destined to slip into calamity, thereby converting a genuinely calamitous second nature into first nature. Such an ahistorical view simply inverts the logic of endless progress into one of endless regression. Reading Adorno and Horkheimer in this way cuts their argument in half.[55]

Their interpretation does not ascribe our ongoing participation in the natural history of suffering to some calamitous principle of history but ties it to the *form* our relationship with living nature has taken on. Because this form has *historically* developed, it can and must be changed by historical practice. Such a dialectical interpretation opens up the possibility of escaping the natural history of suffering and of dissolving the nexus of guilt among the living. Viewed in this light, the metaphor of the speaking animal shows itself to be ambiguous as well: only on the one hand does it illustrate the actual failed humanization of the animal forced to speak. On the other hand, it serves as an allegory of a possible successful humanization. It would count as successful if it allowed for our own animality to become an integral part of human life. Furthermore, the metaphor of the speaking animal is not simply *ambiguous*: its use proves *dialectical* insofar as both meanings contradict and condition each other. Perceiving human beings as animals, that is, recognizing their participation in the natural history of suffering, is the precondition of escaping it. In turn, invoking an idea of humanity's reconciliation with inner and outer nature is the precondition of judging the lives of really existing humans as subject to *deformation*, not as the invariant form of human life.

Now, what does such an idea encompass? As it entails a reconfiguration of humanity's metabolism with nature, such a future outcome can hardly be spelled out in factual terms. However, one can formulate the conditions of the possibility of reconciliation. The early Marx provided such a formulation in his reference to an altered *humanization of nature* that would no longer be aimed exclusively at the domination of nature but would incorporate *the naturalization of man*.[56] Still, what this could mean remains rather vague. Thus, Adorno, whose concept of natural history turns Marx's formulation into a critical programme, employs metaphors and images to render what is possible more concrete without predetermining it. The following passages unfold how the speaking animal serves as a metaphor which concretizes both aspects of reconciliation: in its first meaning, it expresses the naturalization of man by shedding light on man's 'likeness to animals' (AT, 119). It teaches us to see *humans as animals* and thereby points beyond the reduction of animality to creaturely suffering. This, in turn, implies the second meaning, which expresses the *true* humanization of nature by exposing the animal's 'likeness to man' (AT, 119, trans. modified). Becoming able to see *animals as humans* means acknowledging their unredeemed potential for humanity.

What does our likeness to animals render visible? In regard to Circe's spell, Adorno and Horkheimer remark that the epic attempts to gloss over the traces of the aforementioned ambiguity of threat and lure. The scrutinizing gaze of ideology critique rediscovers them in the image of metamorphosis. That is, the mythical spell that traps the sailors in animal form 'at the same time liberates the very nature which is suppressed in them' and revokes 'that which constitutes them as selves and separates them from the beasts' (DE, 55). Unlike in the case of other mythical monsters – think of Scylla and Charybdis or the

Sirens – Circe's spell does not do lethal harm to those who succumb to it. This is confirmed by a few revealing details: as the previous victims she turned into beasts are prowling about Circe's island, they appear as peaceable; they refrain from attacking each other and the visitors, approaching them with curiosity and affection instead, rising on their hind legs, thereby symbolically bridging the gap between the species. Finally, as Odysseus's fellows are transformed back into men, they are actually wistful, despite the fact that, or even because, they appear to be 'confirmed and strengthened in their manhood' (DE, 57). As they had escaped that which rendered their humanization flawed, the purpose-directed, masculine character of the human self, they were no longer forced permanently to suppress their drives, so their purposeless animal existence 'brings about, in however delusive a form, a semblance of reconciliation' (DE, 55).

One searches in vain for such a happy, peaceful and friendly animal existence on the island of Moreau. Or so it seems. Turning the same scrutinizing gaze on the fable, one can make out at least one exception. Recurring without ever playing a major part in the story is a little pink sloth creature. Both in appearance and behaviour, it stands out from the rest of the Beast People. Just like the rest, however, it is a figure charged with symbolic meaning. The creature, resembling a very particular animal, bearing the name of a cardinal sin, is perceived by Prendick to look 'like a flayed child'.[57] It thus represents the violated innocence of the vivisected animals. Its appearance, especially its 'mild but repulsive features', reminds the gentleman of a child. Moreover, its behaviour towards him is, like that of Circe's beast men, curious and affectionate, but it is also childlike; in the beginning, it shyly but ingenuously stares at him and touches his hand. As Prendick is alone with the Beast Men, the sloth creature displays what the superior can only label as an 'odd affection' and follows him around without the malicious intent of its carnivorous peers.[58] But the crucial moment arrives only after it has returned to animal existence and left Prendick's side, as it reappears once more to warn him of his mortal enemy, the Hyena-Swine.

1. Zweizehenfaultier, Unau (Choloepus didactylus). 1/7. (Art. *Faultier*.)

FIGURE 3 *Zweizehenfaultier, Unau (Choloepus didactylus)*, Meyers Konversations-Lexikon. 5th edition (1893–1897/1901). Public domain. Private scan: Sebastian Tränkle

Being an animal, it displays sympathy without deriving any evident benefit or seeking some purpose. Thus, the pink sloth creature is the closest to achieving a semblance of reconciliation of all those one finds in the island's symbolic universe.

The figure of the sloth calls to mind Adorno's interpretation of animals as allegories of an existence devoid of 'any purpose recognizable to man'.[59] The essence of such slothful existence Adorno expresses in the aphorism 'Sur l'eau', which manages to condense quotes from Maupassant, Proust and Hegel in one sentence: '*Rien faire comme une bête*, lying on water looking peacefully at the sky, "being, nothing else, without any further definition and fulfilment"' (MM, 157). It is a common misunderstanding to interpret such images as defining a utopian vision of pure contemplation, resembling life on the islands of Circe or the lotus eaters. Instead of positively identifying the properties of a reconciled human existence, they provide counter-images to the actually existing: not a conceptual but a metaphorical expression of that which has not been subject to rigorous rational character formation. The animalistic purposelessness they illustrate is counterposed to the universal purpose-direction of human beings living in late modern society, defined, in the words of Adorno, by the compulsion to be 'operating, planning, having one's way, subjugating' (MM, 157). This purposelessness is only a negative expression of the possible freedom from the imperatives of instrumental reason and bourgeois work ethics. At the same time, the happiness falsely promised by the images is thus in reality only attainable 'through historical work' whose objective is 'suffering removed' (DE, 49). Hence, regaining the purposeless nature of animal existence only bears reconciliatory meaning as symbolic anticipation, stricken with *semblance*.

Accordingly, through the childish and clownish figure of the pink sloth, the fable takes part in the 'condemnation of empirical rationality' (AT, 119) Adorno associates with art's own ridiculousness (*Albernheit*).[60] Moreover, animals such as sloths – or rhinos and hippos – provoke an experience that Adorno, citing an old army joke, articulates through the exclamation of the young soldier who visits the zoo for the first time: 'Animals like that do not exist!' (AT, 82) In his unpublished 1961/62 lectures on aesthetics, Adorno interprets this scene as the experience of utopian splendour, one aspect of the semblance character of artworks. This semblance character is constituted by 'the contradiction of something not existing, which [momentarily] appears as if it existed, thereby promising that which does not exist'.[61] Thus, in truly unreal figures, such as the pink sloth creature making its random appearances on the island of horrors, the possibility of reconciliation momentarily *flashes up* in the calamitous course of natural history.

Moreover, the ridiculous and childlike sloth figure is a distant relative of the intellectual animals entering the stage in Adorno's correspondence. In a fashion not at all unusual in intellectual circles in the early twentieth century,[62] Adorno signs his letters with 'Archibald, the hippo king', as his wife Gretel becomes 'Giraffe Gazelle'.[63] The mostly exotic animal characters are chosen according to the idea that 'for every person there is an original [*Urbild*] in a fairy tale' (MM, 87). The letters play with the perceived properties of the respective animals, which are taken to resemble the appearance or habits of the person to whom they are assigned. The contrast produced by the often philosophically charged content the letters present so eloquently and their playful framing by salutations and signatures using animal names is not just humorous. In the intellectual self-understanding articulated here, the utmost mastery of rational thought and linguistic expression coalesces with the idea of an existence that allows these to blossom independently of predetermined demands. The eloquent animal represents a relation to the world (and ourselves) that is defined by the same mimetic curiosity and affection towards the objects and other subjects encountered that we find in the pink sloth creature.

Redeeming not *reversing* the violent process of humanization, Adorno's eloquent animal represents man who recognizes his likeness to animals without abandoning his humanity. This implies drawing on the expressive force of language and the reflexive force of reason in a way that transcends their instrumental application. The eloquent recognition of one's own animality belongs to what Adorno and Horkheimer call the 'remembrance of nature within the subject' (DE, 32) and consider the precondition for constituting what would actually be human. Adorno goes as far as defining the only possible moral sense of 'being human' under inhuman social conditions as the attempt 'to live so that one may believe himself to have been a good animal' (ND, 299). Being a *good animal* encompasses both the eloquent recognition of being an animal and the possibility of animality and morality, nature and freedom, no longer being opposites.

Moreover, only human beings who recognize their likeness to animals are able to recognize the animal's likeness to man and thereby open up the perspective of an altered and actual humanization of nature. Seeing animals as humans does not simply mean projecting human properties onto them. Rather, it implies locating the animal's likeness to man in features of its very own existence. Leaving aside common physiological traits, this is without a doubt a speculative undertaking. Adorno hints at such features in the context of discussing art's 'likeness to speech' (*das Sprachähnliche*) (AT, 112, trans. modified). He introduces examples from the realms of both art and nature of non-linguistic expression which, at the same time, resembles speech. In a manner comparable to Etruscan vases, 'the rhinoceros, that mute animal, seems to say: "I am a rhinoceros."' (AT, 112). Such expression Adorno differentiates from common predication. Instead of using language like a purpose-driven human being attributing properties to an object, the mute and purposeless animal expresses something by its *appearance* alone (see AT, 329): 'Here I am' or 'This is what I am' (AT, 112). Through such expression, animals represent nothing but 'their own name, utterly impossible to exchange' (MM, 228). The name for Adorno symbolizes a kind of selfhood that is not defined by external or practical purposes. Obviously, he introduces the rhinoceros as a metaphor for the expression of the non-identical, of which only art is capable, a kind of expression through which the artwork 'closes itself off to being-for-another [...] and becomes eloquent in itself' (AT, 112).

But in turn, the metaphor also reveals the rhinoceros's animal existence in a certain limited sense as *eloquent in itself*. It implies Adorno's understanding of natural beauty as an encounter with a natural object which we experience not merely as an exemplar of brute nature but as something that seems to *say* more than it *is* (see AT, 78). Of course, such eloquence is stricken by semblance, as the rhinoceros only *seems to say* something in the eyes of its human beholder. Yet there is good reason for such an anthropomorphic assumption, as we experience the form of such expression as *objective*, compelling and binding, but its content as something unintelligible, as something that 'questioningly awaits its solution' (AT, 71) by our *subjective* spontaneity. The assumption, for Adorno, is rendered irrefutable by the encounter with animals, provoking him to concede that 'there is nothing so expressive as the eyes of animals – especially apes – which seem objectively to mourn that they are not human' (AT, 113). It is as if the eyes of the apes were speaking a non-significative language older than our significative one, thereby expressing an earlier stage of our own not-yet-human existence. Thus, their eyes objectively express their lack of means of expression, and so their inability to articulate their suffering. While the apes are still awaiting their liberation from the muteness imposed upon them by their lack of full subjectivity, their gaze demands it from us, from our subjective agency.

The mournful eyes of the apes serve as a reminder of what reconciliation would also entail: humanizing nature implies that human beings, who are alone capable of it, give the animal's suffering a voice and break it free from its eternal captivity. Yet this does not at all imply something like the current calls for an 'animal liberation', which actually aim to reinstate the animal's eternal captivity in the happy family cage left by the tamer, that is, to reinstate wild nature. The trenchant images provided by Wells's fable should cure us once and for all of any longing for 'original' or 'authentic' natural existence. 'As a model and goal', write Adorno and Horkheimer, nature signifies nothing but 'bestiality' (DE, 212). In contradistinction, true liberation would mean freeing animals, along with humans, from their dumb, purposeless and bestial existence. As Adorno aptly puts it, 'what accedes to language enters the movement of a humanness that does not yet exist' (AT, 117). As much as the faculties of reason and language might have been complicit in the triumph of calamity, it is at the same time by these two faculties, and by them alone, that true humanization for any living being is rendered possible. As much as they might have served the process of burning out the animal, it is by them alone that 'man, who is one with it through his past, can find the redeeming formula and through it soften the stony heart of infinity at the end of time' (DE, 206). In order to provide the formula for redeeming suffering and liberating all living beings from their confinement in natural history, however, rational thinking must be freed from its instrumental limitation, just as language must be salvaged from its communicative deformation. In other words, the power to think beyond the existing calamities and the capacity to express such thought must be cultivated. We must become more than the cleverest animals: eloquent animals.

Notes

1   Max Horkheimer and Theodor W. Adorno, *Dialectic of Enlightenment*, trans. Edmund Jephcott (Stanford: Stanford University Press, 2002), 203–12. Hereafter cited in text as 'DE'.

2   Theodor W. Adorno, *Aesthetic Theory*, trans. Robert Hullot-Kentor (Minneapolis: University of Minnesota Press, 1997), 119. Hereafter cited in text as 'AT'.

3   See Theodor W. Adorno, 'The Idea of Natural History', trans. Robert Hullot-Kentor, in Robert Hullot-Kentor, *Things Beyond Resemblance: Collected Essays on Theodor W. Adorno* (New York: Columbia University Press, 2006), 252–69.

4   The negativistic and allegorical nature of Adorno's method marks the difference from both Charles Taylor's conceptual and Michael Tomasello's empirical enquiries into the origins and the nature of 'the language animal'. See Charles Taylor, *The Language Animal: The Full Shape of Human Linguistic Capacity* (Cambridge, MA: Harvard University Press, 2016); Michael Tomasello, *Origins of Human Communication* (Cambridge, MA: MIT Press, 2008). For further discussion of the overlap and the parting of ways with Tomasello's rather harmonious 'cooperation model of human communication' (Tomasello, *Origins of Human Cooperation*, 71ff.), see Philip Hogh, *Communication and Expression: Adorno's Philosophy of Language*, trans. Antonia Hofstätter (London: Rowman & Littlefield, 2017), 28.

5   See Alfred Schmidt, *The Concept of Nature in Marx* (London: Verso, 2014), 76–93.

6   Albeit with a polemical twist, in this respect the concept conforms to its Darwinian use. As a historical formation, capitalist society actually reinstates the 'natural' principle: the survival of the fittest. See Theodor W. Adorno, 'Theory of Pseudo-Culture', trans. Deborah Cook, *Telos* 95 (1993): 17.

7   H. G. Wells, *The Island of Doctor Moreau* (London: Penguin, 2005), 78.

8   See Margaret Atwood, 'Introduction', in Wells, *The Island*, xiii–xxvii.

9   Jorge Luis Borges, 'The First Wells', in Jorge Luis Borges, *Other Inquisitions 1937–1952*, trans. Ruth L. C. Simms (Austin: University of Texas Press, 1975), 86–8.

10 See Hans Blumenberg, *Paradigms for a Metaphorology*, trans. Robert Savage (Ithaca: Cornell University Press, 2010), 77–80.

11 Wells, *The Island*, 67.

12 Ibid., 71.

13 Ibid.

14 Ibid.

15 Friedrich Nietzsche, *Beyond Good and Evil*, trans. Walter Kaufmann, in *Basic Writings of Nietzsche* (New York: The Modern Library, 1992), 264.

16 Wells, *The Island*, 82.

17 Ibid., 74.

18 See ibid., 50, 62.

19 Ibid., 72.

20 Ibid., 73.

21 See ibid., 58.

22 Ibid., 59.

23 Ibid., 60.

24 Ibid., 59.

25 Walter Benjamin, 'Goethe's Elective Affinities', trans. Stanley Corngold, in *Selected Writings: Volume 1 1913-1926*, ed. Marcus Bullock and Michael W. Jennings (London: The Belknap Press, 2002), 307.

26 Wells, *The Island*, 78.

27 Ibid.

28 Ibid., 75.

29 Ibid., 78.

30 Theodor W. Adorno, 'Offener Brief an Max Horkheimer', in *Gesammelte Schriften*, ed. Rolf Tiedemann, vol. 20 (Frankfurt am Main: Suhrkamp, 2003), 156. My translation.

31 See Wells, *The Island*, 73.

32 Ibid., 32.

33 See ibid., 119.

34 Ibid., 122.

35 See Franz Kafka, 'A Report to an Academy', trans. Willa and Edwin Muir, in *The Complete Stories by Franz Kafka* (New York: Schocken, 1995), 281–91.

36 Theodor W. Adorno, *Negative Dialectics*, trans. E. B. Ashton (London: Routledge, 1973), 17. Hereafter cited in text as 'ND'.

37 Wells, *The Island*, 38.

38 Ibid., 122.

39 Ibid., 7ff.

40 Ibid., 80.

41 Ibid., 123.

42 See ibid., 90ff.

43 See ibid., 126.

44 Ibid., 95.

45 Ibid., 60.

46 Ibid., 131.

47 Ibid., 130.

48 Ibid., 131.

49 Ibid.

50 Ibid.

51 Ibid., 97.

52 Ibid., 96.

53 Ibid., 124.

54 Jürgen Habermas, *The Philosophical Discourse of Modernity*, trans. Frederick Lawrence (Cambridge: Polity Press, 1990), 106–29.

55 Carrie Rohman reads *Dialectic of Enlightenment* as confirming the utter 'unreasonableness' of the Enlightenment reason presented by *The Island of Doctor Moreau* in her 'Burning Out the Animal: The Failure of Enlightenment Purification in H.G. Wells's *The Island of Doctor Moreau*', in *Figuring Animals: Essays on Animal Images in Art, Literature, Philosophy and Popular Culture*, ed. Mary Sanders Pollock and Catherine Rainwater (New York: Palgrave Macmillan, 2005), 132. The fact that Adorno and Horkheimer also – and for good reason – cling to the 'perverse' (Rohman, 'Burning Out the Animal', 127) idea of enlightenment as elevating all creatures beyond animality by rendering them reasonable remains unmentioned.

56 See Schmidt, *The Concept of Nature*, 76.

57 Wells, *The Island*, 57.

58 Ibid., 122.

59 Theodor W. Adorno, *Minima Moralia: Reflections on a Damaged Life*, trans. E. F. N. Jephcott (New York: Verso, 2005), 228. Hereafter cited in text as 'MM'.

60 Certainly, the fable's undeniable ridiculousness also qualifies it as raw material for the 'calculated fun' (AT, 119) of the Culture Industry. The 1932 movie adaption *The Island of Lost Souls*, with its clichéd exoticism, attests to such a functionalizing of art's ridiculousness.

61 Theodor W. Adorno, 'Ästhetik (1961/62)', lecture, 2 June 1962, Theodor W. Adorno Archiv, Frankfurt am Main, Vo 7111 f. My translation. I would like to thank the Adorno Archiv for the permission to cite from the unpublished typescript.

62 I owe this insight to Magnus Klaue, who brought to my awareness the *locus classicus* for this practice: Franz Blei's *Das große Bestiarium der Modernen Literatur* (Hamburg: EVA, 1995), first published in 1920, is a who's who of modern writers that assigns animal characters to each.

63 See in particular Theodor W. Adorno, *Letters to his Parents 1939–1951*, trans. Wieland Hoban (Cambridge: Polity Press, 2007).

Bibliography

Adorno, Theodor W. *Aesthetic Theory*. Translated by Robert Hullot-Kentor. Minneapolis: University of Minnesota Press, 1997.

Adorno, Theodor W. 'Ästhetik (1961/62)'. Lecture, 2 June 1962. Theodor W. Adorno Archiv, Frankfurt am Main.

Adorno, Theodor W. 'The Idea of Natural History'. Translated by Robert Hullot-Kentor. In Robert Hullot-Kentor, *Things beyond Resemblance: Collected Essays on Theodor W. Adorno*, 252–69. New York: Columbia University Press, 2006.

Adorno, Theodor W. *Letters to his Parents 1939–1951*. Translated by Wieland Hoban. Cambridge: Polity Press, 2007.

Adorno, Theodor W. *Minima Moralia: Reflections on a Damaged Life*. Translated by E. F. N. Jephcott. New York: Verso, 2005.

Adorno, Theodor W. *Negative Dialectics*. Translated by E. B. Ashton. London: Routledge, 1973.

Adorno, Theodor W. 'Offener Brief an Max Horkheimer'. In *Gesammelte Schriften*. Vol. 20, edited by Rolf Tiedemann, 155–63. Frankfurt am Main: Suhrkamp, 2003.

Adorno, Theodor W. 'Theory of Pseudo-Culture'. Translated by Deborah Cook. *Telos* 95 (1993): 15–38.

Benjamin, Walter. 'Goethe's Elective Affinities'. Translated by Stanley Corngold. In *Selected Writings: Volume 1 1913–1926*, edited by Marcus Bullock and Michael W. Jennings, 297–360. London: The Belknap Press, 2002.

Blei, Franz. *Das große Bestiarium der Modernen Literatur*. Hamburg: EVA, 1995.

Blumenberg, Hans. *Paradigms for a Metaphorology*. Translated by Robert Savage. Ithaca: Cornell University Press, 2010.

Borges, Jorge Luis. 'The First Wells'. In Jorge Luis Borges, *Other Inquisitions 1937–1952*, translated by Ruth L. C. Simms, 86–8. Austin: University of Texas Press, 1975.

Habermas, Jürgen. *The Philosophical Discourse of Modernity*. Translated by Frederick Lawrence. Cambridge: Polity Press, 1990.

Hogh, Philip. *Communication and Expression: Adorno's Philosophy of Language*. Translated by Antonia Hofstätter. London: Rowman & Littlefield, 2017.

Horkheimer, Max and Theodor W. Adorno. *Dialectic of Enlightenment*. Translated by Edmund Jephcott. Stanford: Stanford University Press, 2002.

Kafka, Franz. 'A Report to an Academy'. Translated by Willa and Edwin Muir. In *The Complete Stories by Franz Kafka*, 281–91. New York: Schocken, 1995.

Nietzsche, Friedrich. *Beyond Good and Evil*. Translated by Walter Kaufmann. In *Basic Writings of Nietzsche*, 179–436. New York: The Modern Library, 1992.

Rohman, Carrie. 'Burning Out the Animal: The Failure of Enlightenment Purification in H.G. Wells's *The Island of Doctor Moreau*'. In *Figuring Animals: Essays on Animal Images in Art, Literature, Philosophy and Popular Culture*, edited by Mary Sanders Pollock and Catherine Rainwater, 121–34. New York: Palgrave Macmillan, 2005.

Taylor, Charles. *The Language Animal: The Full Shape of Human Linguistic Capacity*. Cambridge, MA: Harvard University Press, 2016.

Tomasello, Michael. *Origins of Human Communication*. Cambridge, MA: MIT Press, 2008.

Wells, H. G. *The Island of Doctor Moreau*. London: Penguin, 2005.

7

The Gaze of the Rhinoceros and the 'It' of *Aesthetic Theory*

Daniel Steuer

'It'

The enigmatic nature of the passage from *Aesthetic Theory* to which the present volume responds is compressed in the phrase 'Here I am or This is what I am'. The formulation does not repeat Exodus 3:14 verbatim, but the likeness is close enough for us to believe that it is not just a coincidence. The Lord is the one who can truthfully say, 'I am that I am', 'I am who I am' or 'I will be what I will be' – even 'I create what I create.' The Lord can simply say to Abraham: go, tell them 'I am hath sent you.' But what the rhinoceros 'seems' to say is not so literal. It can be read as a secularized version of the biblical passage, but while the biblical passage marks some absolute underlying all that is, the passage from *Aesthetic Theory* – not a religious or theological text, though also not a traditional philosophical one – marks the absence of anything absolute and the presence of something enigmatic.

To all philosophy, Adorno says in the fourth of his *Philosophische Terminologie* lectures, 'if it is true philosophy, and not philology or a purely mechanical game, language, that is, presentational form, is essential'.¹ The point is repeated in the introduction of *Negative Dialectics*: 'An idiosyncratic precision in the choice of words, as if they were to designate the things, is one of the major reasons why presentation is essential to philosophy.'² Against traditional philosophy, which has always been 'allergic to expression' (ND, 55), Adorno thus links the task of true philosophy to the literary and expressive use of language: true philosophy's 'integral, non-conceptually mimetic moment of expression is objectified only by presentation – by language' (ND, 18, trans. modified).

And, just to make the task of philosophy even more difficult, the heartbeat that motivates true philosophy is a paradox: the attempt to say what cannot be said. Without that motivation, philosophy 'must capitulate, and all spirit with it. We could not conceive the simplest operation; there would be no truth; emphatically, everything would be just nothing' (ND, 9, trans. modified). The 'utopia' of philosophy, by contrast, would be 'to use concepts to open up the non-conceptual, without making it their equal' (ND, 10, trans. modified).

This innermost core also connects true philosophy to art, more precisely to the 'yearning that animates art, art as something non-conceptual, and whose fulfilment shuns the immediacy of art as semblance. The concept – the organon of thinking, and yet the wall between thinking and the thought – negates that yearning. Philosophy can neither circumvent such negation nor submit to it. It must strive, by way of the concept, to transcend the concept' (ND, 15, trans. modified). As a result, there is a play of mimesis between philosophy and art, and there is a paradox at the heart of both.

The paradoxical nature of Adorno's philosophy and aesthetic theory, I shall try to show, is an inheritance from his negative theology, which, in *Aesthetic Theory*, veers towards an apocalyptic messianism. In order to defend Adorno against the claim that the negative theology that informs his thought renders it liable to charges of irrationalism, mysticism, incoherence and emptiness, Gordon Finlayson has argued that the 'significant and striking parallel between Adorno's thought and negative theology' is rather to be explained in terms of 'the existence of a specifically philosophical dimension in apophatic theology', the 'paradox of the ineffable'.[3] Adorno, he writes, actually had 'virtually no interest' in such theology.[4] Elements such as the ban on images and the prohibition of naming, he says, are pressed 'into the service of [Adorno's] own theoretical agenda'. Thus, Finlayson takes Adorno 'at his word when he claims that philosophy "secularizes theology" insofar as the *Bilderverbot* pervades [his] thought'.[5] For Finlayson, the critics are right in their strong reading of 'non-identity' as the wholly other of discursive thought but wrong in assuming that this justifies the charges they level against Adorno.

In what follows, I shall not attempt to find out how interested Adorno was in negative theology and the Kabbalah, or whether his critics are right or wrong in accusing him of irrationalism because of the presence of motifs such as a messianic light, the Lurianic breaking of vessels, the grass angels of the Zohar, the ban on images – or indeed because of his idea that the redeemed world would be *presque rien* different from the present one. My approach will be to chart some of the tracks that these motifs and – crucially – their secularized forms create in the textual fabric of *Aesthetic Theory* and some of Adorno's other works. For if we grant Adorno's assumption that presentational form is essential to true philosophy, then his true philosophy will inherit certain features from his use of these motifs. My own assumption is that Adorno's secularized adaptation of these elements imbued his writing with strong centrifugal forces that always had to be contained through the construction of constellations, thinking in models, and essayistic strategies of circling, and thereby partly constituting textual objects. But ultimately, as I shall suggest, it relied on something somatic: the resistance of the senses, especially the eye, Adorno's katechontic gaze.

In his preface to the English edition of *Prisms*, Adorno says that 'matters of fact' appear to him as 'processes of *infinite* mediation'.[6] He therefore distrusts presentations of this infinite mediation in terms of literal meanings. Literal meanings are the counter-model not only to essayism and constellations but also to Adorno's gaze, while essayism, constellations and the gaze lead into a process of infinite mediation. 'The literal', as Adorno bluntly puts it, 'is barbaric' – full stop.[7] This may go some way towards explaining why it is not easy to read Adorno: what would a 'process of infinite mediation', or the presentation of it, look like on paper? Could there ever be a linguistic score for it?

Even taking into account the fact that 'Adorno completed' but 'did not finish it',[8] *Aesthetic Theory* appears more bewildering and unwieldy than most of his other writing. The closer a reader looks at a particular passage of this text, the more she is sent adrift to other places, the more she feels all at sea. The text points forwards and points backwards without an overall direction emerging. There may be signposts, but there are no clear paths connecting them on the textual surface.

Adorno mentioned in a letter that a book's

> almost ineluctable movement from antecedent to consequence proved so incompatible with the content that for this reason *any organization in the traditional sense* – which up until now I have continued to follow (even in *Negative Dialectics*) – proved impracticable. The book must, so to speak, be written in equally weighted, paratactical parts that are arranged around a midpoint that they express through their constellation.[9] (AT, 364, my emphasis)

The notion of a 'constellation' is familiar enough to take the sting out of the impracticability of 'any organization in the traditional sense'. Nevertheless, Adorno apparently saw himself forced to go beyond all the principles of form and procedure he previously practised. While elsewhere in Adorno's essayism the 'reflection extends outwards but is nevertheless contained',[10] in

Aesthetic Theory 'sources of orientation', Shierry Weber Nicholsen writes, 'are largely absent' and 'the "centre" that the textual configuration "expresses" [...] becomes the only source of orientation'.[11] But what if on this occasion Adorno's writing was actually catapulted out of the orbit around its centre? What if the attempted mimesis of the object was driven into a centrifugal dynamic, taking the mimetic reader, possibly even the author, with it?[12]

Robert Hullot-Kentor suggests that the 'book's stylistic peculiarities derive' from its orientation towards 'the thing-in-itself' (AT, xi). And this orientation entails a reversal of roles: it is the thing-in-itself that speaks, while 'subjectivity's own voice' can only interfere (AT, xii).[13] What is this thing-in-itself, which is usually considered unapproachable? How does it speak? How does Adorno try to make it speak? Hullot-Kentor's answer is that he does this by paratactically presenting aesthetic concepts as the memory of 'nature sedimented in art', which takes shape 'as the unconscious, mimetically written history of human suffering' (AT, xiii). Adorno's initial answer might have been that he did it by determinate negation. Ultimately, *Aesthetic Theory* courts 'it', and we shall come across 'it' in various places. In his lectures on negative dialectics, Adorno defends himself against criticism of his 'negative' method by saying that the negativity is correlated to a positive '*movens* of thought', something fixed and positive: 'if you do *not* want it – and I say intentionally "it", because it is impossible to say, to express the "it" – well, then there is no determinate negation, then there is really nothing at all.'[14] Despite this inexpressibility of the 'it', Adorno nevertheless says something about it: it 'balks at being abstractly, rigidly, statically fixed into an unmoving state once and for all'. Thus, 'it' is ever moving and at the same time the fixed positive *movens* of negative dialectics. 'If', Adorno says,

> it is true that any philosophy that can make some claim to truth lives off the old fire, meaning that it secularizes not only philosophy but actually also secularizes theology, then, I believe, we have here a prominent moment in

the process of secularization, namely: that the ban on images, which takes a central place in those religions promising salvation, that this ban on images reaches right to the level of thoughts and the most subtle ramifications of thought.[15]

Thus, the 'it' – situated on the threshold between what is communicated and what is expressed – becomes the plenipotentiary of, or linguistic variable that represents, secularized revelation. We will come across it again in this role in a crucial passage of *Aesthetic Theory*.

The Paradox of Secularization

Secularization is an unclear yet central notion in Adorno. In art, he says, form

> secularizes the theological model of the world as an image made in God's likeness, though not as an act of creation but as the objectivation of the human comportment that imitates creation; not *creatio ex nihilo* but creation out of the created. (AT, 143)

Form is thus 'the law of the transfiguration of the existing, counter to which it represents freedom' (AT, 143). Art is the secularized sacred sphere.[16] Its semblance character – which frees it of the 'lie' of the sacred sphere, namely that it is 'actually real' – makes the work of art 'a secularization'. Its theological heritage is the secularization of revelation (AT, 106). Metaphysics and transcendence are secularized into history and decay (ND, 360). Artworks produce their own transcendence (AT, 78).[17] The theological ban on images is secularized (ND, 207). Art, as a non-conceptual language, reflects that of divine creation (AT, 78); magic,[18] mana,[19] epiphanies (AT, 80), the apocalypse (AT, 85) and, arguably, salvation (AT, 2) are also secularized. Then, there is also the idea of a general 'progressive secularization' (AT, 3) and art's position in relation to this development.

In his *The Legitimacy of the Modern Age*, Hans Blumenberg demonstrates that the term 'secularization' was and is used with various meanings. 'The world', Blumenberg says, 'that became ever more worldly was a subject whose extension was about as obscure as that of the impersonal "it" in the proposition "It's raining".'[20] An all-encompassing process of secularization swept the world. What kind of 'secularization', then, does Adorno have in mind? Where the term occurs in his writings it is mostly used in accordance with Blumenberg's formula 'B is the secularized A'.[21] This specific use carries with it a moment of transformation: the transcendent becomes immanent, and we get either a blunt immanence that refuses to address any question of transcendence or the paradox or aporia of some immanent transcendence. As Blumenberg elaborates, the use of the 'B is the secularized A' formula comes at the price of introducing a 'paradox' into our 'understanding of history'.[22] For now the worldly items must be comprehended in terms of precisely those qualities they are meant to lack qua secular items. In other words, the notion of secularization combines two irreconcilable ideas: the 'radical discontinuity of belonging, together with, at the same time, identity of that which belongs'.[23] The secularized item is, and is not, the same as before. And this makes it possible to judge the result of such 'transitively qualitative transformations' as a loss or a gain. But in either case 'the later phase is possible and intelligible only in relation to the earlier phase assigned to it'.[24]

Adorno, to my knowledge, nowhere offers a positive discursive identification or a determinate negation of what secularization is or how it takes place. But in a prominent place, he speaks of it as a 'transmutation', evoking the world of alchemy and arguably – at least by analogy – the Christian concept of transubstantiation. The context is the introduction of the logic of decay in *Negative Dialectics*. Having quoted the passage from *The Origin of German*

Tragic Drama in which Walter Benjamin speaks of 'history' being inscribed on the countenance of nature in the pictograph of transience, Adorno comments:

> This is the transmutation of metaphysics into history. It secularizes metaphysics in the secular category pure and simple, the category of decay. Philosophy interprets that pictography, the ever new Mene Tekel, in microcosm – in the fragments which decay has chipped, and which bear the objective meanings. No recollection of transcendence is possible any more, save by way of perdition; eternity appears, not as such, but diffracted through the most perishable. (ND, 360)[25]

Benjamin's ruin, which represents 'history' physically merging into the stage (*Schauplatz*), is expanded into the 'transmutation of metaphysics into history', and the result of this operation is a process of universal   in Benjamin's words 'irresistible' – decay without any transcendence, except through the immanent reading of the Mene Tekel, that is, of the ever smaller fragments left behind by decay: *Zerfall*, literally a falling apart into ever tinier particles.[26]

Transmutation secularizes. The secularization of metaphysics and transcendence into decay cannot, however, be based on a complete transformation of the former into the latter. Otherwise, the micrological results of decay would not bear objective meanings, and it would not be possible to recollect the transcendent from the fragments. But the transmutation, however it may have come about, creates a paradoxical situation for philosophy. It needs to read the ever new Mene Tekel, the ever smaller chips of decay, the most perishable (*das Vergänglichste*). Thus, what must be read gets smaller and smaller, the decay and transience get ever more intense, and yet this is the only way the recollection of transcendence might succeed. But what will happen at the extreme end point of this process of negative – even 'apocalyptic' – messianism?[27]

The micrological reading suggested by Adorno in 'Meditations on Metaphysics' drives the hermeneutic efforts of philosophy ever deeper into the minute details of the decaying material – in a search of transcendence among ruins.²⁸ Art is secularized revelation, and artworks, we may say, are like burning bushes, except that it is not the angel of the Lord who appears but 'it'. But like the bush of the Bible they burn – maybe even explode – yet are 'not consumed'.²⁹ Under secular conditions there is no stopping point; artworks burn down and explode, and the process of micrological decay and disappearance continues.

It is therefore fitting that *Aesthetic Theory* explicitly takes fireworks to be 'prototypical for artworks' (AT, 81). But the logic of a firework loses one of the three temporal dimensions: it is what it is, and was what it was, but one cannot really say that it will be what it will be. If truth requires duration, then truth will diminish to the extent that fleetingness increases. Thus, in *Aesthetic Theory* fireworks correspond to the question posed in and by the 'Meditations on Metaphysics': 'Is it still possible to have a metaphysical experience?' (ND, 372) *Aesthetic Theory* poses the question of whether aesthetic theory is still possible. But it also asks whether genuine or authentic artworks are still possible: those which, while not 'literally' being epiphanies, gesture towards the ineffable and absolute.³⁰

The counter-movement to decay is art as secularized revelation, gesturing towards the open, that which lies beyond identity thinking. It is difficult not to imagine this as a rearguard action, the interpreter, like Klee's Angelus Novus, having her back turned against the future and being blown by the storm of decay into the ruins, with less and less space left as the amount of rubble increases, while the pieces of rubble get smaller and smaller. And unlike Goethe's Melusine, she has no box into which to escape. Maybe, then, in *Aesthetic Theory*, the antagonism between centripetal and centrifugal forces opens up a rift that threatens to explode the textual fabric and to sever Adorno's method from 'the realm of facticity – without which there can be no true knowledge'.³¹

The counter-movement depends on art's 'inevitable withdrawal from theology, from the unqualified claim to the truth of salvation, a secularization without which art would never have developed' (AT, 2). By itself – without any transcendence – the withdrawal is said to strengthen the spell that art wants to break. In this situation, artworks take on what was formerly the responsibility of theologians and priests: 'In their relation to empirical reality, artworks recall the theologumenon that in the redeemed world everything would be as it is and yet wholly other' (AT, 6). For such a messianic transfiguration to happen, art would need to 'free itself from the once perceived illusion of duration', would need to 'internalize its own transience in sympathy with the ephemeral life' (AT, 28–9). It would thereby become adequate to 'an idea of truth conceived not as something abstractly enduring but in consciousness of its temporal essence' (AT, 29). Because all art is the secularization of transcendence, all art is subject to the dialectic of enlightenment (ibid.). Just as only thinking that '*also*' thinks against itself, and thus transcends itself, is worthy of the name, only art that partakes of the aesthetic conception of anti-art and goes 'beyond its own concept in order to remain faithful to that concept' is genuine art (ibid.). Art is charged, in the same act, with becoming the repository of truth and being the secularization of transcendence, or, at the very least, the secularization of the access to the transcendent. For this it pays a price: it inherits the antinomical structure that characterizes all solidarity with metaphysics at the moment of its fall. The paradox resulting from 'secularization' leads to the final paradox: that the 'one who believes in God cannot believe in God' and that 'the possibility represented by the divine name is maintained, rather, by him who does not believe' (ND, 401–2).

The Telos of Artworks

According to Adorno, artworks not only create '*imagines*', it is as essential to artworks that they also destroy 'their own *imagerie*':

> In the incineration of appearance [*Verbrennen der Erscheinung*], artworks break away in a glare from the empirical world and become the counterfigure of what lives there; art today is scarcely conceivable except as a form of reaction that anticipates the apocalypse. Closely observed, even tranquil works discharge not so much the pent-up emotions of their makers as the works' own inwardly antagonistic forces. (AT, 84–5)

There is thus a strong pyrotechnical presence in *Aesthetic Theory*. Art, Adorno says, 'is profoundly akin to explosion' (AT, 84); fireworks are called 'prototypical for artworks' (AT, 81). New artworks are experienced as shocks, and what causes the shock is 'the explosion of their appearance'. Why do artworks explode? Because of the antagonistic forces at work inside of them and 'the impossibility of bringing these forces to any equilibrium; their antinomies, like those of knowledge, are unsolvable in the unreconciled world' (AT, 85). In exploding, their interiors become exterior. The artworks, as vessels, are no longer able to contain the internal antagonistic forces, and thus 'the outer husk is exploded; their apparition, which makes them an image, always at the same time destroys them as image' (AT, 85).

An artwork as *imagerie* – insofar as it is pictorial, representational – is always its own undoing; it 'bears its own negation embedded in itself as its own telos' (AT, 85). The 'sudden' – explosive – 'unfolding of appearance disclaims aesthetic semblance' (AT, 85). To push the paradoxical aspect of the artwork to its limit: the telos of art, as well as its origin, is its own impossibility.

This is a consequence that Adorno wants to avoid. Invoking Benjamin's reading of Baudelaire, in which 'the demise of the aura' becomes the 'aura itself', perishing and objectivation become one in the shining – *erstrahlen* – of artworks (AT, 85).

The tension between the moment of explosion, which, if not controlled or contained, threatens the possibility of artworks as *imagerie*, and 'the persistence of the transient' (AT, 84) is sustained with the help of Benjamin's notion of a dialectic at a standstill: 'To experience art means to become conscious of its immanent process as an instant at a standstill' (AT, 84). When the appearance of artworks explodes, this 'blasts open' the continuity of their inner temporality: 'To analyze artworks means no less than to become conscious of the history immanently sedimented in them' (AT, 85).

All this can also be looked at from an obverse perspective, that of the artwork as the 'appearance [*Aufgang*: rise] of the nonexistent as if it existed' (AT, 82). Art promises, by its form, 'what is not'; it registers, 'however refractedly, the claim that because the nonexistent appears it must indeed be possible' (AT, 82). Because it might seem to imply that not everything is exchangeable in today's world, this promise risks becoming ideological. It therefore needs a language that brings the exchangeable to 'critical self-consciousness' and that evokes, rather than presents, what is not. The telos of artworks is a language that does not exist, 'whose words cannot be located on the spectrum; a language whose words are not imprisoned by a prestabilized universality' (AT, 83). As an example, Adorno gives 'the color "drommet red"' from a novel by Leo Perutz, an invented name for a colour that is not to be found on the visible electromagnetic spectrum.

This is not a random choice. Perutz's novel is called *Master of the Day of Judgment* and is set in early-twentieth-century Vienna. 'Drommet red' is mentioned in both the narrator's 'Foreword instead of a Postscript' and the editor's 'Postscript'. The colour's central appearance is in a story within the story: in the sixteenth century, the Florentine organist Pompeo del Bene, who once had sought to become a painter, writes, in a book of maps, the truth of what happened to his erstwhile master, Giovansimone Chigi. Having lost his creative imagination, Chigi asks the physician Messer Donato Salimbeni to administer one of his fumigations, which, the physician says, will restore his creative powers. The procedure is not without a certain risk, though. Salimbeni believes that Chigi killed Cino, Salimbeni's brother, which Chigi denies, and

Salimbeni warns him that the fumigation will launch him on a 'stormy sea' and that perhaps it would be better for him 'to stay in harbour'.[32] The weapon used to murder Cino had belonged to a man from Toledo, who claimed to have lost it near Chigi's workshop. He was not believed, and he was sentenced and executed for the murder. When Salimbeni recounts this course of events, Chigi says, 'all honour to the verdict [...] and things that have happened are over and done with', to which Salimbeni replies: 'Things that have happened are never over and done with [...] And those responsible for them have to face divine justice.'[33] In the battle between Chigi's desire to regain his creativity and his fear of the risks involved in the procedure, the former gains the upper hand. Salimbeni prepares the fumigation, but while the actual effects of the drug may heighten the powers of imagination, they do not do so in the way Chigi desires:

> 'There is a terrible fiery sign in the sky that glows in a colour I have never seen before,' the Master cried. 'Woe is to me. It is no earthly colour, and my eyes cannot stand it.'
> 'That colour is drommet red,' Messer Salimbeni called out in a voice of thunder. 'That colour is drommet red, the colour of the sunshine on the Day of Judgment.'[34]

Salimbeni asks Chigi to confess to the murder, whereupon Chigi says only 'Mercy'.[35] But that is enough of an acknowledgement for Salimbeni to save Chigi from death – the certain outcome of inhaling the smoke. Years later, del Bene comes across Chigi in a monastery. His mind, the prior says, is 'clouded': 'We call him the Master of the Day of Judgment, for that is the only thing he paints over and over again.'[36]

Anyone exposed to the smoke sees 'drommet red' and confronts what they take to be the day of judgement. According to the fictional editor, works of art carry with them a faint glimmer of this experience, and through this they engender in their observers a temporary elevation of vision: 'In all the great symphonies of tones, colours and ideas I see a gleam of the marvellous colour drommet red, a faint reflection of the great vision that for a short while raised the Master above the bewildering maze of his tormenting guilt.'[37] The recipe for the fumigation appears at the end of del Bene's story, and in the main story it seems that someone has discovered the recipe, the book having, in the intervening years, made its way from Florence to Vienna. There is a series of suicides, beginning with an actor, Eugen Bischoff, who has lost his powers of imagination. In countless twists and turns, the main story replicates the story embedded within it. On the basis of the stories, the foreword and postscript, it is impossible to decide with certainty what was murder (or, in the case of Cino, who the murderer was) and what suicide. Nor is it possible to say who discovered the recipe in Vienna or whether the recipe actually exists, for when the book finally turns up in Vienna the final page has been ripped out. But by whom? Why? It is not even certain who the Master of the Day of Judgment is. The monks call Chigi the Master. Del Bene makes Salimbeni out to be the 'real Master'.[38] Or is it the recipe itself, which, it is suggested, was brought by Salimbeni from the Far East, that is the Master?

Thus, the story is a drama of the moral life. It is impossible to establish ultimate responsibility for the 'things that have happened' or to distinguish with absolute certainty between good and bad, a certainty that comes only with the Day of Judgement. No one and no thing is the Master of that day, yet the reader is charged with making the judgements. But how can she when she lives in a world in which, despite all the evidence, such questions are undecidable? She lives in the same 'objective-antagonistic society' that Adorno describes in *Negative Dialectics*. And the more 'mercilessly' that society 'will comport itself in every situation, the less can any single moral decision be warranted as the right one' (ND, 243). Everyone is 'infected by the evil of that totality; and no less infected is he who does nothing at all' (ND, 243). And at that point, the text introduces another secularization: 'This is how original sin has been secularized. The individual who dreams of moral certainty is bound to fail, bound to incur guilt because, being harnessed to the social order, he has virtually no power over the conditions whose cry for change appeals to the moral *ingenium*' (ND, 243).

This side of the apocalypse, in a world of secularized and ubiquitous original sin, fireworks are the liminal case of artworks, with just enough form to act as katechon before a final apocalyptic explosion. One might even say, as the most fleeting, they are the least sinful. The very moment the image appears, it disappears. Fireworks border on the purely apparitional. They come closest to heeding the advice that 'one should make no image', 'no image of anything whatsoever': the ban that 'expresses at the same time that it is impossible to make such an image' (AT, 67).[39] Hence, fireworks exemplify in unparalleled fashion that artworks 'are neutralized and thus qualitatively transformed epiphanies' (AT, 80).

Fireworks, whose 'unsurpassable noblesse', according to Ernst Schoen, derives from the fact that they do not aspire to duration but just 'glow for an instant and fade away' (AT, 28), avoid the need for lasting semblance by not excising anything from the web of spatially and temporally dispersed phenomena. There is no reification, just a blending into space and time: fireworks 'are a sign from heaven yet artefactual [*Himmelszeichen und hergestellt in eins*], an ominous warning [*Menetekel*], a script that flashes up, vanishes, and indeed cannot be read for its meaning' (AT, 81). As the prototype of the artwork, they can teach us how these gain independence, emancipatory force, in opposition to the 'fallibly existent': 'by becoming actual, like fireworks, incandescently in an expressive appearance' (AT, 81).

What fireworks share with music is that they are close approximations of 'a pure process of becoming' in which 'fictive elements wither away', including the fiction of a totality: 'In great music such as Beethoven's [...] the so-called primal elements turned up by analysis are usually eminently insubstantial. Only insofar as these elements asymptotically approximate nothingness do they meld – as a pure process of becoming – into a whole' (AT, 100–1). The 'immanent nothingness' of such artworks 'draws integral art down into the amorphous, whose gravitational pull increases the more thoroughly art is organized. It is exclusively the amorphous that makes the integration of the artwork possible' (AT, 101). The very energy put into the attempt at organizing, *durchbilden*, the artwork is redirected – as in some martial arts – against the intended form, and 'the natural element returns as what has yet to be formed, as the nonarticulated' (AT, 101). The closer we look, the more the works turn into pure material: 'paintings metamorphose into a swarming mass and texts splinter into words' (AT, 101). Even mediation only achieves the opposite of what it set out to do: 'Under micrological study, the particular – the artwork's vital element – is volatilized; its concretion vanishes. The process, which in each work takes objective shape, is opposed to its fixation as something to point to, and dissolves back from whence it came' (AT, 101).

The figures Adorno considered as an illustration for '*the metaphysics of musical time*' at the end of his planned book on Beethoven were the grass angels of Jewish mysticism, 'who are created for an instant only to perish in the sacred fire. [...] Their very transience, their ephemerality, is glorification. That is, the incessant destruction of nature. Beethoven raised this figure to musical self-consciousness' by composing 'the absolute transience of music'.[40] The end point of musical composition is thus music as acoustic fireworks. The note from the fragments on Beethoven ends with a reference to the translation of a chapter from the Zohar by Gershom Scholem in which Scholem explains that these angels have 'no shape or form' and thus do not endure: 'they exist for an instant and are consumed by that "fire that consumes fire". And each day they are recreated only to be consumed again.'[41] Adorno's note speaks of 'fire that consumes [nature]' and equates it with the fire that, according to Beethoven, should spark music in a man's soul.[42] In this way, Adorno constructs a connection between three phenomena: the artistic fire; the decay, or consummation, of nature; and the self-referential mystical image of the fire that consumes fire.

The final turning of the screw of the dialectics of aesthetics, then, is the following: by becoming as fully integrated as possible, artworks leave behind subjective themes as well as duration, and instead are returned to the amorphous. The more closely they are looked at, the more they disintegrate into points of colour or light, sounds or isolated words. All mediation was in vain, its only result a realization of the inevitability of the return to the inorganic, disintegrated, non-articulated. In the final instance, artworks – not necessarily their makers – are citizens of the apocalypse; they explode. In this respect, too, the expression of artworks is inherited from theology, and what they reveal at the same time disappears in a flash – or an explosion.

In Adorno's writing, the alternative to this dystopian trajectory is the utopian collection of glimmers of colour that would – who knows? – combine into something like the opposite of 'drommet red', a colour or light as it appears once the spell is broken and the logic of decay suspended.

The Rhino's Gaze: Goosebumps and Rearguard Utopianism

Let us recall the passage that contains our 'one-liner' and contextualize it with the 'twin passage' from *Minima Moralia* that also features a rhino:

> That aspect of the Etruscan vases that most resembles speech touches most closely on a Here I am or This is what I am, a selfhood not first excised by identificatory thought from the interdependence of entities. Thus a rhinoceros, that mute animal, seems to say: 'I am a rhinoceros.' (AT, 112, trans. modified)

The *Minima Moralia* passage introduces an important figure, that of the child, and an important idea, that of non-exchangeability as indicating a utopian moment:

> By existing without any purpose recognizable to men, the expression of animals presents, so to speak, their own name, that which it is utterly impossible to exchange. This makes them so loved by children, their contemplation so blissful. I am a rhinoceros, signifies the figure of the rhinoceros.[43]

These two passages are like two spotlights directed at the same point: the 'it'.

The paradox at the heart of language is its double character: it is both communicative and mimetic, making it constitutive of art and, at the same time, art's mortal enemy. Thus, 'the true language of art is mute' (AT, 112), as becomes apparent in the case of the Etruscan vases at Villa Giulia and in the case of the rhinoceros. Both seem to say: here I am; this is what I am. They *say* nothing but announce their 'selfhood', as something not abstracted, not excised, from the interdependence of beings (*Seiendem*).[44]

Just after the 'mute' animal seems to have spoken through its expressiveness, performing a transition from the particular ('I am') to the general ('a rhinoceros'), Adorno performs a transition to a poem by Rilke: 'denn da ist keine Stelle, / die dich nicht sieht [for here there is no place / that does not see you].' These are two half-lines *excised* from 'Archaic Torso of Apollo'; hence, here we have a fragment from a *Dichtung* that itself concerns a fragment. The lines, Adorno says, codify the non-signifying language of artworks in 'almost incomparable fashion' (AT, 112, trans. modified). At this point, the text pauses for a short moment and puts forward a thesis that brings Rilke, Benjamin and Adorno into a constellation: 'Expression is the gaze of artworks' (AT, 112). Rilke renders the torso poetically as a gaze that speaks.[45] And what does it say? 'You must change your life' – a completely indeterminate ethical demand. That is the poem's final word, not quoted by Adorno, and it addresses both the poet and the reader, who is left wondering why, how and with what aim she and the poet should change their lives.

If we turn to *Minima Moralia*, we find that it is the gaze of children that is able to transform the objects of a commodified world into something like artworks. Figures of animals, like the rhinoceros, offer particularly little resistance to such transformation: 'The relation of children to animals is based entirely on the fact that Utopia is wrapped up [*vermummt*] in them' (MM, 228, trans. modified). Here, too, the expression of an animal presents its name, so to speak: that which is 'utterly impossible to exchange' (MM, 228). The gaze of children and the gaze of the rhinoceros transform the world into one in which absolutely nothing is interchangeable. For such a world to appear to adults, perhaps they would need to change their lives.

As a utopian figure the rhinoceros brings about the aesthetic moment in whoever beholds it. Like music, the utopian rhino is a riddle.[46] Music, Adorno says, 'gazes at its listeners with empty eyes' and calls for an answer, a response, that lies in interpretation, not contemplation: 'the only person who can solve the riddle of music is the one who plays it correctly, as something whole. Its enigma apes the listener by seducing him into hypostasizing, as being, what is in itself an act, a becoming, and, as human becoming, a behavior. In music, what is at stake is not meaning, but gestures.'[47]

But of course, a rhinoceros is a natural object, whereas a piece of music, like any artwork, is an artefact. What unites them may be the primacy of the object in subjective experience, but in the case of the artwork there is, in addition, the artwork's domination over its material. Everything depends on the form this domination takes. It must at the same time enable the counter-movement: the release or liberation of the material. If the semblance produced by domination is mistaken for something naturally given, as the very thing itself, then the artwork becomes pure ideology. If the artwork tries to be fully honest either by openly admitting to being constructed or by reducing itself to its material – if it tries to become only subjective or only objective – it will miss its … well, what can we say at this point without violating the prohibitions on positive identification and graven images? Let us say, it misses the 'it' it *expresses*: the gesture of the 'here I am', or 'this is what I am', is the expressive gesture – *Ausdrucksgeste* – of the natural animal and of the genuine work of art alike.

In that gesture they *express* something that cannot be *said*, something that Adorno, in the original German, puts in the subjunctive mood: 'What radiates wordlessly from artworks is that *it is* [*daß es sei*], against the background that *it* – the unlocatable grammatical subject – *is not; it cannot be referred demonstratively to anything that exists in the world*. In the utopia of its form, art bends under the burdensome weight of the empirical world from which, as art, it steps away' (AT, 105, trans. modified; emphasis following semicolon added).[48] This *uneinlösbare*, unlocatable, *it* – pronoun without referent – is the common utopian yet unapproachable moment in natural objects and artworks alike. *It* cannot be cashed; *it* cannot be exchanged; *it* cannot be fulfilled; *it* is an endless demand or promise never to be met. It is and it is not – so long, that is, as the spell does not end.[49]

What is more than what is literally there, in the case of both nature and the artwork, is given through expression. 'Expression is a phenomenon of interference' between artistic 'technical procedures' and the 'mimetic': 'Mimesis is itself summoned up by the density of the technical procedure, whose immanent rationality indeed seems to work in opposition to expression' (AT, 114). Where the consciously applied and rational technical procedure crosses over with the mimetic, which in turn, is *herbeizitiert* (summoned) by the *density* of the former, there emerges expression. The liminality of this phenomenon is given by the fact that pure procedure would result in pure form that 'rattles mechanically' (AT, 114). The density depends on the degree to which artworks are 'fully integrated' (AT, 114) – *durchgebildet* – and, the more they are, the more they can carry the mimetic dimension: (spontaneous) imitation, not (intentional) representation. Only because of the inextricable mediation between procedure (the rational) and the mimetic (spontaneous imitation) can artworks develop their moment of truth – expression. And this 'leads to a subjective paradox of art: to produce what is blind, expression, by way of reflection, that is, through form [...] "To make things of which we do not know what they are"' (AT, 114).[50]

The artwork is the manifestation of a process that, like psychoanalysis, brings to light what otherwise would remain unexpressed, invisible. Just as technology, if used differently, might 'under transformed relations of production [...] be able to assist nature and on this sad earth help it to attain what perhaps it wants' (AT, 68), so the ideal artwork – at least from the perspective of what was 'formerly called *Sachlichkeit*' – is 'an artwork that, by refusing in any way to appear as other than it is, would become formed [*durchgebildet*] in such a way that what it appears to be and what it wants to be would potentially coincide' (AT, 107). Thus artworks help the material move to where the material wants to go by itself – the construction would cease to be domination at the point where it became fully mimetic, where the interference between technical procedure and the mimetic turned into *it*.

At the point where the gaze of the subject is returned by the object (artwork or animal) – the moment of mimesis – both are infinitely close and infinitely distant; both become fully themselves and fully other. The onlooker does not subsume the rhinoceros under the concept 'rhinoceros'; instead, the rhinoceros, like an artwork, becomes its own resemblance, and the onlooker – as in the case of the child – becomes that self-resemblance (see AT, 104). Without such moments of enigmatic gaze, all conversation, all human practice, would turn into a world of 'mechanical rattle' inhabited by what Adorno calls the 'aesthetically insensible [*Amusische*]', who exemplify a particular pathology: 'They concretize' (AT, 330). As opposed to those whose 'thought is no more than projection', they are those 'who do not project at all' and 'instead repeat and falsify' reality 'by crushing out what glimmered however distantly to preanimistic consciousness: the communication of all dispersed particulars with each other' (AT, 330).

Both these possibilities miss the mutual dependence of rationality and mimesis: '*Ratio* without mimesis is self-negating. Ends, the raison d'être of *raison*, are qualitative, and mimetic power is effectively the power of qualitative distinction' (AT, 331). But a world that is 'objectively losing its openness, no longer has need of a spirit that is defined by its openness; indeed, it can scarcely put up with the traces of that spirit' (AT, 331). The stalled dialectic between ratio and mimesis is what prohibits aesthetic comportment, for which Adorno – hesitantly and cautiously – offers a hint of a definition: ultimately, maybe, aesthetic comportment could be defined as 'the capacity to shudder, as if goosebumps were the first aesthetic image' (AT, 331). Adorno characteristically chooses an instantaneous physical reaction to describe the primordial moment of aesthetic sensibility. 'Aesthetic comportment [*ästhetisches Verhalten*]' is not intentional, not acting. It is something you cannot help but do or display. You do not decide to have goosebumps – it is you, and then again not you, who has them: 'That shudder in which subjectivity stirs without yet being subjectivity is the shudder of being touched by the other. Aesthetic comportment assimilates itself [*bildet sich an*] to that other rather than subordinating it. Such a constitutive relation of the subject to objectivity in aesthetic comportment is a marriage of eros and knowledge' (AT, 331, trans. modified). This is one of the few places where Adorno comes close to spelling out his utopia.

Adorno's Katechontic Gaze and the Work of the Grass Angels

As art cannot but aim at utopia, it shares utopia's fate which, under present conditions, is that of being riddled with antinomies. Fulfilment would be failure, success art's end. Adorno expresses it succinctly in another one-liner: 'Antitraditional energy becomes a voracious vortex' (AT, 23). The same energy that works to overcome the false life sucks art and utopia into an inescapable aporia:

> At the center of contemporary antinomies is that art must be and wants to be utopia, and the more utopia is blocked by the real functional order, the

more this is true; yet at the same time art may not be utopia in order not to betray it by providing semblance and consolation. If the utopia of art were fulfilled, it would be art's temporal end. Hegel was the first to realize that the end of art is implicit in its concept. (AT, 32)

Is there a way out of this predicament? Possibly the clearest expression of Adorno's negative theology can be found in the last section of *Minima Moralia*, which limits responsible philosophy to a contemplation of all things 'as they would present themselves from the standpoint of redemption' (MM, 247). Such philosophy needs to fashion perspectives 'that displace and estrange the world, reveal it to be, with its rifts and crevices, as indigent and distorted as it will appear one day in the messianic light' (MM, 247). Micha Brumlik remarks on this section that it is suffused with the certainty 'that even the distinction between good and evil only derives from the idea of another, better world', though it 'must remain uncertain if this idea can ever be realized. The capacity to make this distinction, and what it points to, Adorno calls "transcendence"'.[51]

This transcendent capacity for distinguishing between good and evil we shall find located in Adorno's gaze. And even though 'gaze', in this context, is not limited to the sense of sight, if Adorno had an epistemological model, it was an optical one. As the motto for his programmatic essay on essayism he chose a line from Goethe: we are 'destined to see what is illuminated, not the light'.[52] The model of refraction can also be found at central points in *Negative Dialectics*, such as the very end of the introduction, which speaks of the 'inextinguishable color' that 'comes from nonbeing': 'Thought is its servant, a piece of existence extending – however negatively – to that which is not. The utmost distance alone would be proximity; philosophy is the prism in which its color is caught' (ND, 57).

Thus, the full colourless light – the transcendent that is never given to us as immanent being – nevertheless can be experienced in refracted form, the scattered colours collected by the prism of philosophy. 'The transcendent is, and it is not' (ND, 375). The transcendent light is only there in the scattered colours: 'Grayness could not fill us with despair if our minds did not harbor the concept of different colors, scattered traces of which are not absent from the negative whole' (ND, 377–8). Artworks are given a revelatory power because they receive their semblance from non-semblance; they are mediations of immanence and transcendence, and thus their semblance promises non-semblance. What they say

> in refraining from judgments is that everything is not just nothing. If it were, whatever is would be pale, colorless, indifferent. No light falls on men and things without reflecting transcendence. Indelible from the resistance to the fungible world of exchange is the resistance of the eye that does not want the colors of the world to come to ruin. (ND, 404–5, trans. modified)

The resistance of the eye, but surely also of the ear and the other senses, is at the heart of Adorno's work. On this resistance rests the distinction between the spell and what would break it, between the grey in grey of the eversame and utopian moments. In a discussion with Max Horkheimer on 13 October 1939, Adorno said about himself: 'I also do not have a secret doctrine. But I believe that the kind of gaze I have is such that it finds in things the reflections of that source of light which cannot be the object of intentions or thoughts.'[53] Not a doctrine but a particular kind of gaze is the non-conceptual precondition for his writing and its methodological centre. Does that make him a secularized katechon? In any case, Adorno still held on to the idea of a gaze that 'secularizes metaphysics' in *Negative Dialectics*, where it is the 'gaze that interprets which becomes aware of more in a phenomenon than it is – and solely because of what it is' (ND, 28, trans. modified). But is this gaze secularized metaphysics or does it secularize the object of metaphysics?

Adorno's solidarity with metaphysics, his courting of 'it' and of the ineffable, seems itself torn between a radical materialist immanence, in which even transcendence is, paradoxically, immanent and a more classical transcendence that would locate the 'wholly other' even beyond the wholly other of a social world that has broken the spell. Just as philosophy shares art's yearning for the non-conceptual, materialism longs to 'grasp [*begreifen*] the thing', a longing that is itself paradoxical, as only without images can 'the full object […] be conceived': 'Such absence concurs with the theological ban on images' (ND, 207). Here secularization is pictured as an asymptotic process in which two sides approach each other. The next sentence, however, makes materialism the more active part: 'Materialism secularized it by not permitting Utopia to be positively pictured; this is the substance of its negativity' (ND, 207). Then, however, the perspective is again reversed. Now it is not a case of materialism pulling the ban on images into the secular, but rather materialism moving towards theology: 'Where it is the most materialist, materialism agrees with theology' (ND, 207). And the next sentence declares – suggesting that this is the point of agreement – that materialism yearns for 'the resurrection of the flesh' (ND, 207, trans. modified). Thus, finally, even resurrection is secularized.

In his lectures on aesthetics of 1958/59, Adorno says that the work of art is a 'secularization' because the separate sphere it constitutes does not continue the lie of the 'sacred sphere', which claims 'that this special, separate area, which is set apart from the world, is actually real'. The 'aesthetic circle, as it were, no longer appears as a magical agency', giving it 'an entirely immediate relationship with the truth'.[54]

Such passages operate with a distinction between the illusion of dishonest religious magic and the relationship to truth of honest artistic semblance. A similar distinction is required for the categories of positivist thinking and thinking that thinks against itself, or *Selbstbesinnung*. The capacity to make such distinctions is not immanently available. The string of paradoxes attached to negative dialectics and especially aesthetic theory, the indistinct zone required for the distinction between colourful reflection and the world of grey in grey, and, finally, the ineffable 'it', these are all the result of a notion of secularization that oscillates between various meanings, even within one and the same passage. If 'the total subjective elaboration of art as a nonconceptual language is the only figure, at the contemporary stage of rationality, in which something like the language of divine creation is reflected, with the paradox that what is reflected is blocked' (AT, 78, trans. modified), then there are at least three ways of understanding the 'language of divine creation': it may refer to a formerly transcendent language that, in its secularized form, is now reflected and blocked; it may still be transcendent, and so reflected and blocked; or it may never have been transcendent and instead may be only a blocked immanent possibility to be unlocked. In that last case, the theologumena can be no more than rhetorical means for expressing what – perhaps only – Adorno's gaze was able to perceive. That would make his writing perilously close to a mirror image of the jargon of authenticity, whose 'dignified mannerism is a reactionary response toward the secularization of death', except that in Adorno's case it would not be 'naked death' but 'the resurrection of the flesh' that 'becomes the meaning of such talk'. But in both cases, without 'something transcendent', the result would be the presentation of 'nothingness as something' and thus 'linguistic mendacity'.[55]

But, independently of those three possibilities, the topos of secularization carries with it what could be called secularization prohibitions. There is an ontological prohibition on saying what something is, and there is a teleological prohibition on saying which way history should move. The limitation to negativity makes such judgements impossible. You might say that a universalized ban on images makes them secularized acts of sin. Artworks may well suspend judgement, but in practical life it is impossible to do so. Is Adorno's aesthetic theory perhaps best characterized as a secularized apocalypse, the Day of Judgement but without the judgement? Such an unattractive conclusion can only be avoided by the material of the theory, which must give the theory a form that saves the measure of understanding the text well from being reduced to the self-referential criterion of 'having been a good reader of Adorno'. Aesthetic theory cannot limit itself to an external rational analysis; it must also follow its object mimetically. And thus understanding aesthetic theory, in turn, means going beyond its explicit statements and establishing what it expresses involuntarily. The unattractive conclusion is unavoidable if 'the end of art implicit in its concept' is the decay of all form and if the 'it' is sucked into the 'voracious vortex' of 'antitraditional energy', along with the fragments. Whether the grass angels are purely rhetorical entities or whether they point to a genuine transcendence, there would be nothing left for them to do.

Epilogue: Fireworks – Ending with a Bang and not a Whimper?

Paradoxes abound. Scripts flash up and disappear. Individual words and sounds convey limited, fragmented meanings. Exploding works discharge antagonistic forces into the amorphous. 'And this *is* the writing that was written', 'this *is* the interpretation of the thing': 'Thou art weighed in the balances, and art found wanting.'[56]

The world, we have been told, will end with a whimper, not a bang. But as the penny for the guy, as we also know, will be spent on fireworks, might it not end with a bang after all?

Mista Kurtz, meanwhile, is not quite dead, his principles live on.

With a bang with this the world thine horror spent not with is the way for thine he dead.

Thine is *it*.

Do fireworks have a gaze?[57]

Notes

1. Theodor W. Adorno, *Philosophische Terminologie*, ed. Henri Lonitz (Berlin: Suhrkamp, 2016), 70. My translation.

2. Theodor W. Adorno, *Negative Dialectics*, trans. E. B. Ashton (London: Routledge, 2004), 52. Hereafter cited in text as 'ND'.

3. James Gordon Finlayson, 'On Not Being Silent in the Darkness: Adorno's Singular Apophaticism', *The Harvard Theological Review* 105, no. 1 (2012): 9.

4. Ibid., 7.

5. Ibid., 8.

6. Theodor W. Adorno, *Prisms*, trans. Samuel and Shierry Weber (Cambridge, MA: MIT Press, 1967), 7, emphasis added.

7. Theodor W. Adorno, *Aesthetic Theory*, ed. Gretel Adorno and Rolf Tiedemann, trans. Robert Hullot-Kentor (London: Continuum, 1997), 86. Hereafter cited in text as 'AT'.

8. As Robert Hullot-Kentor puts it in his preface. AT, xviii.

9. Unfortunately neither the letter's addressee nor the date is given.

10. Shierry Weber Nicholsen, *Exact Imagination, Late Work: On Adorno's Aesthetics* (Cambridge, MA: MIT Press, 1999), 124.

11. Ibid., 130.

12. Finlayson offers another reading of the form of *Aesthetic Theory*. The text, he says, is arranged 'according to principles drawn from musical composition, an arrangement which deliberately frustrates the demands of theory. [...] it enacts the same "success" achieved by successful works of art, on Adorno's account of art: it resists assimilation into a *single*, unified whole, and thus deliberately *fails* as a theory'. James Gordon Finlayson, 'The Work of Art and the Promise of Happiness in Adorno', *World Picture* 3 (Summer 2009): 16, http://www.worldpicturejournal.com/WP_3/TOC.html. What I would describe as an accident that, because of the original theoretical layout, was always waiting to happen is here read as intentional. That is not necessarily a contradiction. As an admirer of Beckett, Adorno may have moved on from failing better to failing best – and finally to failing perfectly.

13. The following applies not just to music but to all of art: 'We do not understand music – it understands us. [...] When we think ourselves closest to it, it speaks to us and waits sad-eyed for us to answer.' Theodor W. Adorno, *Beethoven*, trans. Edmund Jephcott (Cambridge: Polity, 1998), xi.

14. Theodor W. Adorno, *Vorlesung über Negative Dialektik*, ed. Rolf Tiedemann (Frankfurt am Main: Suhrkamp, 2003), 46. My translation.

15 Ibid. My translation.

16 See e.g., Theodor W. Adorno, *Aesthetics*, trans. Wieland Hoban (Cambridge: Polity, 2018), 45.

17 Though the last point requires immediate qualification: 'Aesthetic transcendence and disenchantment converge in the moment of falling mute' (AT, 79). And: 'If transcendence were present in [artworks], they would be mysteries, not enigmas; they are enigmas because, through their fracturedness, they deny what they would actually like to be' (AT, 126).

18 Adorno, *Aesthetics*, 46.

19 Ibid., 45. 'Totality is the grotesque heir of mana' (AT, 84).

20 Hans Blumenberg, *The Legitimacy of the Modern Age*, trans. Robert M. Wallace (Cambridge, MA: MIT Press, 1985), 4.

21 Ibid.

22 Ibid., 10.

23 Ibid.

24 Ibid., 4.

25 A note appended to *Negative Dialektik* calls the 'logic of decay' one of Adorno's earliest philosophical ideas from his times as a student. Theodor W. Adorno, *Negative Dialektik*, (Frankfurt am Main: Suhrkamp, 1997), 409. The note is omitted in the English edition. Immediately following the passage quoted by Adorno, Benjamin introduces the notion of 'decay' himself. In the figure of the ruin, 'history does not assume the form of the process of an eternal life so much as that of irresistible decay'. Walter Benjamin, *The Origin of German Tragic Drama*, trans. John Osborne (London: Verso, 1998), 177.

26 The occurrence of the Mene Tekel in key passages of *Negative Dialectics* and *Aesthetic Theory* suggests at least some relationship between micrological readings and apocalyptic final judgements. Though not part of the Book of Revelation, the Mene Tekel stands for a final judgement made by God. Micrological readings are final judgements which have become self-reflexive, undoing their finality and thus sustaining an ongoing apocalyptic process.

27 For a presentation of not only Adorno's theology but 'his overall philosophy' as a 'version of apocalyptic messianism', see Micha Brumlik, 'Theologie und Messianismus', in *Adorno Handbuch*, ed. Richard Klein, Johann Kreuzer, and Stefan Müller-Doohm (Stuttgart and Weimar: Metzler, 2011), 296. In Brumlik's reading, Adorno was only able to maintain his negative micrology, the search for the unnamed, unnameable absolute among the most minute fragments of decay, by 'not distinguishing clearly between the regulative idea of truth […] and its metaphysical, so to speak Platonic, meaning' ('Theologie und Messianismus', 307).

28 'That which recedes keeps getting smaller and smaller, as Goethe describes it in the parable of New Melusine's box, designating an extremity. It grows more and more insignificant; this is why, in the critique of cognition as well as in the philosophy of history, metaphysics immigrates into micrology. Micrology is the place where metaphysics finds a haven from totality. No absolute can be expressed otherwise than in topics and categories of immanence, although neither in its conditionality nor as its totality is immanence to be deified' (ND, 407).

29 Exod. 3.1-4.

30 See e.g., AT, 82 and 103–4.

31 Adorno, *Prisms*, 7. 'If death were that absolute which philosophy tried in vain to conjure positively, everything is nothing […] Without any duration at all there would be no truth, and the last trace of it would be engulfed in death, the absolute' (ND, 371).

32 Leo Perutz, *Master of the Day of Judgment*, trans. Eric Mosbacher (London: Pushkin Vertigo, 2015), 163.

33 Ibid., 164.

34 Ibid., 168, trans. modified. 'Drommetenrot' is translated as 'trumpet red' in the English edition, missing Adorno's point and, arguably, that of the novel (AT, 83).

35 Perutz, *Master of the Day of Judgment*, 169.

36 Ibid., 170.

37 Ibid., 187.

38 Ibid., 171.

39 Adorno explicitly gives the biblical ban an 'aesthetic as well as a theological dimension' (AT, 67). It expresses humanity's necessary ignorance not only of God but also of the immanent world: 'thou shalt not make unto thee any graven image, or any likeness of *any* thing that *is* in heaven above, or that *is* in the earth beneath, or that *is* in the water under the earth' (Exod. 20.4). 'Any thing that is': this includes His ultimately unknowable creation, *it*.

40 Adorno, *Beethoven*, 176–7.

41 Gershom Scholem, *Die Geheimnisse der Schöpfung: Ein Kapitel aus dem kabbalistischen Buche Zohar* (Frankfurt am Main: Insel, 1971), 82. My translation. See Adorno, *Beethoven*, 24–5, note 305.

42 This remark may or may not be correctly ascribed to Beethoven. See Adorno, *Beethoven*, 201, note 19.

43 Theodor W. Adorno, *Minima Moralia*, trans. E. F. N. Jephcott (London: Verso, 2005), 228, trans. modified. Hereafter cited in text as 'MM'.

44 See Daniel Herwitz in this volume for a convincing critique of this claim.

45 Apollo's torso 'still glows like a candelabra/in which his gaze, even though dimmed down now,/still lives and shines'. Rainer Maria Rilke, *The Selected Poetry of Rainer Maria Rilke*, trans. Stephen Mitchell (New York: Vintage, 1982), 61.

46 There is also a dystopian rhino in Adorno's writings, the one that is so aggressive probably because of the armour that secures its survival (see ND, 180). That rhino illustrates what Adorno calls 'peephole metaphysics'. In Western metaphysics the subject 'was locked up in its own self by that metaphysics, imprisoned for all eternity to punish it for its deification. As through the crenels of a parapet, the subject gazes upon a black sky in which the star of the idea, or of Being, is said to rise' (ND, 139–40). The artwork and the rhino, by expressing 'it', by saying 'here I am', try to lure the subject out of the fortress of which this parapet is a part.

47 Theodor W. Adorno, 'On the Contemporary Relationship of Philosophy and Music', in *Essays on Music*, trans. Susan H. Gillespie, ed. Richard Leppert (Berkeley: University of California Press, 2002), 139.

48 This is related to the way in which artworks produce their own transcendence by way of the nexus of their elements (a nexus they both seek to establish and to which they adapt): 'Their transcendence is their eloquence, their script, but it is a script without meaning or, more precisely, a script with broken or veiled meaning [*gekappter oder zugehängter Bedeutung*]' (AT, 78).

49 Artworks, too, mourn: 'Because meaning, whenever it is manifest in an artwork, remains bound up with semblance, all art is endowed with sadness [*Trauer*]; art grieves all the more, the more completely its successful unification suggests meaning, and the sadness is heightened by the feeling of "Oh, were *it* only so"' (AT, 105, my emphasis).

50 The quotation within the quotation is the final line of 'Vers une musique informelle'.

51 Micha Brumlik, 'Verborgene Tradition und messianisches Licht: Arendt, Adorno und ihr Judentum', in *Arendt und Adorno*, ed. Dirk Auer, Lars Rensmann and Julia Schulze Wessel (Frankfurt am Main: Suhrkamp, 2003), 84. My translation.

52 Theodor W. Adorno, *Notes to Literature*, vol. 1, trans. Shierry Weber Nicholsen (New York: Columbia University Press, 1993), 3.

53 Max Horkheimer, *Nachgelassene Schriften 1931–1949*, ed. Gunzelin Schmid Noerr (Frankfurt am Main: Fischer, 1985), 506. My translation.

54 Adorno, *Aesthetics*, 46–7.

55 Theodor W. Adorno, *The Jargon of Authenticity*, trans. Knut Tarnowski and Frederic Will (Evanston: Northwestern University Press, 1973), 163.

56 Dan. 5.25-7.

57 I would like to thank the following friends and colleagues for their valuable comments on drafts of this chapter: Gilbert Carr, Camilla Flodin, Antonia Hofstätter,

Gregor Noll, Philipp Schönthaler and Ernest Schonfield. Thanks are also due to Leo, our cat, who, during the last stages of writing and for reasons of his own, decided to perch on my desk, behind the laptop, and from time to time get up, raise his head above the screen and gaze at me. Finally, thanks go to my partner, Birgit Illner, for her trademark moral support of the project.

Bibliography

Adorno, Theodor W. *Aesthetic Theory*. Edited by Gretel Adorno and Rolf Tiedemann. Translated by Robert Hullot-Kentor. London: Continuum, 1997.

Adorno, Theodor W. *Aesthetics*. Translated by Wieland Hoban. Cambridge: Polity, 2018.

Adorno, Theodor W. *Beethoven*. Translated by Edmund Jephcott. Cambridge: Polity, 1998.

Adorno, Theodor W. *The Jargon of Authenticity*. Translated by Knut Tarnowski and Frederic Will. Evanston: Northwestern University Press, 1973.

Adorno, Theodor W. *Minima Moralia*. Translated by E. F. N. Jephcott. London: Verso, 2005.

Adorno, Theodor W. *Negative Dialectics*. Translated by E. B. Ashton. London: Routledge, 2004.

Adorno, Theodor W. *Negative Dialektik*. Frankfurt am Main: Suhrkamp, 1997.

Adorno, Theodor W. *Notes to Literature*. Vol. 1. Translated by Shierry Weber Nicholsen. New York: Columbia University Press, 1993.

Adorno, Theodor W. 'On the Contemporary Relationship of Philosophy and Music'. In *Essays on Music*, edited by Richard Leppert and translated by Susan H. Gillespie, 135–61. Berkeley: University of California Press, 2002.

Adorno, Theodor W. *Philosophische Terminologie*. Edited by Henri Lonitz. Berlin: Suhrkamp, 2016.

Adorno, Theodor W. *Prisms*. Translated by Samuel and Shierry Weber. Cambridge, MA: MIT Press, 1967.

Adorno, Theodor W. *Vorlesung über Negative Dialektik*. Edited by Rolf Tiedemann. Frankfurt am Main: Suhrkamp, 2003.

Benjamin, Walter. *The Origin of German Tragic Drama*. Translated by John Osborne. London: Verso, 1998.

Blumenberg, Hans. *The Legitimacy of the Modern Age*. Translated by Robert M. Wallace. Cambridge, MA: MIT Press, 1985.

Brumlik, Micha. 'Theologie und Messianismus'. In *Adorno Handbuch*, edited by Richard Klein, Johann Kreuzer and Stefan Müller-Doohm, 295–309. Stuttgart and Weimar: Metzler, 2011.

Brumlik, Micha. 'Verborgene Tradition und messianisches Licht: Arendt, Adorno und ihr Judentum'. In *Arendt und Adorno*, edited by Dirk Auer, Lars Rensmann and Julia Schulze Wessel, 74–93. Frankfurt am Main: Suhrkamp, 2003.

Finlayson, James Gordon. 'On Not Being Silent in the Darkness: Adorno's Singular Apophaticism'. *The Harvard Theological Review* 105, no. 1 (January 2012): 1–32.

Finlayson, James Gordon. 'The Work of Art and the Promise of Happiness in Adorno'. *World Picture* (Summer 2009), http://www.worldpicturejournal.com/WP_3/TOC.html.

Horkheimer, Max. *Nachgelassene Schriften 1931–1949*. Edited by Gunzelin Schmid Noerr. Frankfurt am Main: Fischer, 1985.

Nicholsen, Shierry Weber. *Exact Imagination, Late Work: On Adorno's Aesthetics*. Cambridge, MA: MIT Press, 1999.

Perutz, Leo. *Master of the Day of Judgment*. Translated by Eric Mosbacher. London: Pushkin Vertigo, 2015.

Rilke, Rainer Maria. *The Selected Poetry of Rainer Maria Rilke*. Translated by Stephen Mitchell. New York: Vintage, 1982.

Scholem, Gershom. *Die Geheimnisse der Schöpfung: Ein Kapitel aus dem kabbalistischen Buche Zohar*. Frankfurt am Main: Insel, 1971.

8

The Muted Animal

Daniel Herwitz

Part I

He's a lazy dog; she's sweet as a lamb; he's a goat; underneath it all she's a lioness; stop monkeying around, you birdbrain; no it isn't – it's a pure case of animal magnetism, you silly goose; when we stop acting like sitting ducks, we will be safer than this bear of a problem suggests; don't go to the dogs tonight even if it is a dog day and I'm dog-tired; he's an albatross but she's a minx; please ferret out the truth unless it turns out to be the elephant in the room, in which case bury it like an ostrich. And so on. Subtract the animal from our language and language becomes as shorn as a sheep. Everyone relies on animals in their sentences. In this spirit Theodor Adorno writes in the passage from his *Aesthetic Theory* that serves as the Talmudic stimulus of this book: 'So seems a rhino, the mute animal, to say: I am a rhinoceros.'[1] ('So scheint ein Nashorn, das stumme Tier, zu sagen: ich bin ein Nashorn.')[2]

Adorno's remark is deeply interesting and has a meaning far more complex, and utopian, than it might appear. Let's approach that meaning gradually, for I also think there is an important way in which his remark is not special, not philosophically prepared but ordinary, part of ordinary language use. Adorno is inserting the animal with the instinctive naturalness of a speaker of language wishing to find an analogy or metaphor or synecdoche, in this case for art. From this point of view there is nothing special about Adorno making a point by relying on an image of an animal. Everyone does it. The animal chronically lives a second life as a *stand-in-for*.

Let's leave the animal aside for the moment before it tramples back on to the page. For Adorno the muteness of the rhino is meant to be an exemplar of the condition of art. A work shows itself, like the rhino, mutely. Being mute is its way of being expressive of its identity. Muteness is a kind of eloquence. The work of art is expressive of what it is in a way that eludes propositional knowledge of its meaning and identity. It does not speak, it intimates, as was said of the Oracle. A work of art is oracular. Whether, if and how it might assert itself/speak/be brought to speech through interpretation: these are matters to be determined in the course of the encounter with it (and we may disagree).

A work of art is, if respected, something the experience of which is at odds with the claim of conceptual control so deep in the history of modern Europe, with its demands for certainty, certainty being the efficient cause of the power to control. Art solicits immersion, subtlety of feeling, imaginative connection rather than certainty. When treated as yet another form of certainty art is reduced to an instrument or brand. This is often how the modern bourgeois has treated art, and more often how it is treated by markets. In response, modern art has often aimed to flout the claims of the bourgeois viewer to extract meaning and pleasure from it in the manner of payment owed. This desire on the part of modern art to interrupt the viewer's experience, challenging his expectations, is perhaps datable to Édouard Manet. The more we gaze at Manet's famous *Olympia* of 1863, the less we feel entitled to say exactly whether Olympia, its underage main character prone and naked before the viewer, is bored, disgusted, indifferent, just doing her job, repressed, empty or enraged. Her figure is foreshortened to the point where her nudity will be unappetizing to those who expected a limpid female from Titian, all passive allure and soft readiness. This challenging of the viewer's expectation of deriving exactly the kind of content he seeks and doing so in a way that confirms his concept of the world (with him at the centre) is even more true of Manet's famous series of paintings of 'philosophers', which includes *The Ragpicker*. In those works old men appear in full-frontal theatre directly facing the viewer. However, their eyes are averted; they are lost in their own thought or mental ramblings. The more we study these figures, the more elusive they become. Is the old man before us a wizened Diogenes, preferring his cave to humanity? Is he drunk, mentally shredded by a lifetime of booze and hardscrabble living? Is he bored? Deadened? We do not know. Manet's intent is to place a full stop to the bourgeois French viewer's claim that the world is his oyster, that his ability to extract pleasure from what he sees should be immediate and unbridled. Since the extraction of pleasure always depends on knowledge claims about what the object of extraction is, Manet's challenge is also conceptual, or epistemological.

Modern art actively challenges claims to viewer certainty but the elusiveness of art is for Adorno a general characteristic. The more we find ourselves absorbed in a work, feeling through its expressive frissons and intimations of depth, the more we know that we don't exactly know what is in it. The claim of control is replaced by a more sceptical desire for immersion and experience. (This I think the eighteenth century got right with its turn towards non-conceptual aesthetics, even if it went too far, as is so often the case with new ideas.)

The work of art is mute for Adorno in its elusiveness. *Being-mute* is of course a metaphor. For neither a work of art nor anything else can literally be mute if it did not have the possibility of speech in the first place. Muteness is, meant literally, the dampening of speech, its inability or disability. The violin or the trumpet is muted only because it can sound out full register. Subtract the musical instrument's ability to sound out and you subtract the possibility of its being muted. Muteness is what happens to speech, and therefore assumes it.

Muteness in Adorno's *Aesthetic Theory* is converted from disability into ability: the ability for the work to stand against conceptual intrusion, generating wonder rather than certainty, challenging in its quiet way the modern demand on objects that they fulfil the demand of utility or what is often called instrumental reason. However, the work of art's ability is highly fragile, since it depends on the success of the encounter between persons or groups and works of art: a recognitional success ideally leading to respect for the work's otherness, and more than that, the ability of the viewer to transfer that sense of respect to other contexts, contexts where otherness is similarly repressed, such as markets, nationalism, racism and, importantly, nature. Should this enlightened state of recognition not eventuate from the encounter with the work of art, that work is unable to do anything more; it is as mute as a sheep, that poor animal unable to advocate on its behalf. As J. M. Coetzee's narrator quips about two such sheep being prepared for the feast table in his great novel *Disgrace* of 1999: 'Twins, in all likelihood, destined since birth for the butcher's knife ... When did a sheep last die of old age? Sheep do not own themselves, own their own lives. They exist to be used.'[3]

As one would expect of a book about aesthetics, Adorno is less interested in animals than in the aesthetic representation of nature: in the question of how nature has been represented since the eighteenth century vis-à-vis the turn from the aesthetics of nature to those of art in the early nineteenth. In the section of *Aesthetic Theory* about natural beauty Adorno speaks of the need to vindicate 'what capitalism has oppressed, animal, landscape, woman' (AT, 63). As nineteenth-century aesthetic theory turns from natural beauty to art, it takes nature over, leaving the dregs to exist in a state of 'negativity' (AT, 67). Nature turns into 'nature reserve', 'tourist industry', something 'insignificantly neutral' (AT, 68). One might add, nature then lives a second life in the Museum of Natural History in the solitary confinement of the vitrine, that vivisected scene of lion in wild and naked hunter poised to spear it as bird and tree linger in the background like the background to portraiture. Nature, having originally been imitated in art, is now that which imitates art as a kind of epiphenomenon or alternative. This is by the way also true in the various 'naturalist' movements that have from time to time arisen in Europe and America as antidotes to the ills of modernity, alternatively imagined paradises where natives freely make love on tropical islands (Gauguin), where human life and nature are happily one (Max Pechstein), where nudism, life without electricity, veganism or adoration of plants is meant to prompt recovery of the spiritual whole. Today we call this 'new age'. The point is, nature returns only in opposition to society as corrective culture. Or only as five-star hotels beautifully set in feng shui. This is of course vastly oversimplified if only because since the Renaissance urban design has equally sought to remake nature in harmony with cities and societies (from Palladio to Central Park in New York City) but there is a lot to it. The horrifying confinements of zoos have modulated into theme parks more user-friendly to the animal. But nature as *wild* is always replaced by nature as contained, if also beautiful and child-friendly.

Is this sufficient? Adorno says not: 'The dignity of nature is that of the not-yet-existing; by its expression it repels intentional humanization' (AT, 74). I am not sure what 'not-yet-existing' means, but the tenor of the sentence is clear. Nature's muteness is a silent cry even against the most user-friendly humanizations of it.

The way nature is re-presented in modern life and aesthetics is a deep question that goes way beyond the purview of this essay. But the animal does not, and it is time to introduce again what is not in *Aesthetic Theory*, namely the animal itself.

Part II

Extracting an animal from the wild is usually a form of violence done to it. But is it similarly violent, or morally faulty, when the animal is extracted from the wild on to the philosophical page, especially when the figure of the animal on the page is meant to stand as a poignant reminder of the power of art on the one hand, and the loss of nature on the other? The muted animal is meant to speak volumes about these matters, making it exalted, even utopian, as Adorno means it to be. I think this is a question which can only be approached by examining the relationship between those pages of text and the wider culture in which they are written. When the rhino gets on to the page of a philosophy text, it turns into a stilled image. It has become an object of use all the same: philosophical use.

What is wrong with such philosophical use? Some forms of use are all to the good. And the use Adorno makes of the rhino *is* to the good. The rhino becomes a symbol of identities elusive to the clutches of conceptual control, an object beautiful in its elusiveness. A utopian reminder. The problem arises when the real animal ceases to be of public concern and we prefer, we readers of Adorno, the Adorno rhino. When a philosopher participates in the culture of removal or extraction, a culture preferring animals as stand-ins rather than animals in themselves, in their own habitats and worlds, …. That is like what happens to black people when they come to occupy the pages of a novel wholly sympathetic to them but finally part of a culture that turns away from their real lives. When our relation to nature is more figural than actual, this is a lack of interest, even a form of disrespect, even on the part of those who celebrate the figure, turning it into something sepulchral. The judgement about whether a philosopher is participating in the repression of real things by turning to their second lives as figures is not an easy one to make. And, to repeat, that judgement can only be made *relationally*, in terms of whether the individual writer is participating in a larger ideological form of uninterestedness perhaps in spite of his or her best intentions. Whether Adorno should be accused of the repression of the actual rhino or not therefore is a judgement that goes beyond him to the larger culture in which he writes. I leave this judgement open, preferring just to raise the question of how to make it.

Here is some possible context for making it. Placing a rhino on a page might, in the context of colonialism and its legacies, be considered a form of extraction. To mute an animal is to take it away from its sources of life, from the world in which it is expressive of itself in all movement and animation, and to still it as a now-muted trophy. We extract the animal from its place in the world – from the site of its life – and turn it into a sight within our institutional and linguistic systems. This is what colonialism did with everything, making colonialism a politics of extraction. It extracted labour from native populations for little or no compensation, sometimes enslaving whole villages, in the case of King Leopold and the Belgian Congo, in order to force men to work the rubber trees. It extracted gold, diamonds and everything else it could tear out of the earth. It extracted artefacts.

There is no clearer example of the colonial extraction process than the museum, itself an institution created by the eighteenth century to house and display what was understood to be national patrimony. The colonial artefact which had lived its original life in ritual, religion, on the street corner or in the temple was stolen by the French or British conqueror, purchased at negligible prices or otherwise heisted away from the site of its enmeshment with 'native' life. Once relocated to the halls of the Louvre, British Museum or Hermitage, the 'native' object was given a second life as a mere sight, an object denuded of meaning and use, there for the contemplative gaze of the museum-goer. As such it lost all social meaning and acquired a new one: that of *national heritage*. Napoleon went to Egypt and returned with pyramids which monumentalized his nation by becoming 'French', a part of national patrimony.

The museum was a space of autonomy, where objects 'freed' from their original social meanings (in which Europe was not interested) were now there simply to be contemplated. In the museum the object became mute, like an animal. Here Adorno's rhino may be found. A work of African art might have been mute, but declared itself as 'African Art' as if the rhino were declaring its identity. This identity was either empty, with no one interested in filling it, or contained all the usual colonial stereotypes.

Animals were thought inert, permanently muted, with or without horns. The violence perpetrated on them is too well known to recite here; let me only add one iota of which you may not be aware. Every year in South Africa rhinos are sold to the highest bidders, who may do with them what they like. About a decade ago a big controversy erupted when a famous rock star bought one at auction only to then say: 'I'm now going to kill it with a high-powered rifle.' When challenged, he replied: 'It's mine now. I can do what I like with it.'

This is real mutation, not any literary variety. The literary variety is eloquent for sure, but really quite disconnected from life on the ground. Utopia is all too often an excuse not to take things as they are seriously in direct form. Perhaps Adorno might be accused of that, under what might be called the charge of benign neglect.

FIGURE 4 *Still from* Mine, *1991.* © *William Kentridge*

The very act of turning from a live being (a rhino) to a figure of it is a turn away, even if, Janus-like, the head is pointing back. This is a form of extraction. Extraction mutes because it deracinates the object from its original meaning, purpose, instinct, world, turning it into an empty cipher for whatever purpose it may now have, for aesthetic contemplation, for politics, for philosophical books like *Aesthetic Theory*. Since colonialism was first and foremost about the extraction of labour (from the native) and of (thanks to native labour) materials from the earth such as gold and diamonds, it is fitting that William Kentridge's work of genius, *Mine*, a film from 1991, ends with Soho Eckstein, the heavy European capitalist who owns the mine (it is his, meaning from his point of view: all mine), hulking over his huge desk. From a tiny 'animal home' at the front of the desk saunters out a miniature rhino which Soho strokes like a pet dog. This taming of the rhino is funny, since size and power are reversed. The rhino has become Soho's pet, while Soho is the rhino in a heavy gaberdine suit. But in fact the rhino is among the most powerful and untameable animals in the world.

I was once driving in a Jeep through the Kruger Park, that vast tract of wild land stretching between South Africa and Mozambique, when upon turning a corner on the dirt road we encountered a black rhino. It couldn't have been more than twenty metres from our vehicle and faced us, snorting. Now, there are two kinds of rhino, white and black, and the black one is by far the more aggressive. It can be hard to tell the difference since white rhinos are usually covered in mud, their whiteness concealed. But we knew this one was black. The black rhino is so volatile that guides at the game park will tell you to run to the nearest tree and climb if you come across one while walking – and this when the trees are the home of the green mamba and the boomslang, both snakes with a fatal bite. You are less likely to grab on to a snake while climbing than to be battered by the fierce black rhino. So to tame a rhino into a pet is for a South African truly funny. It is also a complete expression of the extraction from the wild of the animal, which becomes 'mine', by the man who owns and controls the labour of the natives and the gold they extract. The muteness of the labourer, the muteness of the pet rhino: these are part of a single system.

Fortunately, the rhino snorted and turned away.

The figure of the animal speaks eloquently in its muted form. But real animals are not mute at all, unless disabled. To state the obvious, they communicate incessantly. The roar of the lion, the song of the bird – these are ways in which the species is bonded in its collective response to the world. Communication is central to the animal's form of life. If you have had the joy of seeing elephants in the wild, watched female elephants slowly moving in a circle around their babies to protect them as the herd approaches the river, you will probably also know that these mothers are in constant communication. It is simply that their decibel level is too low for the human ear to pick up. They vocalize continually, hear and respond to one another. This is hardly muteness. While their communication may not be language, it is certainly intelligent communication that refers to and responds to the world – *their world* as they sense it and are embodied in it, not our world, and the way we take ourselves to live in relation to its truth conditions. Elephants respond to signals which are addressed to them. They are in sync. Each elephant is prompted to grasp the sounds from the other as a form of address to it. They are primed to 'expect' signals from each other. That is hardly muteness. It looks a lot like rudimentary language. The question of what counts as language is at issue given their form of communication.

Now, if we consider animals in the wild directly, they present us with a kind of elusiveness other than the figural. It is the otherness of a being whose form of communication is very hard to understand, and with respect to which we lack conceptual control in spite of much good work by animal behaviourists. If one has the privilege of visiting animals in the wild, their utter liminality is breathtaking. In the wild it is our own liminality which is experienced. We are the intruders. It is we who become mute before them, unable to decode signals passed between them, astonished at our irrelevance.

This failure to understand is reflected in an oracular remark of Ludwig Wittgenstein's, which appears late in Part II of his *Philosophical Investigations*: 'If a lion could talk we couldn't understand him.'[4] What does this mean? For Wittgenstein, to understand a language is to be part of a form of life, an organically interconnected set of ways of responding, reading, knowing, sharing, parsing, stating what is true and so forth. Words only take on meaning and use in the context of this organic whirl of life. Since the lion's form of life is too different from ours, Wittgenstein believes we will never be able to understand any language the lion might have. His use of the subjunctive (if a lion *could* talk) leaves it open as to whether the lion actually does talk (but we can't understand), or if the lion's capacity for language is a condition contrary to fact (the lion *cannot talk but even if it could* ...). Either way, our form of life is too far from that of the lion for us to grasp its words, if words are what it roars.

The remark occurs in the context of a discussion of various failures of understanding. Earlier on the same page Wittgenstein says:

> one human being can be a complete enigma to another. We learn this when we come into a strange country with entirely strange traditions; and, what is more, even given a mastery of the country's language. We do not understand the people. (And not because of not knowing what they are saying to themselves.) We cannot find our feet with them.[5]

Elizabeth Anscombe's translation of the passage is here quite colloquial. The German reads: 'Wir können uns nicht in sie finden', which more literally translates: we cannot find ourselves in them. That is, we cannot find our form of life in their words. They are too different, so the words are given meaning by a life form that eludes us.

The proximity of Wittgenstein's pair of remarks, the one about animals (the lion), the other about distant peoples, is not I think accidental. The two categories have gone together in the modern European imagination: the strangeness of the animal (along with its muteness) and the strangeness of primitive peoples. We can no more find ourselves in the lion and its world than in the world of an anthropologically distant tribe, imagined to be so distant as to preclude the sense of a shared world encountered as part of the same form of life. This is what the late colonial European standardly believed.

In point of fact I doubt Wittgenstein is right. It is very hard to find a people with whom we share so little that we utterly fail to understand them and they remain permanently enigmatic. Indeed, the idea that we can understand their language but still find them *completely enigmatic* may be a less than coherent possibility. Conversely, the lion is *less far from us* than Wittgenstein surmises. We share many features with the lion beyond eating and procreation. To consider but one: a male lion sleeps up to eighteen hours a day. But young adolescent boys may sleep nearly as much as the male lion. (I did anyway at that age.) The male lion sleeps while the female does the hunting. He then pushes the females aside to eat first. He is a *fresser*. How many men do you know who have lived happy and fulfilling lives doing exactly that to their womenfolk? The pages of history are full of this.

But Wittgenstein's sense of the otherness of other people, and of animals, is, like Adorno's, a crucial corrective to the Enlightenment ideal of sameness, and assimilation – the idea that because we know distant peoples and also the animal, we may bespeak them unproblematically and at will.

By bespeaking them, assuming we know what they are and who they are, we fail to listen, and fail to acknowledge how hard it is to listen. Since we don't listen, we mute them. And here I use the word 'mute' in its ordinary sense. This is the paradox. *By calling them mute, we mute them.* And once muted, they can now live second lives, like works of art, as mute beauty in Adorno's sense. But the crime remains, namely the initial muting, which is a form of destruction. You might say, 'Well, given that nature has disappeared from modern life, this utopian hope of return now redolent in the expressive cast of the rhino, on the pages of Adorno, is the best we can have.' I do not believe this. I believe it is far better, today anyway, simply to write about animals and their fate and leave the silent eloquence to the past. But you may disagree. This is, however, I believe, the right question to ask, however it is best answered.

Part III

That Adorno's text can give rise to questions of this moral urgency is a sign of its excellence. It is absolutely well intentioned in its desire to vest the rhino with a utopian voice or expressivity. But if there is one more criticism to be made of Adorno's fascinating and moral use of the concept of the muted animal, it is that Adorno never thereby takes up the question of anthropomorphism straightforwardly. And here I return to the opening paragraph of my essay, where it is raining cats and dogs.

I love my pets. I have three beloved dogs, all Pomeranians. Before that I had dachshunds, but they passed away. I still grieve for those beauties, so full of uppity, intransigent personality, so demanding of affection, not to mention food. I happen to consider dogs as a whole more noble than people. Dogs have far better character. I talk to them as most dog owners do. Am I then yet another instance in the history of anthropomorphism, yet another projecting muteness and then identity (as I understand it) onto my animals? Or do dogs really have character, or what in the dog industry is called 'temperament'? Both, I think. So perhaps there is a place, an indelible place, in language for such humanizing turns of phrase addressed to the dog. Perhaps anthropomorphism is so deeply rooted in our form of life (and hence our language) as to be indelible, even if anthropomorphism mutes, or mutates, the animal into our system of linguistic signs, on to the pages of our texts. When I use language with my animals it is part of my aspiration for intimacy with beings with whom I feel privileged to share my life. But I also recognize that anthropomorphism is a genuine mutation of the animal from its habitat, courtesy of fiction. This is the *mutability* of language in use.

The animal is and is not part of our form of life. It is a limit case for our understanding. We do and do not know it. We do and do not understand it. This paradox is insuperable, built into our way of understanding the world. And so, let the animal mutate on to the page with interest, but also with trepidation. Adorno, like most modern Europeans, simply mutates the animal without intellectual trepidation. And this is a person whose thought is dedicated to unravelling and critiquing the instrumentalist urge to dominate nature.

When we reach into the wild and domesticate what we extract thanks to language, we also mute it. Without anthropomorphism there could be no art, and little imagination. Yet we should treat this capacity with fear and trembling even as we rely on it.

Notes

1 Theodor W. Adorno, *Aesthetic Theory*, trans. and ed. Robert Hullot-Kentor (London: Continuum, 1997), 112, trans. modified. Hereafter cited in text as 'AT'.

2 Theodor W. Adorno, *Ästhetische Theorie, Gesammelte Schriften 7* (Frankfurt am Main: Suhrkamp, 1997), 171–2

3 J. M. Coetzee, *Disgrace* (New York: Penguin, 1999), 123.

4 Ludwig Wittgenstein, *Philosophical Investigations*, trans. Elizabeth Anscombe (New York: Macmillan, 1953), 223.

5 Ibid.

Bibliography

Adorno, Theodor W. *Aesthetic Theory*. Translated and edited by Robert Hullot-Kentor. London: Continuum, 1997.
Adorno, Theodor W. *Ästhetische Theorie*. In *Gesammelte Schriften*. Vol. 7, edited by Rolf Tiedemann. Frankfurt am Main: Suhrkamp, 1997.
Coetzee, J. M. *Disgrace*. Penguin: New York, 1999.
Wittgenstein, Ludwig. *Philosophical Investigations*. Translated by Elizabeth Anscombe. New York: Macmillan, 1953.

FIGURE 5 *Rhino on Lake, Lake Nakuru, 2007*. © *Nick Brandt, Courtesy of Edwynn Houk Gallery, New York*

9

Epilogue: On the Actuality of Adorno's Rhinoceros – Extraction, Extinction, and Dignity

Daniel Steuer

On 4 December 1958, at the beginning of one of his lectures on aesthetics, Adorno addressed a question that had arisen in a previous conversation with one of his listeners: 'Why does art express only what has been destroyed in us?'[1] In his response, he said: 'there is really no art that does not have, as a substantial element, the aspect of giving a voice to what has been muted or suppressed – not necessarily destroyed – in the process of the progressive control of nature.' He also mentioned that Samuel Beckett, 'barely a week ago', had said to him that the task of art is almost entirely 'to express the powerless and oppressed parts of humans', or, in Adorno's own parlance, 'what has been damaged'. What was specific to the moment in which Adorno was speaking, however, is expressed in the following correction to the statement on art in general: 'Probably *only in our time* does the perspective of the radically destroyed or damaged become the signature of any art that can be taken seriously.'[2]

Truth, as Adorno saw it, has a temporal core, and theory must respond to the theorist's own historical times. We thus need to see his writing as a response to the condition of human history in the early and mid-twentieth century. In fact, the theme of actuality, together with the 'logic of decay', was at the centre of Adorno's thought from at least the time of his inaugural lecture. His work, one might say, constitutes a theoretically reflected seismographic recording of the actual ongoing process of decay. If that is right, and if *Aesthetic Theory* in particular raises the question of the historical conditions of its own possibility, we need to ask what Adorno's *Aesthetic Theory* would look like today. What point would the recording of decay have reached by now? If the point of radical destruction had already been reached in 1958, what can we say about the kind of intensified destruction that has taken place since then? And, in the face of the intensifying crises of today's world of destruction, is Adorno's perspective still useful?

Two general methodological recommendations can certainly be gleaned from his thought: we should not try to identify the crises by name, and we should try to understand them as historically produced rather than fixed. The first of these may seem odd: why not call a spade a spade and, for example, a climate crisis a climate crisis? Well, maybe because calling the crisis one of the 'climate' may already occlude certain aspects of it by excising it from the web of factors that produce it. And the same applies to the now popular talk of the 'Anthropocene', according to which the human race is a global epochal force, as underlying the current mass extinction. One could push the point to the extreme: to speak of a climate crisis denies the real crisis that we want to criticize; to speak of the 'Anthropocene' expresses the same human hubris that we want to criticize.[3] Today's very real crises are a question of politics, both formal and informal, but the ways in which they are discussed often reify them. And in this reified form they often lead to futile confrontations: 'Climate change is man made!' – 'No, it's not!' 'Only technology can save us!' – 'No, technology is destroying the planet!' Adorno's well-known aversion to demonstrative forms of activism would then become explicable as a reluctance to fuel the same form of politics that is actually a cause of the false life and not a potential corrective to it. Strict observance of the ban on images and positive ideas of utopia is not necessarily a form of quietism – it could be part of a search for different forms of political activism that might lead to different forms of institutional politics.

It is a staple argument of Adorno's, one that is certainly still valid today, that the continuation of 'real want' is an 'absurdity'.[4] Given the development of the productive forces, scarcity is no longer forced on us by nature. It is an effect of the fact that we lack a rational form of social organization, a form of organization whose telos 'would be to negate the physical suffering of even the least of [society's] members' and 'to negate the internal reflexive forms of that suffering' (ND, 203–4). Within that parallel between the material and the intellectual, the priority of the object – 'no Being without beings' (ND, 135, trans. modified) – remains: 'If no man had part of his labor withheld from him', then society would also 'have transcended the identifying mode of thinking' (ND, 147).

In *Aesthetic Theory*, technological and artistic forces of production are blended into each other in the discussion of the 'ugly' and of 'beauty'. A 'devastated industrial landscape or a face deformed by a painting' are not 'just plain ugly', and the 'ugliness of technology and industrial landscapes' cannot be avoided by using 'aesthetically well-integrated functional forms'.[5] Ugliness, like beauty, defies definition, but Adorno explains both within the context of the violence done to nature: 'The impression of ugliness stems from the principle of violence and destruction' (ibid.). And this violence consists in artistic and productive forces being used to pursue aims that 'are unreconciled with what nature, however mediated it may be, wants to say on its own' (ibid.). The *differentia specifica* of technology is that, in technology, 'violence toward nature is not reflected through artistic portrayal, but it is immediately apparent. It could be transformed only by a reorientation of technical forces of production that would direct these forces not only according to desired aims but equally according to the nature that is to be technically formed' (ibid.). In other words, just as an artwork may carry its material to where it wants to go, so technology may help nature to move where it wants to go.[6] But such a transformation of technological possibilities cannot be effected by means that are themselves technological. It would require social change, namely, again, the abolition of want: 'After the abolition of scarcity, the liberation of the forces of production could extend into other dimensions than exclusively that of the quantitative growth of production' (AT, 46).

There can be little doubt that Adorno was an egalitarian. But his idea of equality was less a matter of the equal distribution of material goods than of a social organization that at least minimizes, and at best eradicates, suffering. If we disregard his aversion to labels and 'isms', we might call his thinking a kind of sufficientarianism, one that takes not material goods, however defined, but the corporeal well-being of (human) animals, all of them, as its currency.

Perhaps more surprisingly, we can also see that he viewed technology as not necessarily in opposition to the arts. Rather, the almost Aristotelian motif of helping nature and helping the artistic material move to where it wants to go suggests that Adorno – in contrast to Heidegger and in line with Jean-Luc Nancy – thought of modern technology, as well as the arts, as a version of Greek *techne*.[7] The culprit is not technology; it is the exchange principle.

The practices of modifying nature that we call 'art' and 'technology' are thus bound up with critique. If they intensify the formal social nexus of exchange, they strengthen the hold of the eversame; if they listen to their material (in the widest sense) and allow it to express itself, they open up gaps in the context of delusion. The evidence we might use in distinguishing between these two possibilities are phenomena of suffering. It is in physical suffering that what is 'specifically materialist' converges with critique, that is, with a 'practice that brings social change' (ND, 203).

Extraction: Colonialism and Logisticality

Two types of immediate presence: fragile Etruscan vases, the massive figure of the rhinoceros – not exactly a case of a bull in a china shop, but a striking enough juxtaposition to stir the reader of *Aesthetic Theory* and to suggest to us that both artefacts and nature have surprises in store for us, surprises that require our *response*. The responses of the contributors to this volume have sometimes seen the vases and the rhino taken to unexpected places, places from where there may be no 'returning home', unlike for Ulysses who, as Levinas puts it, in 'all his peregrinations is only on the way to his native island'.[8] There is, for instance, as Sebastian Tränkle makes clear, no return home for Prendick after he has been on Dr Moreau's island and has realized that 'not just the Beast Men, but we as well are "grotesque caricatures of humanity"'. If movement without return is a condition for breaking the spell of the eversame, then any writing wishing to heighten the chances for such an escape cannot know in advance where it is heading – or, as Adorno might have put it: it must both know it and not know it. In order to remain faithful to this spirit, a concluding chapter to the excellent contributions that make up this volume cannot simply extract from them the most intriguing places that have been visited. Still less should it use them to illustrate foregone conclusions. It can only be a journey inspired by them, a journey with an unknown destination, a journey that carries some risk that we will end up as castaways.

The idea of breaking the ban of the eversame leads straight to one of Adorno's central motifs, maybe *the* central motif: that of rescuing, of the hope we are given, as Benjamin puts it at the end of his essay on Goethe's *Elective Affinities*, only for the sake of the hopeless. Who these hopeless are is historically specific and depends on the form which humankind's metabolism with nature takes (though in this formulation a first abstraction – or extraction – has already taken place, that of humans from the remainder of nature).[9] Were

Dürer's rhinoceros to make his fateful journey, carefully charted by Antonia Hofstätter, today, it would probably be electronically tagged, and we would be able to track its progress on the shipping company's website. Would the signal disappear upon sinking? We live in an age of surveillance capitalism, and nothing goes unnoticed.[10] Although its details are complex, the fundamental features of this age are few: any part of life – mechanical, physical, mental, emotional – is increasingly being made dependent on digital data processing, and the analysis of data, increasingly monopolized, is used to predict and manipulate future behaviour and – crucially – to extract value. Insofar as the term 'data mining' suggests a connection to colonial practices that reach back in an unbroken chain to the extraction of natural resources and the extraction of labour from human bodies, it is not just a metaphor. What unites these practices is the forceful removal of elements from their original context, whether products from their producers, labour from bodies or bodies from their homeland. Mezzadra and Neilson sum it up thus: 'The extractive zeal of European imperialism emptied the world's pits and mountains and lined the mints and museums of the metropole with metals and artefacts that barely conceal the scars of slavery and indentured labour.'[11] They add, following Achille Mbembe, that 'the connection between forced labour and extraction is so strong that it allows an understanding of the slave trade in extractive terms. Mbembe writes of a process by which "African peoples are transformed into living minerals from which metal is extracted", giving rise to a transition from "*homme-minerai* to *homme-métal* and from *homme-métal* to *homme-monnaie*".'[12] Just as with minerals and other natural resources, there is a long history to the extraction of labour. Lewis Mumford, in his *Technics and Human Development*, dates it to at least the Pyramid Age in ancient Egypt, around 4500 BC, and to the invention of what he calls the megamachine, an 'archetypal machine composed of human parts'.[13] The megamachine combines a labour part with an army and a bureaucratic and communicative part. The distribution of these parts makes the overall machine invisible. It is designed for 'mobilizing a large body of men and rigorously coordinating their activities' – which, in the case of the labourers, consists of no more than limited, routinized tasks – 'in both time and space for a predetermined, clearly envisaged and calculated purpose'.[14] William Kentridge's film *Mine*, discussed by Herwitz, makes visible one such megamachine. In the end, the calculating head is sitting at his desk when he is surprised by nature: a tiny rhinoceros is lifted up a mine shaft right on to the desk.

The common denominator between the analyses of extractive capitalism and the concept of the megamachine is that they reveal social organization to be at the root of a situation in which neither things nor people move to where they want to go but are moved under compulsion – man-made compulsion.

Against this background, surveillance is only one aspect of the escalating logic that is inherent in colonialism and capitalism. Contemporary surveillance capitalism is not a corruption of liberal democracy; it has been part of the logic of liberal and imperial economics from the very beginning.[15] Alfred Sohn-Rethel, who was an important influence on Adorno, gave this a very clear theoretical formulation in his derivation of the exchange abstraction from the colonization of *whole* forms of life and their production. In his early exposition of his theory, the so-called 'Lucerne Exposé', he describes the transition from 'natural' (*naturwüchsige*) forms of society to functionally integrated societies. The former, he assumes, exhibit a form of organization made up of gens. People's existence is based on their own labour. The break happens when

> such a natural community subjugates another one in order to base its existence on the surplus from the labour of the subjugated community. This is what we call 'primary social exploitation'. Its crucial characteristic is that the conquering community neither destroys the conquered community in order to incorporate the vanquished as slaves in its own labour structure, nor simply kills its members. Rather, the conquering community preserves the one it conquers, at least as an organism of production, and establishes

its relation of domination with this organism. Thus, the result is a complete superimposition of two natural communities in their entireties and as social orders.[16]

Primary social exploitation is violent 'unilateral appropriation', not exchange. Only between the members of a group that has violently subjugated another can pure exchange value emerge. Among those producing the necessities of subsistence within a common form of life, all exchange remains bound up with use value. In short, colonial extraction is the common origin of colonialism, imperialism, slavery and the various stages of capitalism.[17]

The intensification of extraction and circulation leads to what Stefano Harney and Fred Moten call 'logisticality', the world conceived as a gigantic supply chain, a just-in-time machine.[18] Shipping is the universal form of movement within this regime, a movement that is directed entirely by other movements. It is a directionless movement within which there is neither a return home nor a setting off to nowhere, a movement within which anything may end up being shipped, be they things, humans or rhinoceroses. Under the heading 'Logisticality, or The Shipped', they ask: 'Where did logistics get this ambition to connect bodies, objects, affects, information, without subjects, without the formality of subjects, as if it could reign sovereign over the informal, the concrete and generative indeterminacy of material life?' And their answer is: 'modern logistics was born that way. Or more precisely it was born in resistance to, given as the acquisition of, this ambition, this desire and this practice of the informal. Modern logistics is founded with the first great movement of commodities, the ones that could speak. It was founded in the Atlantic slave trade, founded against the Atlantic slave.' And ever since logistics has been unable to 'contain what it had relegated to the hold'. In the words of Robert F. Harney, the historian of migration, 'once you crossed the Atlantic, you were never on the right side again'.[19]

'Never on the right side again', or, in a possibly more Adornian formulation, 'never just on the right side again, always also on the wrong side', and likewise, 'never just on the wrong side but always also on the right side'. Logisticality, one might say, contains, or sets in motion, a negative dialectic: after the original displacement, no entity will be in the position it wants to be. Adorno's idea of art could then be described as a counter-force to logisticality.

This connection places a heavy burden on presentational form. If, in Adorno, philosophical substance is inseparable from textual form, then it is even less legitimate to excise passages, sentences, formulations from the fabric of his texts, or indeed any text, as quotations. Suddenly, the mere act of quoting appears to be a colonial procedure of extraction. Does this, in turn, make the charge levelled against Adorno by one of our contributors, that of extracting the rhino and, so to speak, leading it on to the page, bound like a circus animal, even more serious? Is Adorno's use of the rhinoceros the result of colonial impulses? Adorno's texts, in the end, do not bear analysis, as every element taken out of the configuration assumes a false meaning, but as an author he nevertheless makes the configuration of elements his method. Do his readers mute his texts' rustling by taking them apart, turning their substance into a mechanically rattling argumentative machinery? Is this way of writing, which does not bear disassembly, a special form of armour? Is the intention behind his rhetorical tool of the one-liner, set out so eloquently by Lydia Goehr, to force the reader to move along with him, from line to line, instead of assuming resting places, philosophical positions that can only ever be wrong? For here there is no line that does not see you.

What exactly does the actuality of today's digital abstraction and extraction amount to? Decay's end point? Is there a point at which a negatively proceeding critical theory and logisticality become indistinguishable in the manner in which they destroy any fixed structure? Or is the negativity that refuses to take any fixed position an inheritance from forms of resistance to the logisticality of modernity?

Never on the right side again – that applies as much to the refugees who want to come to Europe in the twenty-first century, whether they succeed or not, whether they are sent back, allowed in or able to hide, as it did to the slaves crossing the Atlantic at the dawn of modern times. The theme of extraction has always been tied to that of being bound, being tied to a mast, handcuffed to rafters in the hold. Dürer's rhinoceros was a contemporary of those – millions of them – who perished in the sunken ships of the Atlantic slave trade and an ancestor of those who today find themselves in overloaded dinghies and boats on the Mediterranean and elsewhere.[20] Odysseus, at least, enjoyed the song of the sirens while tied to the mast. No music for the slaves, no song for the refugees, no pleasure for the dislocated animal. Just the bottom of the sea.

From Extraction to Extinction: The Last-Ever Rhino

The protagonist of our book, the rhinoceros, is close to extinction. And the historical reasons for this reach back to colonial practices of trophy hunting and the horn trade.

When Theodore Roosevelt, the twenty-sixth president of the United States, left office in 1909, he went on an African expedition. This is the same president who was well known for being a conservationist, who created close to a million square kilometres of parks and nature reserves. But rhinos did not fare well in the presidential naturalist's judgement, especially when compared to the elephant. The late Miocene or early Pliocene ancestors of the elephant and rhino, he assumes, 'were substantially equal in brain development'. But in the rhino, increased size led to 'lethargy and atrophy of brain power'; in the elephant 'brain and body have both grown'. Today, 'the elephant learns by experience infinitely more readily than the rhinoceros. The former no longer lies in the open plains, and now even crosses them if possible at night. But those rhinoceros which formerly dwelt in the plains for the most part continue to dwell there until killed out'.[21]

Roosevelt and his son, who accompanied him, 'shot and killed more than five-hundred animals of seventy different species'. Among those were twenty rhinos, including nine square-lipped, or white, rhinoceroses, a species that had been discovered only a few years earlier. Over the course of the expedition, 'more than five-thousand mammals, four-thousand birds, five-hundred fish and two-thousand reptiles were killed and in the end shipped to American museums'.[22] Another hunter – by name and vocation – John Alexander Hunter, killed 996 rhinoceroses within the space of three months. He was acting on behalf of the Kenyan government, which wanted to clear the land for agriculture. It later turned out that the land was not suitable for crops.[23]

In his account of his African adventures, Roosevelt points out that efforts to protect the rhinoceros, as well as other large species, failed because of the 'damage to property' they caused and, especially in the case of the rhinos, because of their 'repeated and wanton attacks on human beings'.[24] Roosevelt also defended, as Patricia O'Toole puts it, the 'mounting pile of skins and skulls [...] in the name of science: a single specimen might be anomalous, but with eight or ten a zoologist could begin generalizing about the species'.[25] She quotes Roosevelt: 'I can be condemned only if the existence of the National Museum, the American Museum of Natural History, and all similar zoological collections are to be condemned'.[26] From today's perspective, his defence seems weak. His frequent resort to this kind of argument – e.g. 'Hitherto we had not obtained a bull hippo, and I made up my mind to devote myself to getting one, as otherwise the group for the Museum would be incomplete'[27] – makes it clear that the museum, that clearest 'example of the colonial extraction process', as Herwitz puts it, was more important to him than its exhibits.

Roosevelt's aim as a conservationist was not conservation for conservation's sake. Rather, he subscribed to the utilitarian principle expressed in the definition of the 'purpose of Forestry' given by his close collaborator, the first Head of the United States Forest Service, Gifford Pinchot: 'to make the forest produce the largest amount of whatever crop or service will be most useful, and keep on producing it for generation after generation of men and trees. [...] the forest rightly handled – given the chance – is, next to the earth itself, the most useful servant of man'.[28]

The intention behind mentioning these facts and stories is not to bash the individuals involved, who lived in times different from ours, but to show how an impulse to safeguard nature, a presumably genuine interest in animals and an anthropocentric utilitarianism according to which the earth is the servant of man can go hand in hand. And yet fundamental criticisms of such all-consuming utilitarianism were being advanced around the same time. Pinchot's *Breaking New Ground* was published in 1947, three years after Karl Polanyi's *The Great Transformation*, which spells out that land, next to human labour and money, is one of the three things that cannot be commodified. They may be 'essential elements of industry', but they are 'obviously *not* commodities [...] Labor is only another name for a human activity which goes with life itself'.[29] And life, Polanyi was still able to believe, 'is not produced for sale but for entirely different reasons'. 'Land is only another name for nature, which is not produced by man; actual money, finally, is merely a token of purchasing power'.[30] Thus, none of the three 'is produced for sale. The commodity description of labor and money is entirely fictitious'.[31] It says a lot about the three-quarters of a century that have since elapsed that it demands some imaginative effort on our part today to remember that Polanyi's analysis is not naive, and that talk of 'financial products', 'data mining' (where the mined product is us, our habits, thoughts and feelings) and 'property development' are just rhetorical window dressing for the further expansion of value extraction.

Of course, no species can avoid engaging in a metabolism with the rest of nature and thus using some of it for its own purposes. But Polanyi nevertheless raises important questions: at what point does such use become commodification? What should the limits of commodification be? In order to begin to answer them, something like the sensibility Adorno called 'aesthetic comportment' is needed. And this sensibility certainly seems to have diminished rather than deepened over the past sixty years. The logic of extraction is a logic that disintegrates, isolates and makes fungible. In the case of the rhino's horn, this is complicated by powerful myths about its efficacy as a drug and by its symbolic value as a signifier of social status. Financial and symbolic values cross over in the horn of the rhinoceros. On the black markets of China and Vietnam, a kilogram of rhino horn costs about $100,000, making it financially more valuable than gold or cocaine.[32] A campaign by the Vietnamese government in 2016 that aimed to make it 'culturally unacceptable' to buy, give or receive rhino horn was only a partial success. Some Hanoi businessmen say they would only stop buying it if it proved detrimental to their 'health or status'; one of them says 'he would happily buy a horn from the last-ever rhino'.[33]

Dignity as Utopia: Who Can Say 'Here I Am'?

Only by developing our sense of responsibility towards non-human nature can we hope to take responsibility for others, as Camilla Flodin makes unmistakeably clear. The metabolism between humanity and nature must be de-colonialized; technology must be used to help nature to go where it wants to go by itself. These suggestions shine a particular light on discussions around animal rights, even rights of nature, in the strong sense, that is, on the question of whether beings other than human beings should be treated as legal persons. If we do not see nature as the wholly other, as that which constitutes human dignity through its fundamental lack of dignity, then such a discussion can focus on criteria for making gradual, rather than absolute, distinctions between entities with different degrees of legal personhood. This is in line with the point Peter Singer – more precisely his fictionalized self – makes in his response to the argument J. M. Coetzee's character Elizabeth Costello advances in *The*

Lives of Animals: to say that 'normal humans have capacities that far exceed those of non-human animals' and that this is 'morally significant' does not yet commit one to speciesism.[34] And to compare the destruction of humans by humans to the destruction of animals by humans is not euphemistic as 'a comparison is not necessarily an equation'.[35] What is needed is the complicated work of articulating the family resemblances between humans and animals, and between other parts of nature. Maybe it would then be even easier to hear the personhood in Camilla Flodin's irresistible *Stefanorhinos etruscus*. ('What is your name?' 'Stefanorhinos Etruskus.') But, as Alexander García Düttmann reminds us, the threshold between the human and non-human animal 'is the site of conflicting and indomitable forces' and Adorno therefore must 'separate them as much as he can'. If the reified form of political discussion mentioned above is to be avoided, similarities and differences must neither be ignored nor exaggerated. Only then can the 'It is thus' attributed by Adorno to Schubert's music appear, as Düttmann puts it, 'in the gap that the movement of self-reference leaves open when it does not come full circle and turn selfhood into an identity'.

Adorno knows that untamed nature can be terrifying. If the task is the remembrance of nature in the subject, then this cannot be remembrance of the brute nature that figures as the antipode to the industrial culture of the human species; it would be the remembrance of a nature that never was, a remembrance that gives something back to nature that was nipped in the bud, something without which, as Camilla Flodin tells us, the affinity between man and animal cannot be acknowledged, to the detriment of both. In Adorno's observations on aesthetics, animals therefore do not merely serve an illustrative purpose. They have a systematic place and value that is central: 'If the case of natural beauty were pending, dignity would be found culpable for having raised the human animal above the animal' (AT, 62). If there were an appeal in the case of natural beauty, dignity would be found to be the culprit: the reason for the self-exaltation, the hubris, of the human species over animal life as such, *Tierheit*, animality. This animality, sentenced to its fate not by a single errant judge but by a judiciary that is systematically skewed, is also something the gaze of the rhino asks us to think. And just as the nature to be remembered perhaps never was, so dignity never was: 'Human beings are not equipped positively with dignity; rather, dignity would be exclusively what they have yet to achieve' (AT, 62). On both sides, the objective and subjective, the present condition is one of being under the spell. And the only way to break it is through what Adorno calls *Selbstbesinnung*, reflecting on one's own assumed selfhood instead of indulging in a false sense of superiority over nature, over the animal.[36]

Dignity as a symptom of erroneous self-elevation is a recurring theme in Adorno. It concludes the *Jargon of Authenticity*. The jargon's schema, its 'dignified mannerism', is 'a reactionary response toward the secularization of death. Language wants to grasp what is escaping, without believing it or naming it.'[37] This is a secularization that falsely claims to have done away with theology, but only substitutes its own immanent, souped-up trivialities for the transcendent: 'Naked death becomes the meaning of such talk – a meaning that it could have only in something transcendent. The falseness of giving meaning, nothingness as something, is what creates the linguistic mendacity.'[38]

Adorno's analysis of the jargon of authenticity is thus much more than just a critique of a linguistically inflated philosophical style. It demonstrates that that jargon is the result of a particular reaction to the historical process of secularization, namely the arrogation of transcendent functions to the secular *without* this takeover being acknowledged. The alternative, for Adorno, would not be an open and honest takeover, because this would be an impossibility: we *do not*, and cannot, know the transcendent. Determinate negation is therefore the only option that allows us to retain an aspiration to the transcendent without contaminating it with traces of the profane. Human dignity is a test case for this. According to Adorno, Kant, despite his distinction between price and dignity, was close to realizing that 'dignity contains the form of its decadence within itself', as becomes apparent as soon as intellectuals opt for power rather than *Selbstbesinnung*: 'The Kantian dignity finally disintegrates into the jargon of authenticity. With it goes that humanity which has its basic nature not in self-reflection [*Selbstbesinnung*] but in its difference from a suppressed animality.'[39] Such suppression cannot but show itself in an instrumental attitude towards animals and nature at large. Depriving the natural of dignity reduces it to a realm of things, each of which has its price. It may therefore have been more than politeness when Adorno wrote to the director of the Frankfurt zoo, Bernhard Grzimek, about his sympathy for Grzimek's campaign against the 'nonsense of "big-game hunting"'. This sympathy, he said, had nothing to do with the 'official tasks of an institute for social research but all the more with the deeper *impulses* followed by such an institute if it wants to do justice to its humane task [*menschliche Aufgabe*]'.[40] Maybe we can conclude that humane tasks tend to be unofficial, and to require affective as well as rational responses.[41]

External nature becomes a target for the rage of idealism, the sublimated aggression that has its roots in the need of beasts of prey to muster the courage for attack. Thus, it is not just the human mind that imagines itself to be sovereign. Human dignity, understood in Adorno's terms, 'has its primal history in the pre-mental, the animal life of the species' (ND, 22). The hungry predator needs additional impulses if it is to find the courage to mount an attack:

> These impulses and the unpleasantness of hunger fuse into rage at the victim, a rage whose expression in turn serves the end of frightening and paralyzing the victim. In the advance to humanity this is rationalized by projection. The 'rational animal' with an appetite for his opponent is already fortunate enough to have a superego and must find a reason. The more completely his actions follow the law of self-preservation, the less can he admit the primacy of that law to himself and to others; if he did, his laboriously attained status of a *zoon politikon* would lose all credibility. (ND, 22)

But, crucially, this status of humans as political animals also remains unfulfilled as long as its implicitly negative foundation – *unlike* animals, humans have speech, hence know the difference between good and bad and are political, i.e. have a form of life, not just bare life – is not itself negated. It is a double injustice: it is not true that having more developed linguistic and reasoning capacities than other animals is sufficient to realize the potential of a political life that aims at justice, and it is wrong to ascribe to animals a deficiency on the basis of a standard that is alien to them.

Roosevelt's account of his African expedition is exemplary of a certain colonial form of rationalization through projection, applied to both other peoples as well as animals. He was travelling on the Uganda railway, built by the British. To him, the railway was 'the embodiment of the eager, masterful, materialistic civilization of to-day'. It led straight through 'a region in which nature, both as regards wild man and beast, did not and does not differ materially from what it was in Europe in the late Pleistocene'. The 'wild creatures, the stupendous size of some of them, the terrible nature of others, and the low culture of many of the savage tribes, especially of the hunting tribes, substantially reproduced the conditions of life in Europe as it was led by our ancestors ages before the dawn of anything that could be called civilization'.[42] Thus, without resorting to a fundamental difference between civilized nations and savages, or man and animal, he can maintain the superiority of the colonialist by pointing to the evolutionary backwardness of people, animals, even the land.

It is the cycle of such self-justificatory explanations, which are blind to the violence all about them, that *Selbstbesinnung* must break. And maybe *Selbstbesinnung* sets in at the very moment we find ourselves, in Daniel Herwitz's words, 'astonished at our irrelevance' in the scheme of things, in the face of a planet and its surroundings whose vastness seems to laugh at us and our self-importance – even if mutely.

Notes

1. Theodor W. Adorno, *Aesthetics*, trans. Wieland Hoban (Cambridge: Polity, 2018), 54; trans. modified.

2. Ibid. My translation; emphasis added.

3. Howard Caygill has demonstrated that the concept of the 'Anthropocene' is based on 'human exceptionalism'. For the earth, the sixth mass extinction is business as usual, while in our blindness we do not see that 'we have destroyed ourselves but not the earth'. 'Anthropokenosis and the Emerging World of War', in *War and Algorithm*, ed. Max Liljefors, Gregor Noll and Daniel Steuer (London: Rowman & Littlefield, 2019), 53–74; here: 68–9.

4. Theodor W. Adorno, *Negative Dialectics*, trans. E. B. Ashton (London: Routledge, 2004), 121. Hereafter cited in text as 'ND'.

5. Theodor W. Adorno, *Aesthetic Theory*, ed. Gretel Adorno and Rolf Tiedemann, trans. Robert Hullot-Kentor (London: Continuum, 1997), 46. Hereafter cited as 'AT'.

6. The formulation is borrowed from Adorno: 'Following a schema ultimately borrowed from bourgeois sexual morality, technology is said to have ravished nature, yet under transformed relations of production it would just as easily be able to assist nature and on this sad earth help it to get to where, perhaps, it wants to go' (AT, 68).

7. See Jean-Luc Nancy, 'Of Struction', *Parrhesia* 17 (2013): 1–10; see especially 10, note 2.

8. Emmanuel Levinas, 'The Trace of the Other', in *Deconstruction in Context: Literature and Philosophy*, ed. Mark C. Taylor (Chicago: University of Chicago Press, 1986), 345–59; here: 346. Levinas opposes to Ulysses Abraham, who 'leaves his fatherland forever for a yet unknown land'. '*A work*', Levinas says, '*conceived radically is a movement of the same unto the other which never returns to the same*' (Levinas, 'The Trace of the Other', 348). Such good work, such goodness must not ask for gratitude nor recompense. It is a free movement into a void that does not seek 'the triumph of its cause'; it aims 'at a time beyond the horizon of my time' (Levinas, 'The Trace of the Other', 349).

9. Adorno, of course, did not accept the distinction between humankind and nature: 'The division of social and extra-social Being, a division that takes its bearings from the arrangement of the sciences, deceives us about the fact that heteronomous history perpetuates the blind growth of nature' (ND, 141).

10. See Shoshana Zuboff, *The Age of Surveillance Capitalism: The Fight for a Human Future at the New Frontier of Power* (London: Profile Books, 2019).

11. Sandra Mezzadra and Brett Neilson, 'On the Multiple Frontiers of Extraction: Excavating Contemporary Capitalism', *Cultural Studies* 31, nos. 2–3 (2017): 7.

12. Ibid.

13 Lewis Mumford, *Technics and Human Development* (London: Harvest/HBJ, 1966), 11.

14 Ibid., 191.

15 See Megan Archer, 'Logistics as Rationality: Excavating the Coloniality of Contemporary Logistical Formations' (PhD diss., University of Brighton, 2020).

16 Alfred Sohn-Rethel, *Soziologische Theorie der Erkenntnis* (Frankfurt am Main: Suhrkamp, 1985), 45. My translation. See also his *Intellectual and Manual Labour: A Critique of Epistemology* (London: MacMillan, 1978), esp. 86–8.

17 In *Negative Dialectics*, Adorno condenses Sohn-Rethel's theory of exchange abstraction, which provides the background to his utopia of the non-identical, hence non-exchangeable, in one sentence: 'The process of abstraction – which philosophy transfigures, and which it ascribes to the knowing subject alone – is taking place in the factual barter society [*Tauschgesellschaft*]' (ND, 178). On the notion of exchange abstraction, see Sohn-Rethel, *Intellectual and Manual Labour*, 13–79.

18 Stefano Harney and Fred Moten, *The Undercommons: Fugitive Planning & Black Study* (Wivenhoe: Minor Compositions, 2013).

19 Ibid., 92–3.

20 An online transatlantic slave trade database says that, during the period 1500–1875, there were 10,015,607 embarkations and 8,706,771 disembarkations. See www.slavevoyages.org. Worldwide, an estimated 21 million 'men, women and children today are in a form of slavery'. Kenneth Morgan, *Transatlantic Slavery* (London: I. B. Tauris, 2016), 2.

21 Theodore Roosevelt, 'African Game Trails: An Account of the African Wanderings of an American Hunter-Naturalist', *Scribner's Magazine* 47, no. 6 (June 1910): 654. Roosevelt's account appeared as several articles in editions of *Scribner's Magazine*. These were later published as a book.

22 Lothar Frenz, *Nashörner* (Berlin: Matthes & Seitz, 2017), 68.

23 See ibid., 69.

24 Roosevelt, 'African Game Trails', 658.

25 Patricia O'Toole, *When Trumpets Call: Theodore Roosevelt after the White House* (New York: Simon & Schuster, 2005), 67.

26 Ibid.

27 Roosevelt, 'African Game Trails', *Scribner's Magazine* 47, no. 5 (May 1910): 536.

28 Gifford Pinchot, *Breaking New Ground* (Washington DC: Island Press, 1998), 32.

29 Karl Polanyi, *The Great Transformation: The Political and Economic Origins of Our Time* (Boston: Beacon Press, 2001), 75.

30 Ibid.

31 Ibid., 76.

32 See Frenz, *Nashörner*, 83.

33 James Fair, 'The Other Side of Rhino Conservation', *BBC Wildlife*, October 2016, 64–5.

34 See Peter Singer's 'Reflection', in J. M. Coetzee, *The Lives of Animals* (Princeton: Princeton University Press, 1999), 87.

35 Ibid., 86.

36 On Adorno's notion of critique as *Selbstbesinnung*, see Antonia Hofstätter, *The Fabric of Critique: 'Lending Voice to Suffering' in the Work of T. W. Adorno*, D. Phil. University of Brighton, 2017.

37 Theodor W. Adorno, *The Jargon of Authenticity*, trans. Knut Tarnowski and Frederic Will (Evanston: Northwestern University Press, 1973), 163.

38 Ibid., trans. modified.

39 Ibid., 165.

40 Theodor W. Adorno, Letter of 1 February 1955, Theodor W. Adorno Archiv, Frankfurt am Main, Br 518/1. My translation; emphasis added.

41 For an account of political philosophy's long-standing aversion to feeling and affect as unreliable, and critical theory's corrective attempts, see Simon Mussell, *Critical Theory and Feeling: The Affective Politics of the Early Frankfurt School* (Manchester: Manchester University Press, 2017).

42 Theodore Roosevelt, 'African Game Trails', *Scribner's Magazine* 46, no. 4 (October 1909): 386.

Bibliography

Adorno, Theodor W. *Aesthetic Theory*. Edited by Gretel Adorno and Rolf Tiedemann. Translated by Robert Hullot-Kentor. London: Continuum, 1997.
Adorno, Theodor W. *Aesthetics*. Translated by Wieland Hoban. Cambridge: Polity, 2018.
Adorno, Theodor W. *The Jargon of Authenticity*. Translated by Knut Tarnowski and Frederic Will. Evanston: Northwestern University Press, 1973.
Adorno, Theodor W. Letter of 1 February 1955. Theodor W. Adorno Archiv, Frankfurt am Main, Br 518/1.
Adorno, Theodor W. *Negative Dialectics*. Translated by E. B. Ashton. London: Routledge, 2004.
Archer, Megan. 'Logistics as Rationality: Excavating the Coloniality of Contemporary Logistical Formations'. PhD diss., University of Brighton, 2020.

Caygill, Howard. 'Anthropokenosis and the Emerging World of War'. In *War and Algorithm*, edited by Max Liljefors, Gregor Noll and Daniel Steuer, 53–74. London: Rowman & Littlefield, 2019.

Mezzadra, Sandra, and Brett Neilson. 'On the Multiple Frontiers of Extraction: Excavating Contemporary Capitalism'. *Cultural Studies* 31, nos. 2–3 (2017): 1–20.

Fair, James. 'The Other Side of Rhino Conservation'. *BBC Wildlife*, October 2016, 64–5.

Frenz, Lothar. *Nashörner*. Berlin: Matthes & Seitz, 2017.

Harney, Stefano, and Fred Moten. *The Undercommons: Fugitive Planning & Black Study*. Wivenhoe: Minor Compositions, 2013.

Hofstätter, Antonia. 'The Fabric of Critique: "Lending Voice to Suffering" in the Work of T.W. Adorno'. PhD diss., University of Brighton, 2017.

Levinas, Emmanuel, 'The Trace of the Other', in *Deconstruction in Context: Literature and Philosophy*, edited by Mark C. Taylor, 345–59. Chicago: University of Chicago Press, 1986.

Morgan, Kenneth. *Transatlantic Slavery*. London: I. B. Tauris, 2016.

Mumford, Lewis. *Technics and Human Development*. London: Harvest/HBJ, 1966.

Mussell, Simon. *Critical Theory and Feeling: The Affective Politics of the Early Frankfurt School*. Manchester: Manchester University Press, 2017.

Nancy, Jean-Luc. 'Of Struction'. *Parrhesia*, no. 17 (2013): 1–10.

O'Toole, Patricia. *When Trumpets Call: Theodore Roosevelt after the White House*. New York: Simon & Schuster, 2005.

Pinchot, Gifford. *Breaking New Ground*. Washington DC: Island Press, 1998.

Polanyi, Karl. *The Great Transformation: The Political and Economic Origins of Our Time*. Boston: Beacon Press, 2001.

Roosevelt, Theodore. 'African Game Trails: An Account of the African Wanderings of an American Hunter-Naturalist'. *Scribner's Magazine* 46, no. 4 (October 1909): 384–406.

Roosevelt, Theodore. 'African Game Trails: An Account of the African Wanderings of an American Hunter-Naturalist', *Scribner's Magazine* 47, no. 5 (May 1910): 515–538.

Roosevelt, Theodore. 'African Game Trails: An Account of the African Wanderings of an American Hunter-Naturalist'. *Scribner's Magazine* 47, no. 6 (June 1910): 640–70.

Singer, Peter. 'Reflections'. In J. M. Coetzee, *The Lives of Animals*. Princeton: Princeton University Press, 1999, 85–91.

Sohn-Rethel, Alfred. *Intellectual and Manual Labour: A Critique of Epistemology*. Translated by Martin Sohn-Rethel. London: MacMillan, 1978.

Sohn-Rethel, Alfred. *Soziologische Theorie der Erkenntnis*. Frankfurt am Main: Suhrkamp, 1985.

Zuboff, Shoshana. *The Age of Surveillance Capitalism: The Fight for a Human Future at the New Frontier of Power*. London: Profile Books, 2019.

NAME INDEX

Because of their presence throughout the volume, '*Aesthetic Theory*' and 'Theodor W. Adorno' have not been included in the subject and name index respectively.

Locators followed by "n." indicate endnotes

Adorno, Gretel 110
Aesop 91
Anscombe, Elizabeth 163
Aprà, Adriano 83 n.3
Archer, Megan 187 n.15
Arendt, Hannah 149 n.51
Aristotle 172
Atwood, Margaret 113 n.8

Baudelaire, Charles 49, 129
Beckett, Samuel 70, 83 n.8, 146 n.12, 169
Beethoven, Ludwig van 59, 133–4, 148 n.42
Benjamin, Walter 8, 13, 16 n.16, 47–9, 54 n.7, 54 nn.11–13, 65, 96, 114 n.25, 126, 129–30, 136, 147 n.25, 173
Berger, John 3, 15 n.5
Blei, Franz 116 n.62
Blumenberg, Hans 114 n.10, 125, 147 n.20
Borges, Jorge Luis 90, 113 n.9
Brecht, Bertolt 70
Brehm, Alfred 10
Bruce, James 62, 71 n.7
Brumlik, Micha 141, 147 n.27, 149 n.51

Carr, Gilbert 149 n.57
Carroll, Lewis 31, 38 n.24
Caygill, Howard 186 n.3
Cerdeño, Esperanza 39 n.26
Clarke, Timothy H. 60–1, 71 n.5
Codrea, Vlad 39 n.26
Coetzee, J. M. 156, 166 n.3, 181, 188 n.34
Colman, Andrew M. 36 n.3
Crystal, David 37 n.15

Dali, Salvador 1, 63
Darwin, Charles 91, 113 n.6
Dürer, Albrecht 1, 6, 12–13, 43–6, 48, 51–3, 53 n.1, 54 n.16, 61–4, 81, 174, 178
Düttmann, Alexander García 5, 13, 29, 83 n.2, 83 n.8, 182

Eco, Umberto 15 n.2

Fair, James 188 n.33
Falconer, Hugh 38 n.26
Fatu (rhinoceros) 35
Fieschi, Jean-André 83 n.3
Finlayson, James Gordon 121, 146 n.3, 146 n.12
Flodin, Camilla 4, 12, 16 n.10, 36 n.6, 37 n.14, 38 n.23, 39 n.27, 39 n.34, 47, 149 n.57, 181–2
Frenz, Lothar 15 n.2, 187 n.22, 188 n.32
Freud, Sigmund 88
Friis, Elisabeth 38 n.24

Gauguin, Paul 157
Geulen, Eva 16 n.8, 36 n.1, 37 n.10
Goehr, Lydia 11, 13, 20, 29, 33, 177
Goethe, Johann Wolfgang von 23, 37 n.10, 60, 64, 127, 141, 148 n.28, 173
Grzimek, Bernhard 7, 16 n.14, 184

Habermas, Jürgen 105, 115 n.54
Harney, Robert F. 176
Harney, Stefano 176, 187 n.18
Hawks, Howard 83 n.4

NAME INDEX

Hegel, Georg Wilhelm Friedrich 21, 57, 60, 62, 67, 108, 141
Heidegger, Martin 172
Herwitz, Daniel 9, 14, 54 n.17, 148 n.44, 175, 179, 185
Hofstätter, Antonia 12–13, 29, 37 n.11, 149 n.57, 174, 188 n.36
Hogh, Philipp 113 n.4
Horkheimer, Max 8, 16 n.17, 26, 37 n.13, 85–6, 88–9, 91, 94, 96–7, 103, 105–6, 110, 112, 113 n.1, 115 n.55, 142, 149 n.53
Hullot-Kentor, Robert 83 n.8, 85, 123, 146 n.8
Hunter, John Alexander 179

Illner, Birgit 150 n.57
Ionesco, Eugène 1, 63, 66–8, 70, 71 n.11, 71 n.13, 81

Kafka, Franz 85, 99, 114 n.35
Kant, Immanuel 20–1, 23, 34, 36 n.5, 39 n.27, 65, 183–4
Kentridge, William 1, 53 n.1, 54 n.16, 62, 161, 175
Kierkegaard, Søren 69
Klaue, Magnus 116 n.62
Klee, Paul 66, 127
Kolbert, Elizabeth 39 n.30
Kotsakis, Tassos 39 n.26
Kundera, Milan 68

Leo (cat) 150 n.57
Leopold, King 159
Leo X, Pope 44
Levinas, Emmanuel 173, 186 n.8
Longhi, Pietro 1

Mahler, Gustav 7, 11, 15 n.4
Manet, Édouard 154–5
Manuel of Lisbon, King 44
Marco Polo 15 n.2
Marx, Karl 29, 47, 87, 106
Maupassant, Guy de 108
Mbembe, Achille 174

McDonald, Joseph F. 15 n.7
Mezzadra, Sandra 174, 186 n.11
Morgan, Kenneth 187 n.20
Moten, Fred 176, 187 n.18
Mozart, Wolfgang Amadeus 62
Mumford, Lewis 174, 187 n.13
Mussell, Simon 188 n.41

Najin (rhinoceros) 35
Nancy, Jean-Luc 172, 186 n.7
Napoleon 159
Neilson, Brett 174, 186 n.11
Nicholsen, Shierry Weber 54 n.13, 123, 146 n.10
Nietzsche, Friedrich 89, 92, 114 n.15
Noll, Gregor 150 n.57

O'Toole, Patricia 179, 187 n.25
Ovid 85

Pandolfi, Luca 38–9 n.26
Panofsky, Erwin 62
Pechstein, Max 157
Perutz, Leo 130, 148 n.32, 148 n.35
Petronio, Carmelo 38 n.26
Phalaris 69
Pinchot, Gifford 179–80, 187 n.28
Pliny the Elder 60–1, 71 n.4
Polanyi, Karl 180, 187 n.29
Ponzi, Maurizio 83 n.3
Proust, Marcel 45, 48, 51, 108

Raphael 61
Renoir, Auguste 45, 51
Riegl, Alois 66
Rilke, Rainer Maria 10, 28, 33, 65, 136, 149 n.45
Robins, Robert Henry 37 n.15
Rohman, Carrie 115 n.55
Roosevelt, Theodore 178–9, 185, 187 n.21, 187 n.24, 187 n.27, 188 n.42
Russell, Bertrand 4, 15–16 n.7

Sartre, Jean-Paul 70
Schelling, Friedrich Wilhelm Josef 23

Schmidt, Alfred 113 n.5, 115 n.56
Schoen, Ernst 133
Scholem, Gershom 134, 148 n.41
Scholze, Britta 5, 16 n.9
Schonfield, Ernest 150 n.57
Schönthaler, Philipp 150 n.57
Schubert, Franz 82, 182
Silberbusch, Oshrat C. 38 n.19
Singer, Peter 181, 188 n.34
Sohn-Rethel, Alfred 175, 187 nn.16–17
Spencer, Clare 39 n.33
Steuer, Daniel 14, 29, 33
Sudan (rhinoceros) 35

Taylor, Charles 113 n.4
Téchiné, André 83 n.3
Thompson, Marie L. 36 n.9

Tomasello, Michael 113 n.4
Tränkle, Sebastian 10, 14, 16 n.17, 34, 173

Valentine, John M. 68–70, 71 n.11
Vermeer, Jan 63
Visconti, Luchino 83 n.3
Von Bothmer, Dietrich 64, 71 n.9

Wells, Herbert George 14, 86, 89–91, 99, 103, 112, 113 nn.7–8, 114 n.11, 114 n.16, 114 n.26, 114 n.31, 115 n.37, 115 n.55, 115 n.57
Werner, Elke Anna 54 n.4, 62, 71 n.8
Wittgenstein, Ludwig 4, 15–16 n.7, 163–4, 166 n.4

Zuboff, Shoshana 186 n.10

SUBJECT INDEX

Abraham 29, 119, 186 n.8
Abraxas grossulariata 37 n.10
Adorno's Philosophy of the Nonidentical: Thinking as Resistance (Silberbusch) 38 n.19
'Adorno's Utopian Animals' (Flodin) 38 n.20, 38 n.23, 39 n.27, 39 n.29, 39 n.34
Aesthetics 1958/59 (Adorno) 49, 54 n.15, 143, 147 n.16, 147 n.18, 149 n.54, 169, 186 n.1
affinity 3, 8, 34, 47, 52, 60, 64, 67, 182
'African Game Trails' (Roosevelt) 187 n.21, 187 n.24, 187 n.27, 188 n.42
afterimage/after-image 51, 53, 80
The Age of Surveillance Capitalism: The Fight for a Human Future at the New Frontier of Power (Zuboff) 174, 186 n.10
Alice's Adventures in Wonderland (Carroll) 31
'Amorbach' (Adorno) 6, 16 n.11
Angelus Novus (Klee) 66, 127
animal
    eloquent 86, 105–13, 162
    forced to speak 86, 90–1, 105
    mute 4–5, 13, 26, 58–9, 63–4, 73–5, 79–81, 86, 111, 135–6, 153, 159
    muted 9, 14, 54 n.17, 158–160, 162, 164–5
    speaking 7–8, 14, 85–6, 91, 93, 105–6
animality 58, 73, 80–1, 85, 89, 97, 99, 101–2, 104–6, 110, 115 n.55, 182–4
animal liberation 81, 112
Animal Life (Brehm) 10
Anthropocene 170, 186 n.3
anthropomorphism 45–6, 62–3, 81, 111, 165–6

apocalyptic messianism 120, 126, 147 n.27
appearance 1–3, 13, 25, 28, 38 n.17, 48, 50, 59–60, 62–4, 69–70, 86, 91, 107, 111, 129–30, 133
'Archaic Torso of Apollo' (Rilke) 33, 65, 136
armour 6, 44–7, 52, 61–3, 67–8, 70, 149 n.46, 177
art/artworks 3–5, 7, 11, 13–14, 16 n.8, 19, 21, 26–7, 29, 33–5, 37–8 n.17, 49–50, 53, 58–65, 68, 73–5, 79–80, 82, 83 n.3, 86, 109, 120, 124, 127, 129–30, 133, 135–9, 142–4, 146 n.12, 149 n.46, 149 nn.48–9, 156, 159, 172, 177
    eloquence of 49, 51, 64, 66, 74
    as *imagerie* 129
    as *imago naturae* 12, 20–5
    modern 59, 63, 154 5
    and nature 12, 20, 24, 111, 138
    as non-conceptual language 120, 124
    as remembrance of nature 28, 52
    as secularized revelation 127
    social situation of 63
    telos of 128–35
autonomy 76, 159

ban on images 121, 124, 143–4, 171
Beast People/Beast Men (*Island of Doctor Moreau*) 90, 92–9, 101, 107, 173
    bestiality 100, 102–3
    cult of the Law 104
    linguistic inability 99–100
Beethoven (Adorno) 146 n.13, 148 nn.40–1
Berlin Childhood around 1900 (Benjamin) 16 n.16, 47–8, 54 n.7, 54 n.11

Between Cultures: Tensions in the Struggle for Recognition (Düttmann) 83 n.2
Beyond Good and Evil (Nietzsche) 114 n.15
big-game hunting 184
black rhinoceros 39 n.31, 161
Breaking New Ground (Pinchot) 180, 187 n.28
Brehms Tierleben (Brehm) 6–8
'Burning Out the Animal' (Rohman) 91–6, 112, 115 n.55
'Butterflies' (Thompson) 23, 36 n.9

capitalism 113 n.6, 156, 161, 174–6
child/childhood 6–8, 30, 47–50, 67, 107, 135, 139
colonialism/colonial 2, 14, 61–2, 91, 158–9, 161, 185
　extraction process 159, 176–7, 179
　and logisticality 173–8
Comment c'est (*How it is*) (Beckett) 83 n.8
communication 27, 59, 74, 98, 113 n.4, 139, 162. *See also* language
Communication and Expression: Adorno's Philosophy of Language (Hogh) 113 n.4
concept 5, 21–3, 27, 30–1, 33, 60, 66, 76–8, 85, 88, 101, 120, 123, 128, 139, 141–2, 145, 155
conceptless 88, 93, 120, 124, 142–4
The Concept of Nature in Marx (Schmidt) 113 n.5, 115 n.56
conceptual 63–4, 76, 109, 113 n.4, 154–5, 158, 162
constellation 6, 12, 28, 38 n.17, 51, 121–2, 136
cooperation model of human communication (Tomasello) 113 n.4
Critical Models: Interventions and Catchwords (Adorno) 54 n.6
Critical Theory and Feeling: The Affective Politics of the Early Frankfurt School (Mussell) 188 n.41
Critique of the Power of Judgment (Kant) 20–1, 36 n.5

'Cultural Criticism and Society' 70 n.3
culture 3, 8–9, 14, 59–60, 67–8, 157–8, 182, 185
culture industry 57, 90, 116 n.60

Das große Bestiarium der modernen Literatur (Blei) 116 n.62
data mining 174, 180
Day of Judgement 131–2
decay 124, 126–7, 134, 145, 147 n.25, 147 n.27, 170, 177
　logic of 125, 135, 147 n.25, 170
Deconstruction in Context: Literature and Philosophy (Taylor) 186 n.8
Dialectic of Enlightenment (Adorno and Horkheimer) 8–9, 14, 22, 26, 37 n.13, 38 n.21, 47, 85–9, 91, 94, 96–7, 100, 101, 104–7, 109–10, 112, 115 n.55
A Dictionary of Psychology (Colman) 36 n.3
Die Geheimnisse der Schöpfung: Ein Kapitel aus dem kabbalistischen Buche Zohar (Scholem) 134, 148 n.41
Die Schriften zur Naturwissenschaft (Goethe) 37 n.10
dignity 10, 157, 181–5
Disgrace (Coetzee) 156, 166 n.3
disintegration 14, 25, 53, 75, 135, 181, 184
domination 2–3, 11, 30, 49–53, 76, 89, 95–6, 137, 139, 176
　of nature 3–4, 10–11, 22, 24–5, 27, 33, 96, 106, 166
Don Quixote 62
Double Vision: Albrecht Dürer/William Kentridge (Werner) 54 n.4, 62, 71 n.8

Elective Affinities (Goethe) 173
elephant 5, 15 n.2, 60–1, 162, 178
eloquence 26–7, 37 n.14, 49–51, 53, 66, 74–5, 86, 99, 105–13, 149 n.48, 154, 160, 165
enigma/enigmatic 1–4, 12, 53, 119, 137, 139, 147 n.17, 163–4

essayism 121–2, 141
Essays on Music (Adorno) 49, 54 n.14, 149 n.47
Etruscan rhinoceros 38–9 n.26
Etruscan vases 4, 13, 26, 33, 38 n.26, 64–6, 74, 82, 111, 135–6, 173
Exact Imagination, Late Work: On Adorno's Aesthetics (Nicholsen) 54 n.13, 146 n.10
exchange 4, 29, 47–8, 58–9, 67, 83 n.7, 98, 111, 136–7, 142, 172, 175–6, 187 n.17
exchangeability 4, 33–4
exchangeable 10, 25, 32, 130
exchange principle 172
exotic/exoticism 2–3, 15 n.4, 61, 110, 116 n.60
expression 4, 16 n.8, 19, 22, 25–30, 33, 35, 38 n.26, 43, 47, 50–2, 64, 76–80, 82, 83 nn.6–7, 86, 99, 106, 109–12, 120, 135–8, 154, 157, 161, 184. *See also* language
  objectivation of 27, 51, 83 n.6, 111–12
  symbolic 86, 99
extinction 2–4, 35, 61–2, 170, 178–81, 186 n.3
extraction 14, 155, 158–9, 161, 178–81

fireworks 14, 127, 129, 133–4, 145

gaze 1, 3, 11, 14, 33–4, 58, 65, 78, 87, 106–7, 112, 122, 135–40, 142, 150 n.57, 154, 159, 183
  anthropomorphic 45–6
  contemplative 32–3, 159
  katechontic 121, 140–5
Geist 20, 65, 87
gesture 5, 7, 11–14, 27–8, 47–9, 52–3, 75, 77–80, 82–3, 127, 137–8
The Great Transformation (Polanyi) 180, 187 n.29

Hatari (Hawks) 83 n.4
hippopotamus 15–16 n.7
history 2–3, 10, 13, 21, 52–3, 58, 80–1, 83 n.3, 87, 89, 104, 124–6, 154, 165

human (*see* human history)
natural (*see* natural history)
prehistory/protohistory 65, 78–81, 83 n.3
Urgeschichte (primordial history) 87–8
human exceptionalism 186 n.3
human history 170
  and animal 2–3
  nature and 11
humanity 10–11, 21, 58–9, 65, 67, 69–70, 85, 87–8, 94, 96–7, 100–2, 104–6, 148 n.39, 173, 181, 184
humanization/humanizing 14, 86–9, 91–3, 96–9, 105, 107, 110, 112, 157, 165
  of nature 106, 111–12

'The Idea of Natural History' (Adorno) 87, 113 n.3
identity 6, 13, 21, 29, 46, 60, 64, 76–8, 82–3, 97, 125, 154, 158–9, 165, 182
  Cartesian 63
identity thinking, identificatory thought/thinking 4, 26, 29, 49–51, 64, 75, 77, 127, 135
image 8, 22–3, 26, 36 n.8, 45, 48–9, 51, 53, 59, 61–3, 70, 80, 82, 103, 106, 108–9, 112, 129, 133, 140
  aspect of language 26
  ban on 121, 124, 143–4, 171
  of God 23, 92, 124, 148 n.39
imago 22–4, 36 n.3
imago ad vivum 62
imago contrafacta 62
Imago Dei 23
imago naturae, art as 12, 20–5
Intellectual and Manual Labour: A Critique of Epistemology (Sohn-Rethel) 187 nn.16–17
The Island of Doctor Moreau (Wells) 14, 85–117 passim, 173
The Island of Lost Souls (film by E. C. Kenton) 116 n.60
'The IUCN Red List of Threatened Species' 39 n.31

The Jargon of Authenticity (Adorno) 144, 149 n.55, 183-4, 188 n.37
Javan rhinoceros 35
judgement 28, 102, 142, 144, 147 n.26, 158, 178

kitsch 68-9
'Kitsch and the Absurd in Eugène Ionesco's Rhinoceros'(Valentine) 68, 71 n.11
Kruger Park 161

Lacemaker (Vermeer) 63
language 13-14, 24-5, 27, 33, 37 n.17, 50, 65, 73, 76-7, 86, 88-9, 111, 120, 130, 153, 163-5, 183
   acquisition 85, 93
   arbitrary 26-8
   character 3, 26, 64, 74-5, 79-80, 136
   communicative 26, 64, 74, 79, 136
   conventional 27-8
   deformation of 104, 113
   of divine creation 124, 144
   expressive 26, 28, 73, 79, 86, 110, 120
   image aspect of 26
   mimetic 26, 28, 50, 120, 136
   non-significative 79, 112, 136
   and rationality 96
   signifying element of 26, 74-5
   sprachlos 26-8, 64, 74
   symbolic 27-8, 86, 99
   of things 26-7, 65
The Language Animal: The Full Shape of Human Linguistic Capacity (Taylor) 113 n.4
Lectures on the Philosophy of History (Hegel) 57
The Legitimacy of the Modern Age (Blumenberg) 125, 147 n.20
Letters to his Parents 1939-1951 (Adorno) 116 n.63
Lied von der Erde (Mahler) 15 n.4
likeness 7, 11, 30, 67, 86, 106, 110-11, 119, 124, 148 n.39
liminality 1, 3, 133, 138, 162

lion 156, 162-4
The Lives of Animals (Coetzee) 181-2, 188 n.34
logistics/logisticality 176-7
'Lucerne Exposé' (Sohn-Rethel) 175

Magic Flute (Mozart) 62
Mahler: A Musical Physiognomy (Adorno) 7, 11, 15 n.4, 16 n.13, 17 n.19
Mammoth 16 n.17
'Man and Beast' (Horkheimer and Adorno) 85, 88
mass extinction 3-4, 35, 170, 186 n.3
Master of the Day of Judgment (Perutz) 130-2, 148 n.32, 148 n.35
mastery of nature. *See* domination, of nature
materialism 143
meaning 22, 58-9, 63, 65, 70, 73, 79, 86, 100, 105-7, 122, 125-6, 133, 137, 144-5, 147 n.27, 149 nn. 48-9, 153-4, 159, 161, 163, 177, 183
megamachine 174-5
memory 8, 12-13, 48, 90, 123
'In Memory of Eichendorff' (Adorno) 44, 53 n.2
Menschenaffe 80
messianism 120, 126, 147 n.27
metaphysics 70, 104, 124, 128, 142-3
   micrology 148 n.28
   of musical time 134
   peephole 149 n.46
   secularization of 126, 128, 142
   transmutation of 126
Mignon (*Wilhelm Meisters Lehrjahre*) 23
mimesis/mimetic 13, 16 n.8, 22-4, 26-8, 37 n.13, 47-51, 54 n.13, 59, 62, 65, 110, 120, 123, 136, 138-40, 145
Mine (Kentridge) 161, 175
Minima Moralia (Adorno) 2, 4, 7, 9-10, 15 n.6, 29, 31-2, 38 n.20, 47, 54 n.10, 58-9, 65, 67, 70-1 n.3, 83 nn.7-8, 99, 108-11, 116 n.59, 135-7, 141, 148 n.43
'Frog King' 7

'Mammoth' 9–10
'Second Harvest' 59
'Toy Shop' 4, 29, 136–7
'Wolf as Grandmother' 7
museum 7, 9, 64, 156, 159, 174, 179
music 7, 26, 49–50, 63–4, 74–5, 82, 133–4, 137, 146 n.13, 182
muteness/mute/muted 4–5, 9, 13–14, 26–8, 30, 35, 50–1, 54 n.17, 58–9, 63–4, 73–5, 78–81, 83 n.6, 86, 111–12, 135–6, 147 n.17, 153–66, 169

name 29–32, 35, 47–8, 67, 83 n.7, 111, 128, 136–7, 180
Nashörner: Ein Portrait (Frenz) 15 n.2, 187 n.22, 188 n.32
natural beauty/beauty of nature 4, 12, 19, 21–2, 24, 27, 36 n.8, 111, 156
　dignity 182
　objective expression 27
natural history 11, 87–9, 91, 97, 101–2, 104–6, 109, 113
Natural History (Pliny) 60, 71 n.4
nature 3–4, 8–12, 20–5, 27–8, 32, 34–5, 36 n.8, 37 n.17, 45–6, 51–3, 59, 61, 63–5, 67, 69, 86–9, 93, 96, 102, 105–6, 110, 112, 123, 126, 134, 138–9, 156–8, 164, 166, 169, 171–3, 175, 180–5, 186 n.6, 186 n.9.
　See also domination, of nature
　aesthetic experience of 36 n.8
　art and 12, 20, 24, 111, 138
　being-in-itself of 12, 34, 39 n.28
　humanity/humankind and 21, 87, 106, 173, 181, 184, 186 n.9
　humanization/humanizing of 87–8, 96, 106, 111–12
　of modern exchange 59
　non-human animals and 32
　rescue of 24–5, 52
Negative Dialectics (Adorno) 6, 11, 14, 15 n.3, 16 n.12, 17 n.18, 25, 29–31, 34, 37 n.12, 45–7, 54 n.5, 66–7, 71 n.10, 81, 83 n.5, 110, 115 n.36, 120, 122, 124–8, 132–3, 141–3, 146 n.2, 147 nn.25–6, 148 n.28, 148 n.31, 149 n.46, 171–2, 184, 186 n.4, 186 n.9, 187 n.17
non-exchangeability 19, 26, 29, 135
non-exchangeable 35, 67, 187 n.17
non-identity/non-identical 5, 38 n.19, 76, 97, 111, 121, 187 n.17
Notes to Literature (Adorno) 37 n.14, 53 n.2, 149 n.52

Odysseus (Ulysses) 100–2, 107, 173, 178, 186 n.8
Odyssey 89
'Offener Brief an Max Horkheimer' (Adorno) 114 n.30
'Of Mice and Men: Adorno on Art and the Suffering of Animals' (Flodin) 36 n.4
Olympia (Manet) 154
one-liners 13, 20, 26, 57–9, 135, 140, 177
'Online transatlantic slave trade database' 187 n.20
'On Some Motifs in Baudelaire' (Benjamin) 49, 54 n.13
The Origin of German Tragic Drama (Benjamin) 125–6, 147 n.25
Origins of Human Communication (Tomasello) 113 n.4
Other Inquisitions 1937–1952 (Borges) 113 n.9

Paradigms for a Metaphorology (Blumenberg) 114 n.10
'Parataxis: On Hölderlin's Late Poetry' (Adorno) 26, 37 n.14
The Philosophical Discourse of Modernity (Habermas) 115 n.54
Philosophical Investigations (Wittgenstein) 163, 166 n.4
Philosophische Terminologie (Adorno) 120, 146 n.1
'In Praise of Mistranslation' (Kentridge) 53 n.1, 54 n.16
presentation 120–2, 144, 177

Prisms (Adorno) 70 n.3, 122, 146 n.6, 148 n.31
progress 14, 20, 86–8, 92, 104–5
purpose 4, 29–30, 33, 47, 62, 76, 83 n.7, 88, 95, 103–4, 107–9, 111, 136, 161, 175, 179–80
purposeless 4, 29, 34, 47, 81, 83 n.7, 88, 107–9, 111–12, 136

The Ragpicker (Manet) 155
rationality 24, 70, 86, 89, 93, 95–8, 103, 109–10, 138–9, 144, 184
rationalization 21–3, 25–6, 184–5
redemption/redeeming 14, 86, 110, 112, 121, 128, 141
reification 33, 45, 51–2
remembrance 5–6, 8, 11, 13, 28, 48–9, 51–2, 110, 182–3
   of nature in/within the subject 5–6, 11, 28, 52, 110, 182
'A Report to an Academy' (Kafka) 99, 114 n.35
representation 43, 61, 65
resemblance 3–5, 8–9, 37 n.17, 47–9, 52, 60, 64, 74–5, 79, 82, 89, 139, 182
Rhinoceros (Dürer) 12–13, 43–5, 61
Rhinocéros (Ionesco) 63, 67–8, 70
Rhinoceros and Other Plays (Eugène) 71 n.13
The Rhinoceros from Dürer to Stubbs, 1515–1799 (Clarke) 60–1, 71 n.5
Rhinoceros Vase 62
rhino horn 2, 15 n.2, 30, 35, 60, 62–3, 68, 181
Rinoceronte vestido con puntillas (Dali) 63

second nature 11, 34, 89, 93, 105
secularization 14, 124–8, 132, 143–4, 183
   of metaphysics and transcendence 126, 128, 142
   progressive 125
Selbstbesinnung 143, 183–5, 188 n.36
The Selected Poetry of Rainer Maria Rilke (Rilke) 149 n.45

Selected Writings: Volume 1 1913–1926 (Benjamin) 114 n.25
self/selfhood/self-identity 4–5, 13–14, 16 n.11, 26, 28–9, 32, 43, 46, 51, 64, 73–82, 83 n.2, 88, 93, 98, 101, 111, 136, 182–3
semblance 2, 4–6, 9–10, 14, 24, 33–4, 46, 51–2, 79, 82, 86, 107–9, 111, 120, 124, 129, 133, 137, 141–3, 149 n.49
Serendipities: Language and Lunacy (Eco) 15 n.2
shudder/trembling 65, 140, 166
sign 26–7, 30–1, 78, 133, 165
The Sixth Extinction: An Unnatural History (Kolbert) 39 n.30
'Some Etruscan Vases' (von Bothmer) 71 n.9
species 11, 19, 30, 32, 35, 37 n.10, 38–9 n.26, 45, 67, 81, 107, 162, 179, 184
speech 4, 26, 59, 62, 64, 74–5, 86, 93, 100, 111, 135, 154–5, 185
speechlessness 25, 27, 50, 64, 74–5, 85, 88, 93
Stephanorhinos etruscus (rhinoceros) 38 n.26, 182
suffering 3, 8, 22–3, 27, 35, 52, 86, 88–9, 95–7, 99, 104, 109, 112, 123, 171–2
   natural history of 97, 101, 105–6
sufficientarianism 172
Sumatran rhinoceros 35
System of Transcendental Idealism (Schelling) 36 n.6

Technics and Human Development (Mumford) 174, 187 n.13
technology 139, 171–2, 181, 186 n.6
theory of exchange abstraction (Sohn-Rethel) 187 n.17
'Theory of Pseudo-Culture' (Adorno) 113 n.6
Third Symphony (Mahler) 7
Through the Looking-Glass and What Alice Found There (Carroll) 31–2, 38 n.24
Toward a Theory of Musical Reproduction (Adorno) 54 n.9

'The Trace of the Other' (Levinas) 186 n.8
Transatlantic Slavery (Morgan) 187 n.20
transcendence 2, 38 n.17, 51, 66, 88, 124–6, 128, 141–5, 147 n.17, 149 n.48, 183
transmutation 125–6
transubstantiation 125
The Travels of Marco Polo: The Complete Yule-Cordier Edition (Marco Polo) 15 n.2
Travels to Discover the Source of the Nile (Bruce) 62, 71 n.7
Triceratops 45, 81
truth, truth content 21–4, 31, 59, 66, 75, 81–2, 89–90, 120, 123, 127–8, 138, 143, 147 n.27, 148 n.31, 170

Unau (Choloepus didactylus) vii, 108
The Undercommons: Fugitive Planning & Black Study (Harney and Moten) 187 n.18
utilitarianism 180

utopia/utopian 8–9, 14, 29–30, 32–4, 36, 47–9, 51, 109, 120, 135, 137–43, 153, 158, 160, 164–5, 171, 181–5, 187 n.17

Vaghe stelle dell'Orsa (Visconti) 83 n.3
violence 13, 24, 34, 82, 88–9, 91, 95–6, 104, 110, 157, 160, 171, 176, 185
vivisection 88–92, 95, 99, 104, 107, 156

War and Algorithm (Liljefors, Noll and Steuer) 186 n.3
When Trumpets Call: Theodore Roosevelt after the White House (O'Toole) 187 n.25
white rhinoceros 35, 39, 161, 179
'Why Look at Animals?' (Berger) 3, 15 n.5
wild boar of Amorbach 6, 15 n.2, 16 n.11
Wilhelm Meisters Lehrjahre (Goethe) 23
woolly rhinoceros 15 n.2

www.ingramcontent.com/pod-product-compliance
Lightning Source LLC
Chambersburg PA
CBHW061828300426
44115CB00013B/2296